Understanding Roberto Bolaño

**Understanding Modern European
and Latin American Literature**

James Hardin, Series Editor

volumes on

Ingeborg Bachmann

Samuel Beckett

Juan Benet

Thomas Bernhard

Johannes Bobrowski

Roberto Bolaño

Heinrich Böll

Italo Calvino

Albert Camus

Elias Canetti

Camilo José Cela

Céline

Julio Cortázar

Isak Dinesen

José Donoso

Friedrich Dürrenmatt

Rainer Werner Fassbinder

Max Frisch

Federico García Lorca

Gabriel García Márquez

Juan Goytisolo

Günter Grass

Gerhart Hauptmann

Christoph Hein

Hermann Hesse

Eugène Ionesco

Uwe Johnson

Milan Kundera

Primo Levi

John McGahern

Robert Musil

Boris Pasternak

Octavio Paz

Luigi Pirandello

Marcel Proust

Graciliano Ramos

Erich Maria Remarque

Alain Robbe-Grillet

Joseph Roth

Jean-Paul Sartre

W. G. Sebald

Claude Simon

Mario Vargas Llosa

Peter Weiss

Franz Werfel

Christa Wolf

Roberto Bolaño

Ricardo Gutiérrez-Mouat

The University of South Carolina Press

© 2016 University of South Carolina

Published by the University of South Carolina Press
Columbia, South Carolina 29208

www.sc.edu / uscpress

Manufactured in the United States of America

25 24 23 22 21 20 19 18 17 16
10 9 8 7 6 5 4 3 2 1

Library of Congress Cataloging-in-Publication Data
can be found at http://catalog.loc.gov/.

ISBN: 978-1-61117-648-3 (hardback)
ISBN: 978-1-61117-649-0 (ebook)

This book was printed on recycled paper with
30 percent postconsumer waste content.

This book is dedicated to my sons, Aidan and Asher Mouat,
both lovers of good literature.

Contents

Series Editor's Preface

Understanding Modern European and Latin American Literature has been planned as a series of guides for undergraduate and graduate students and non-academic readers. Like the volumes in its companion series *Understanding Contemporary American Literature,* these books provide introductions to the lives and writings of prominent modern authors and explicate their most important works.

Modern literature makes special demands, and this is particularly true of foreign literature, in which the reader must contend not only with unfamiliar, often arcane artistic conventions and philosophical concepts, but also with the handicap of reading the literature in translation. It is a truism that the nuances of one language can be rendered in another only imperfectly (and this problem is especially acute in fiction), but the fact that the works of European and Latin American writers are situated in a historical and cultural setting quite different from our own can be as great a hindrance to the understanding of these works as the linguistic barrier. For this reason the *UMELL* series emphasizes the sociological and historical background of the writers treated. The philosophical and cultural traditions peculiar to a given culture may be particularly important for an understanding of certain authors, and these are taken up in the introductory chapter and also in the discussion of those works to which this information is relevant. Beyond this, the books treat the specifically literary aspects of the author under discussion and attempt to explain the complexities of contemporary literature lucidly. The books are conceived as introductions to the authors covered, not as comprehensive analyses. They do not provide detailed summaries of plot because they are meant to be used in conjunction with the books they treat, not as a substitute for study of the original works. The purpose of the books is to provide information and judicious literary assessment of the major works in the most compact, readable form. It is our hope that the *UMELL* series will help increase knowledge and understanding of European and Latin American cultures and will serve to make the literature of those cultures more accessible.

J. H.

Acknowledgments

I wish to express my gratitude to Chris Wait, permissions editor at New Directions Publishing, for allowing me to quote from Bolaño's translated poetry; to Karen Stolley, chair of the Department of Spanish and Portuguese, and Michael Elliott, dean of Emory College, for supporting my work on this book by letting me bank a course in the spring of 2014; to Ángel Díaz Miranda, who as a former graduate student at Emory suggested a connection between Oscar Hahn's poem "Reencarnación de los carniceros" and the title of Bolaño's 2666; and to my fellow scholar Marion Elizabeth Rodgers for taking time from her busy schedule to read and make enlightening comments on my work in progress. Her generosity and encouragement were boundless.

Karen Stolley, who oversaw the editing process in the wake of Ricardo's untimely death, would additionally like to acknowledge the contributions of Amy Linenberger and Sergio Salazar, who reviewed page proofs with meticulous professionalism. Amy also did an impeccable job preparing the index. Their help was invaluable in bringing Ricardo's book on Bolaño to print.

A Note on Translations

All citations from Bolaño's works are from the translations listed in the bibliography. Exceptions are noted in the body of the text. Those of Bolaño's works available in English are referred to by the title in translation throughout the book, unless the reference specifically involves the Spanish original. References in the bibliography to novels, stories, and poems by Latin American authors other than Bolaño are given in English when available and in Spanish otherwise.

Chronology

Bolaño's works are listed in the order of composition. When the date of composition is not known or covers a range of years, the original publication date suffices. Publication dates are given for both the Spanish originals and their English translations.

1953.   Born in Santiago, Chile, but grows up in small towns and cities of south-central Chile (Los Ángeles, Quilpué, Cauquenes).

1968.   Family moves to Mexico. Lives with his family until parental separation in 1973. Then with his father while sister and mother move to Spain.

1973.   Travels to Chile in August and survives Pinochet's coup on September 11. Stays five months after brief imprisonment.

1974.   Returns to Mexico in January and goes back to living with father near the famous basilica of Guadalupe.

1976.   *Reinventar el amor* (Mexico City: Taller Martín Pescador. "Reinventing Love," untranslated poetic work).

Infrarealist manifesto. (Published a year later in a short-lived journal.)

Pájaro de calor: Ocho poetas infrarrealistas (Mexico City: Ediciones Asunción Sanchís. "Bird of Flames: Eight Infrarealist Poets," contains a few poems by Bolaño).

1977.   (January) Leaves Mexico for Barcelona, where his mother lives. Works as a night watchman in a campground near the city for several summers.

1979.   *Muchachos desnudos bajo el arcoiris de fuego* (Mexico City: Editorial Extemporáneos, "Naked Boys under the Rainbow of Fire," Bolaño's anthology of *infrarrealista* poetry).

"Diario de bar" ("Bar Diary," story not included in any of Bolaño's story collections).

1980.   Moves to Gerona (or Girona), in Catalonia, when his married sister returns to Mexico and leaves the writer her house.

   Amberes (Barcelona: Anagrama, 2002; *Antwerp*, 2010).

1981.   Meets Carolina López in Gerona, whom he marries in 1985.

   Monsieur Pain (Barcelona: Anagrama, 1999; *Monsieur Pain*, 2010). Originally published in 1993 by the municipality of Toledo with the title *La senda de los elefantes* ("The Elephant Path").

1983.   "El contorno del ojo" ("The Contour of the Eye," story collected in *Encuentro en Praga*, Valencia: Editorial Prometeo).

1984.   *Consejos de un discípulo de Morrison a un fanático de Joyce* ("Advice from a Disciple of Morrison to a Fan of Joyce," Barcelona: Anthropos).

1985.   Moves to Blanes, on Spain's Costa Brava, and lives there until his death.

1989.   *El tercer Reich* (Barcelona: Anagrama, 2010; *The Third Reich*, 2011).

1990.   Birth of son, Lautaro, named after an indigenous Araucanian leader who fought the Spanish during the conquest of Chile.

1992.   Diagnosed with terminal liver condition.

1993.   *Fragmentos de la universidad desconocida* ("Fragments of the Unknown University," Toledo: Ayuntamiento de Talavera de la Reina). An expanded edition was published in 2007 with the title *La universidad desconocida*.

   La pista de hielo (Alcalá de Henares: Ayuntamiento, 1993; *The Skating Rink*, 2009).

1995.   *Los perros románticos* (Irún: Fundación Kuxta; *The Romantic Dogs*, 2008). A second expanded Spanish edition was published in 2000 with the title *Los perros románticos: Poemas 1980–1998*, Barcelona: Editorial Lumen). *El último salvaje* (Mexico City: Al Este del Paraíso). Poems from *Los perros románticos* and *Fragmentos de la universidad desconocida*.

1996.   *La literatura nazi en América* (Barcelona: Seix Barral; *Nazi Literature in the Americas*, 2008).

   Estrella distante (Barcelona: Anagrama; *Distant Star*, 2004).

1997.   *Llamadas telefónicas* (Barcelona: Anagrama; some of these stories are translated in *Last Evenings on Earth*, 2006; and in *The Return*, 2010).

1998.   *Los detectives salvajes* (Barcelona: Anagrama; *The Savage Detectives*, 2007). Winner of the Herralde Prize in Spain for *The Savage Detectives*.

   Travels to Chile to be a juror in a story contest organized by *Paula* magazine. Stays twenty days.

1999.   *Amuleto* (Barcelona: Anagrama; *Amulet,* 2006).
         Awarded the Rómulo Gallegos prize for *The Savage Detectives.*
         Returns to Chile in November invited by the Santiago book fair.
2000.   *Nocturno de Chile* (Barcelona: Anagrama; *By Night in Chile,* 2003).
         Tres (Barcelona: Acantilado; *Tres,* bilingual edition, 2011).
2001.   *Putas asesinas* (Barcelona: Anagrama; some of these stories are trans-
            lated in *Last Evenings on Earth,* 2006; and in *The Return,* 2010).
         Birth of daughter Alexandra.
2002.   *Una novelita lumpen* (Barcelona: Mondadori; *A Little Lumpen
            Novelita,* 2014).
2003.   *El gaucho insufrible* (Barcelona: Anagrama, 2003; *The Insufferable
            Gaucho,* 2010).
         Dies in a Barcelona hospital on July 15.
2004.   *2666* (Barcelona: Anagrama; *2666,* 2008).
2007.   *La universidad desconocida* (Barcelona: Anagrama; *The Unknown
            University,* 2013).
         El secreto del mal (Barcelona: Anagrama; *The Secret of Evil,* 2012).
2011.   *Los sinsabores del verdadero policía* (Barcelona: Anagrama; *Woes of
            the True Policeman,* 2012).

Chapter 1

Bolaño's Life and Works

Few people in Chile, Mexico, or Spain—his three countries of residence—had heard of Roberto Bolaño before the late 1990s when a series of his fictional works appeared seemingly out of the blue and with stunning regularity, beginning in 1996 with *Nazi Literature in the Americas* and continuing through 1998, the year of *The Savage Detectives,* the watershed novel that received the prestigious Rómulo Gallegos award in 1999 and that almost a decade later (and in English translation) was selected by the *New York Times* as one of the ten most notable books of 2007. Before 1996 Bolaño had published only some poetry in limited editions and three novels in Spain that went mostly unnoticed, though all three were reissued in later years and mostly read retrospectively, from the standpoint of the author's mature work. After *The Savage Detectives* Bolaño continued to make his mark by releasing another series of novels and stories that culminated with the monumental *2666,* published in 2004, a year after his death. This novel appeared in English translation four years later. By then Bolaño's reputation as a world-class author was firmly established in Latin America, Europe, and the United States.

Bolaño was born and grew up in Chile but moved to Mexico with his family when he was fifteen. This was in 1968, the year when the summer Olympic Games were held in Mexico City and an untold number of students were massacred by the army a few days before the opening ceremonies for protesting social and political conditions in the country. The massacre took place in Tlatelolco Square in Mexico City (also known as the Plaza de las Tres Culturas) and it is a recurring theme in Bolaño's *Amulet.* Bolaño was enrolled in a school run by priests but quickly dropped out (or was expelled). He used his time to take long walks around the city and catch up with the movies available at downtown theaters. As he confessed many times thereafter, he fed his addiction to reading by sometimes lifting books from downtown bookstores. At night he often stayed up late reading and writing, and possibly listening to the suggestive noises coming from the apartment upstairs, as the first-person narrator of "Colonia Lindavista" relates in the story by that name (included in *The Secret of Evil*). In 1973 Bolaño took a poorly timed trip to Chile and arrived in the country the month before the military coup of September 11. In November, while he was on his way to see a friend in the southern city of Concepción, he was escorted off the bus by an overzealous policeman who thought he was a foreign terrorist on account of his long hair and Mexican accent. He spent a few days in jail but was freed when his prison guards—who turned out to be two former schoolmates—recognized and helped him. (The incident is told in "Detectives" and in "Cell Mates," stories included in *The Return*.) Upon returning to Mexico, Bolaño gathered a group of young bohemians around him and founded a neo-avant-garde poetic movement known as "infrarealism." The infrarealists claimed the legacy of French symbolism and surrealism and of the U.S. Beat generation but were better known for their disruptive cultural tactics than for their poetic output. The various members of this group are portrayed in *The Savage Detectives,* a novel written about twenty years after the group had dissolved. Bolaño published a thin book of poems in Mexico City in 1976 and then moved on to Barcelona, where he was reunited with his mother, who was by then separated from the author's father. Bolaño never returned to Mexico but imagined such a return in a story called "Death of Ulises" (in *The Secret of Evil*). At this time Bolaño's future preeminence as a writer of fiction was nowhere in sight.

Bolaño's move to Barcelona took place less than two years after General Franco's death, and at a time when Spanish youth were finding a new lease on life after decades of dictatorship. Twenty years after that date Bolaño remembered the city as a place where politics and frequent partying mixed together and sexual liberation was in the air. Barcelona was for the twenty-something that he was at that time a memorable learning experience, a veritable "university" for a Chilean immigrant who had spent the previous ten years of his life in the very different urban atmosphere of Mexico City (Dés 140). In Barcelona, Bolaño fell in with other South American immigrants, some of whom were Chilean political exiles. For a few months he lived with his mother in an apartment on the Gran Vía and later by himself in a small apartment on 45 Tallers Street, doing a variety of jobs to make ends meet. From 1978 to 1981 he worked summers as a night watchman in a campground on the outskirts of the city, an experience that appears often in his fiction and poetry. In 1978 he met Antoni García Porta (A. G. Porta), a young local author with whom he collaborated on some unsuccessful film scripts and short stories that are now lost, but who is also the coauthor of Bolaño's first major publication, the novel *Consejos de un discípulo de Morrison a un fanático de Joyce,* as yet untranslated into English.

Stories such as "Enrique Martín" and "Days of 1978" (both included in *Last Evenings on Earth*) record some of the author's Barcelona experiences.

In 1980 Bolaño moved to Gerona (Girona, in Catalan), in the northeastern Catalonian region, to live in a house previously occupied by his sister and brother-in-law. Bolaño would spend the next five years in Gerona, at the beginning of which—as he writes in one of his semiautobiographical stories—he had lost his job as a night watchman, was "poorer than a rat," lived in a house in ruins, had no friends, got used to taking long solitary walks in the evenings, and did nothing much other than write (see "Sensini," in *Last Evenings on Earth*). What he wrote was mostly poetry and at least one novel (published much later as *Monsieur Pain*), apart from the collaborative projects with A. G. Porta mentioned earlier. Despite these achievements, Bolaño remembers the early years in Gerona as a particularly bleak period in his life, when "literature was a vast minefield occupied by enemies" ("Meeting with Enrique Lihn," *The Return*, 192). In Gerona, nevertheless, Bolaño met Carolina López, his future wife and mother of his two children, whom he married in 1985 and who remains to this day the executor of the Bolaño estate. Bolaño's time in Gerona was not forgotten by the local authorities. In June 2011 the Gerona city hall named a street after the city's now famous onetime resident.

In 1985 Bolaño relocated to the town of Blanes, on Spain's eastern coast, where he would live until his death eighteen years later and compose the bulk of his work. His friend, Spanish author Enrique Vila-Matas, writes that Bolaño had "come to Blanes with Carolina in the summer of 1985 to work as a shop assistant, attending to customers, usually tourists, in a small costume jewellery shop that his mother had opened in carrer Colom . . . [Colom Street]. His friends were fishermen, waiters, young drug addicts (all sentenced to death)—the famous school of life" ("Blanes" 154). While the writer helped his mother with her business, his wife found employment on the local town council. (A local bureaucrat, but a male one, is one of the main characters in *The Skating Rink*.) His son, Lautaro, was born in 1990 and his daughter, Alexandra, in 2001. In 1992 Bolaño was diagnosed with the liver condition that would eventually kill him. At the end of the decade he returned twice to Chile after twenty-five years of absence. He first returned in November 1998 when he agreed to be a juror for a story competition sponsored by a popular local magazine and returned again a year later when he was a guest of honor at Santiago's book fair. In between these homecomings Bolaño wrote an article for a Barcelona review denigrating Chilean literature, society, and politics, an account that made his second return somewhat controversial.[1] Bolaño became an ardent polemicist as he became better known in literary circles. He often provoked the literary establishment as he attempted to impose his own preferences among writers, reviewers, and critics. In the specific case of Chile, he condemned national literature as a whole and showed skepticism toward national icons such as Pablo Neruda and José Donoso but also displayed remarkable empathy with poets and prose writers like Enrique Lihn, Nicanor Parra, and Pedro Lemebel.

Bolaño spent the last years of his life informally separated from his wife and in the company of another Catalan woman, Carmen Pérez de Vega, who was the intimate witness of his final phase. She was with him at the hospital where he died—waiting for a liver transplant that never materialized—and watched him slave over the thousands of pages that would bring the writer's work to a conclusion. They met in 1997 when the author of *The Savage Detectives* was busy correcting the novel's proofs—a labor of love that allegedly left him in a progressively weakened state—and were in close contact when Bolaño started writing *Amulet* and showing interest in the murders of women in Ciudad Juárez, a Mexican border town south of El Paso, Texas. (This city is the Santa Teresa of *2666*.) Pérez de Vega reports that Bolaño was working on *Woes of the True Policeman* near the end of his life and on a novel provisionally called *Corrida* (*Bullfight*) that he later abandoned. She adds that the final stories Bolaño wrote were "The Insufferable Gaucho" and "Police Rat," and that he put a stop to his work on *2666* hoping to complete and revise the novel after having a transplant operation. But he fell ill and had to be rushed to ER on the way back from a congress in Seville and did not survive what would become his last visit to a hospital room. Bolaño died in Barcelona on July 15, 2003.[2]

Understanding Bolaño

Helpful as these facts are in understanding Bolaño's work in general, some points need to be expanded before approaching specific works of poetry and fiction. For example, was Bolaño a poet or a novelist? Was he a Chilean, Mexican, or Spanish writer, and why would this matter? Is the "American" Bolaño the same as the "Hispanic" Bolaño? And what are the great themes of his work?

Regarding the first of these points, conventional wisdom is that Bolaño started out as a poet in Mexico and switched to writing fiction when he moved to Spain in order to support himself and, later, his newborn son. There is no doubt that Bolaño lived on a shoestring budget during his early years in Spain, but his money woes never reached a catastrophic dimension and never deterred him from writing. Getting published, however, was a different matter. In the preface to *The Unknown University* Bolaño includes a poem that attests to his successive failures in this respect and suggests the financial hardships he had to endure until his writing became successful. Bolaño wrote "My Literary Career" in 1990, the year his son was born. In it he portrays himself holding his newborn son on his knee and writing poetry for an indifferent public. In the poem Bolaño also records the many rejection notices he has received over the years from some of Spain's leading publishers (Anagrama, Grijalbo, Planeta) but vows to keep on writing even if a thousand demons were to carry him to hell.

This poem supports the view that writing for money was a priority for Bolaño and would help explain the author's turn to fiction in the early 1980s, a period when Bolaño was entering as many literary contests as he could find announced in the newspapers in order to help support himself (see "Sensini"). It was also the period in which he actually won third prize in a municipal competition and saw his first story in print, "El contorno del ojo." Since until then Bolaño had published only poetry, it is easy to think that not only did he switch from poetry to fiction at that point but that he did so out of concern for his material existence. The fact is, however, that Bolaño was already writing fiction as a recently arrived teen in Mexico City, as he himself hints in "Colonia Lindavista." In that story a semiautobiographical narrator states that during his early days in Mexico City he used to stay up late at night listening to the lovemaking noises coming from the apartment above and writing something "doubtlessly bad, but long" that kept him going. It can be assumed that what the narrator was writing during those long Mexico City nights were the "novelitas" and incomplete stories that the young Bolaño kept handing over to one of his mother's good friends so that she could type them (Maristain, *Bolaño: A Biography* 25). There is no reason to doubt the kindhearted typist's testimony because it is known that Bolaño kept writing stories in his early years in Barcelona, one of which ("Diario de bar") has survived. The Mexican efforts were undoubtedly premature attempts at writing fiction, but they confirm their author's early vocation for storytelling, which coexisted with his penchant for poetry.

Bolaño once stated that the best poetry of our times is written in prose (Boullosa 67). He himself wrote poetry through the rest of his life, and poetry is a constant theme in his fiction. Poetry is also responsible for the narrative logic of novels such as *Amulet* and *By Night in Chile*. Bolaño also said that he confronted the great narrative tradition of Latin American literature from the perspective of a poet, and that if he had approached Latin American fiction from the point of view of a storyteller, he would have learned more about the art of narration and his novels would not have the structural gaps that characterize them (Soto and Bravo 44). It is true that the structure of novels like *Amulet* and *By Night in Chile* shows the imprint of a poetic apprenticeship, for they are both constructed as dramatic monologues whose narrative sequences are loosely strung together and have a semiautonomous character. But the same structural discontinuity is also evident in other novels and stories. Bolaño evolved at least three methods to bridge the gap between ideas, paragraphs, or sequences. One was to use a numerical system to aid the development of a story; another is the diary format in which continuity is created chronologically; and a third is the use of monologue, not necessarily the dramatic kind of monologue typical of *Amulet* and *By Night in Chile* but a more prosaic kind usually headed by the name of the speaker and the date of the speech act. "Dance Card" (*Last Evenings on Earth*) and "Two Catholic Tales" (*The Insufferable Gaucho*) employ the first of these techniques; *The Savage Detectives* has recourse to the last two; and *The Skating Rink* uses a variation of the third. Structural discontinuity creates the impression that Bolaño's writing is made up of set pieces that can stand alone as a short story or poem, or be integrated in a larger narrative context like that of a novel. A good example is the story of the Andalusian woman told in chapter 24 of *The Savage Detectives,* which has significant parallels with "Clara," one of the stories of *Llamadas telefónicas.* "The Grub," another story from this collection, takes the form of a poem in *The Unknown University* ("The Worm") and is briefly evoked in *Woes of the True Policeman* (225–26).

It is not an exaggeration to say that Bolaño's poetry came into view—and quickly retreated—as a consequence of the author's success in the realm of fiction. Since Bolaño's novels and stories began coming out regularly beginning in the mid-1990s, critical interest has overwhelmingly focused on the narrative aspect of the author's production. As a result critics have relegated Bolaño's poetry to the background or have deemed it to be a kind of testing ground for the more important prose works in the making. But Bolaño's poetry cannot be separated from his prose, and his poems are not just a testing ground for his fiction but have a life of their own. It is true that many great and accomplished poems are not likely to be found in *Reinventar el amor* and *The Unknown University,* but there will always be memorable poetic moments, insights, and images strewn along the way. Bolaño's writing is a hybrid of poetry and prose where the accent can be on either of these two components of literary discourse—on the fleeting poetic insight or on the more sustained logic of narrative. In fact attention should be paid to the continuity between the author's poetic beginnings and his later incarnation as a prose writer. In the infrarealist manifesto of 1976 (see chapter 2), Bolaño encourages young poets to subvert official culture, to leave it all behind, and to head off along the roads in search of adventure. These principles do inform Bolaño's early poetry, but they really come to fruition in the poet's fiction. Thus *The Savage Detectives* enacts the call to leave it all behind and head off along the road, just as *Amulet* could be preceded by a disillusioned sentence from the manifesto: "we dreamed of Utopia and woke up screaming." The imprint of poetry appears too in *2666,* although it's a novel about the search for a novelist. Its title (which already appears in *Amulet*) has a marked affinity with an apocalyptic poem by fellow Chilean Oscar Hahn (see chapter 8). And *Antwerp,* a text published as a novel in 2002, was originally a long poetic sequence called "People Walking Away," dating back to 1980.

Poetry and fiction also intersect in Bolaño's idea of the writer and of the literary life. For Bolaño, the prototype of the writer is the doomed poet (the *poète maudit*), and the prototype of the doomed poet is Arthur Rimbaud. The infrarealist manifesto includes a call for Rimbaud to "get back home," and Bolaño's narrative alter ego is Arturo Belano, a character whose given name is a tribute to the French poet. Furthermore one of only two poems quoted at length in *The Savage Detectives* is by Rimbaud, and at the end of the novel Belano abandons literature and disappears in Africa, like the poet from Charleville. In the famous "Lettre du Voyant," Rimbaud takes it for granted that being a poet means being a visionary and explains that becoming a visionary is a risky process of self-invention that involves a search for the unknown through the derangement of the senses and the experiencing of all forms of love, suffering, and madness. Through this process of absorbing all the "poisons" of experience in order to distill their quintessence, the poet becomes the "grand malade, le grand criminel, le grand maudit" (the seriously ill, the great criminal, the doomed one) in the eyes of society but also "le suprême Savant" (the supreme Sage) because he has cultivated his soul more than anyone and explored the unknown.

In characterizing the poet's lot, Bolaño picks up on the outlaw theme sounded by Rimbaud: "If I had to hold up the most heavily guarded bank in Europe and I could choose my partners in crime, I'd take a gang of five poets" ("The Best Gang," *Between Parentheses* 117). And in the same piece he goes on to stress the poet's bravery, pointing out that poets work "in the void of the word, like astronauts marooned on dead-end planets, in deserts where there are no readers or publishers" (117). For Bolaño, who admired the outsize and risky lives of poets but had enough common sense not to recommend it to his son (as he half-jokingly said during the Santiago book fair of 1999), poetry was a youthful gesture typical of vulnerable adolescents who bet the little they have on an uncertain future and usually come out the losers.

Poets populate Bolaño's fiction, and in many of the author's novels and stories poetic courage is put to the test in war or revolution. At various times in his writings Bolaño refers to the Tlatelolco massacre, to the victims of the military dictatorships in Argentina and Chile, and to the internal conflicts that tore Central America apart in the 1970s and 1980s. Poets are participants, witnesses, and victims of these events. Sometimes the term "poet" serves as a blanket metaphor for the idealistic youth who gave their lives for social change in what Bolaño often calls the Latin American *guerras floridas*.[3] By the same token, the Rimbaud of the barricades can serve as a symbol for the fusion of art and life in a revolutionary spirit—even if Rimbaud never actually made it to the barricades. In praising poets for their bravery, Bolaño makes no distinction between choosing the life of a poet—an act that is by itself a measure of courage—and risking it all for a utopian cause. Poets are warriors at odds with history, with society, and even with the literary institution that gives them a place in society. The warrior metaphor is prevalent in "The Private Life of a Novelist" (*Between Parentheses*). In "Dance Card" Bolaño remembers some of the casualties of poetry: "the children of Walt Whitman, José Martí, and Violeta Parra; torn apart, forgotten, in mass graves, at the bottom of the sea" (218).[4] Literature is a dangerous undertaking, warned Bolaño more than once, for it demands that writers peer into the darkness and leap into the void ("Caracas Address," *Between Parentheses* 34). The burden of literature explains Bolaño's bleak prophecy that a time will come when "all poets will live in artistic communities called jails or asylums" ("Dance Card" 219). We may surmise that Bolaño was led to this cheerless vision of the writer's fate by his own decades-long experience as a neglected poet and novelist.

The second point, Bolaño's nationality, concerns the place of his writing in a particular national tradition. Bolaño was a Chilean citizen to the end of his life, but was he a Chilean, Mexican, or Spanish writer? He wrote two "Chilean" novels and several "Chilean" stories. On the other hand, many critics have hailed *The Savage Detectives* as one of the greatest Mexican novels of the late twentieth century. And Bolaño's early novels, written between 1981 and 1993, are basically Spanish novels in terms of their setting and most of their characters. And to complicate the issue further, many see *2666* as a "global" novel. Faced with this rich menu of national and international choices critics have predictably turned to labels like extraterritoriality, postnationalism, transnationalism, or nomadism to try and encapsulate the condition of a writer who lived in three different countries and read indiscriminately across national borders and national languages (mostly in translation). Bolaño was above all a *radicant* writer, "*radicant* being a term designating an organism that grows its roots and adds new ones as it advances. To be radicant means setting one's roots in motion, staging them in heterogeneous contexts and formats, denying them the power to completely define one's identity, translating ideas, transcoding images, transplanting behaviors, exchanging rather than imposing" (Bourriaud 22). Bolaño himself claimed he was a Latin American writer and not specifically Chilean, Mexican, or Spanish (Maristain, "Last Interview" 99). And elsewhere he denied he was an exile and made fun of the confusion caused by his multiple "nationalities."

As a Latin American writer and, particularly, as a Latin American novelist, Bolaño had to deal with the legacy of the Boom. The admiration he felt for the novelists who came of age in the 1960s and took the Latin American novel to new heights was tempered by the fear of imitation and the challenge these novelists posed to an upstart writer. In the 1990s the magic realist style that had become the trademark of Latin American literature in the United States and Europe was discredited by younger writers like Alberto Fuguet and

Jorge Volpi. The former advocated a narrative that captured the experience of middle-class urban youth living in a globally connected world, while the latter argued for a return to the formal daring of the Boom novels after years of the commercially successful but "lite" literature of the "post-Boom." Bolaño was closer in spirit to Volpi. The center of his canon was Borges, the writer whom all the Boom novelists hailed as their precursor, but the canonical authors of the Boom—Cortázar, Fuentes, Vargas Llosa, and García Márquez—all found a place in Bolaño's apprenticeship. Bolaño acknowledges his debt to both Borges and Cortázar in his brief note "About *The Savage Detectives*" (*Between Parentheses* 353), and one of his best stories—"The Insufferable Gaucho"—is an ironic commentary on Borges's "The South." (In a reference to Cortázar's master novel, critics have called *The Savage Detectives* the author's *Hopscotch*.) Elsewhere Bolaño calls García Márquez and Vargas Llosa "gigantic" authors whose work is superior to anything produced by the members of his own generation (Soto and Bravo 43). His evaluation of Fuentes is more qualified. In the last interview he granted, Bolaño admits to not having read anything by the Mexican author "in a long while" (Maristain, "Last Interview" 103); but upon arriving in Mexico City, Bolaño was fascinated by Fuentes's first novel, *Where the Air Is Clear,* which—according to the testimony of a fellow poet and house guest during Bolaño's Mexican sojourn—greatly facilitated the young arrival's introduction to the Mexican capital (Quezada 21).[5]

Bolaño also read José Donoso, Chile's Boom novelist, but his evaluation of his precursor's work is not particularly generous. He agrees that Donoso is the best Chilean novelist of the twentieth century but adds that to qualify him as such is to insult him, given the insignificance of the Chilean narrative tradition. On the other hand, he finds it exaggerated to state that Donoso is on the same level as authors such as Lezama, Bioy Casares, Rulfo, Cortázar, García Márquez, Vargas Llosa, Sábato, Benet, Puig, or Reinaldo Arenas, a company among which Donoso's work would take second place ("The Transparent Mystery of José Donoso," *Between Parentheses* 108–9). Bolaño only gives Donoso credit for three novels: *Hell Has No Limits, The Obscene Bird of Night,* and *The Garden Next Door,* but is far more severe with the "donositos," the younger heirs of Donoso in Chile whose reading of "their master" is deficient and distorts his legacy. Bolaño radically sets himself apart from this crowd of disciples and, in the process, aggrandizes the figure of Donoso, who thus remains available for further reading and interpretation. He ends the piece by advising Donoso's followers to stop writing and spend the time rereading the Chilean master again.[6]

Bolaño was well aware, then, of the burden imposed by the canon. As an unknown author, he must have viewed it as a major obstacle to his own consecration; but after reaching a measure of recognition by fellow writers, critics, and readers he saw a chance to redraw canonical boundaries and place himself on a map of his own making. In a dialogue with Argentine writer Rodrigo Fresán he says, thinking of Rimbaud, that great literature is not a question of style or grammar but of "illumination": "on the one hand it is a lucid and comprehensive reading of the canonical tree and, on the other, a ticking time bomb. A testimony . . . that explodes in the hands of the readers and is projected toward the future" (137). This definition of literature is somewhat cryptic, but it does imply that strong writers do not enter the canon without reordering its priorities. And when asked in a 1999 interview what his relationship was with the writers of the Latin American Boom, Bolaño responded: "Good, very good—as a reader, of course" (Soto and Bravo 43), which presumably means that as a *writer* his relationship with the novels of the Boom was more explosive. Like any major writer, Bolaño simultaneously prolongs and breaks with tradition.

Jorge Volpi renders the relationship between latecomer and precursors as a playful take on the anxiety of influence, arguing that Bolaño read the Boom writers from an early age and that each of his books is a response to their work: "Each morning . . . [he] spent a couple of hours preparing himself for his daily struggle with the authors of the Boom. Sometimes he faced Cortázar . . . ; other times he rushed the team of expert wrestlers formed by Vargas Llosa and Fuentes; and when he felt exceptionally powerful or irritable or nostalgic, he allowed himself to face the heavyweight champion of the world, the ripper of Aracataca, the tough García Márquez, his nemesis." And Volpi concludes by pointing out that the "old-timers" never took their successor into account or did so when it was too late ("Bolaño, epidemia" 193).

The interplay between Bolaño and his Latin American forerunners and, more generally, Bolaño's identity as a Latin American writer is the kind of issue that is easily lost in translation. Concerning the third point—namely Bolaño's reception in the United States, as compared to his reception in the Spanish-speaking world—Latin American and U.S. writers and critics have pointed out a certain dissonance between the "original" or Hispanic Bolaño and Bolaño in English translation. The same Jorge Volpi, for example, argues that Bolaño's reception in the United States had little to do with the Chilean author's reception (and canonization) among his Hispanic readers and fellow writers. In both languages Bolaño quickly became either a canonical figure or an outstanding representative of world literature. But whereas in Spanish Bolaño's work was perceived as responding to certain autochthonous traditions, Bolaño in translation was received in isolation from the relevant background and projected against stereotypes that required a previous reinvention of his image. Thus, for American readers, Volpi argues, Bolaño became a mix of Che Guevara and Jack Kerouac (*El insomnio de Bolívar* 174–75).

This is true as far as it goes. Critic Sarah Pollack develops Volpi's point in reference to the English translation of *The Savage Detectives* when she points out that the design of the dust jacket—specifically aimed at the U.S. market—is meant to evoke "the newly released 'original scroll' version of Jack Kerouac's *On the Road* on the fiftieth anniversary of that book's original publication in 1957" (357). And she adds that the front flap of *The Savage Detectives* does not picture the author as he was when he wrote the novel but as "a young man with long locks and a faint mustache, a nostalgic memento that for U.S. readers evokes the rebellious counterculture of the sixties and seventies" (357). This reinvention of the authorial image does have its own logic. Bolaño was in fact a member of the countercultural generation and the Arturo Belano of the novel may have looked like the author in the mid-1970s. Furthermore, writers like Kerouac, movies like *Easy Rider,* and rock stars like Jim Morrison (whose affinity with Rimbaud has been recognized by literary scholars and whose ghost haunts some of Bolaño's writings)[7] were part and parcel of literary and popular culture in Mexico City in the late 1960s and 1970s. The problem is not that these reference points cannot be assimilated into a total image of Bolaño but that they may occlude other meaningful themes and modes of perception offered by the text. It's a safe bet that "endogenous" readers are more likely to connect the author and characters of *The Savage Detectives* with the Mexican student movement of 1968 than would their "external" counterparts. Of course the distinction between an inside and an outside reading is highly relative and impossible to sustain, but the fact remains that Bolaño was working from within a certain literary tradition—involving, for example, the Mexican avant-garde of the 1920s—as he reconstructed the Mexican neo-avant-garde scene of the 1970s.

Pollack also points out that a certain reified version of Bolaño's personal story often accompanied the reviews of *The Savage Detectives* and contributed to the novel's aura and massive sales. Reviewers' emphasis on issues like the author's drop-out status, his detention in a Chilean jail after the military coup, his itinerant existence in Europe, his bohemian lifestyle, his odd jobs, his putative drug habit, and other bits and pieces of Bolaño's life makes it seem as if the author of *The Savage Detectives* is being read through the vicissitudes of its young protagonist's life rather than on its own terms. It bears repeating that Bolaño was forty-five when the novel was published, comfortably settled in Blanes, and the conscientious father of an eight-year-old child. The temporal distance between the novel's publication and the happenings depicted in its first and third parts (perhaps its most distinctive sections) is reflected in Bolaño's assessment of his work as "a love letter or a farewell letter to my own generation" ("Caracas Address," *Between Parentheses* 35).

Bolaño's life story was also manipulated to contextualize the reception of some of his other novels. Reviewing *2666* for the *New York Times Book Review,* for example, Jonathan Lethem portrays Bolaño as a "rebel, exile, [and] addict" who constructed a remarkable body of stories and novels spurred by the urgency of poverty and the pressing awareness of an early death.[8] It is true that the young Bolaño was a rebel and that he was aware for many years that he needed a liver transplant. But Bolaño was not desperately poor—even in the worst of times he received some financial support from his family—nor a political exile or a committed left-wing militant. And he certainly was no heroin addict. There is no evidence of Bolaño's addiction to heroin, a rumor that seems to have originated in a fictional piece ("Beach") included in *The Secret of Evil* and in *Between Parentheses* but originally published in the Madrid newspaper *El Mundo* in August 2000. (Bolaño, however, did suffer from a temporary addiction to the works of William S. Burroughs.) The "real" Bolaño comes through in stories like "Vagabond in France and Belgium" (*Last Evenings on Earth*) and "I Can't Read" (*The Secret of Evil*). The first of these is a semiautobiographical story in which the narrator states that he has recently sold a novel and that he plans to travel to France and Belgium after depositing 60 percent of the proceeds in his son's bank account. "I Can't Read" is a chronicle of the author's return to Chile in 1998 that focuses on the trivial, everyday experiences of his eight-year-old son. Bolaño's life was simply not as dramatic or adventurous as the lives of some of the poets, rock stars, and revolutionaries he admired (Rimbaud, Jim Morrison, Rodrigo Lira, Roque Dalton, Sophie Podolski, Leopoldo María Panero) or the lives of some of his characters.

Another aspect of Bolaño's reception in the English-speaking world that should be considered in this context is the publication history of his novels, because their order of appearance in English did not follow the publication order of the originals. Whereas in Spanish *The Savage Detectives* followed *Nazi Literature in the Americas, Distant Star,* and some of the stories included in *Last Evenings on Earth*—and was followed in turn by *Amulet* and *By Night in Chile*—this last title was the first novel by Bolaño to be published in English (2003), followed by *Distant Star* (2004), *Amulet* (2006), *Last Evenings on Earth* (2006), *The Savage Detectives* (2007), and *Nazi Literature in the Americas* (2008), published the same year as *2666*. Readers of *Nazi Literature in the Americas* must have noticed that its last chapter was the rough draft for *Distant Star,* though this latter novel had been published four years earlier. A similar impression of anachronism must have taken readers of *Amulet* and *The Savage Detectives* by surprise, since the earlier novel is a full-blown expansion of a brief chapter of the later one. This is not to say that the order of publication of the Spanish-language originals was without problems. Some of Bolaño's novels were published out of sequence with respect to the dates of their composition, or years after their initial publication in obscure presses. *Amberes,* for example, was written (as a kind of poem) in 1980 and published as a novel in 2002; *Monsieur Pain* was written in 1981, originally published (with a different title) in 1993 by a local Spanish press, and reissued by Bolaño's regular publisher (Anagrama) in 1999; *La pista de hielo* was published with the support of a university foundation in Spain in 1993, reissued by Planeta in Chile in 1998, and reprinted later by Seix Barral (2003) and Anagrama (2009); and *El tercer Reich* was written in 1989 but published only in 2010. In English too early novels like *The Third Reich* and *The Skating Rink* were translated and published long after they had been written and after the publication and massive acceptance of Bolaño's "hard-core" works.

It must have been confusing for Spanish-language readers to read *Monsieur Pain,* for example, a year after the publication of *The Savage Detectives,* novels that at first sight seem to be written by two different authors. But what is at risk of getting lost in this disorder, both in Spanish and in English, is that Bolaño's recognition as a major writer really took hold when his work began to display a specifically *Latin American* stamp. The turning point was *Nazi Literature in the Americas,* a work that is basically an intervention in the national literatures of several Latin American countries (Argentina, Chile, Cuba) and that leaves the Spanish and European settings of earlier Bolaño novels behind. *Nazi Literature in the Americas,* furthermore, shows the imprint of Jorge Luis Borges's *Universal History of Infamy,* an early work by the most prestigious Latin American writer of modern times. (Its first edition is from 1935.) Even though both Borges and Bolaño inspired themselves on Marcel Schwob's *Les Vies imaginaires* (1896), the Borgesian signature of Bolaño's book—and the originality of Bolaño's rewriting—signaled the appearance of a worthy heir to the Argentine master.

In the final analysis, how important are these issues for the student of Bolaño in translation? It seems obvious that a full understanding of Bolaño requires that his work be placed in its proper literary context and that his novels and stories be read in a meaningful order. As for the image of the author created by publishers and marketing specialists, one may always hope that readers will be able to deduce their own authorial images from reading the actual texts. Overemphasizing the advertising sleight of hand that attended Bolaño's entrance into the U.S. market has its own dangers. It is true that a half made-up biography of the author was not used to distribute Bolaño's fiction in Spain or Latin America as it was in the United States, but it is equally true that Bolaño's Spanish publisher at times made no great effort to avoid a certain degree of sensationalism in choosing posthumous titles such as *The Secret of Evil* or illustrating the cover of *Amberes* with the picture of a woman posing for sadistic sexual practices. In both instances, the uninformed reader will be disappointed. The title story of *The Secret of Evil* is a truncated two-page account of a late-night meeting between two characters that stops before going anywhere, and *Amberes* is for many critics and Bolaño himself unintelligible (Maristain, "Last

Interview" 117). Editorial common sense prevailed, though, in choosing the evocative title of *Nocturno de Chile* over the original title that Bolaño had proposed—"Tormenta de mierda" ("Shit Storm"). In addition the visual presentation of the first four Bolaño novels to come out in English—especially the cover art of *By Night in Chile* and *Distant Star*—tone down any potential sensationalism. The same is true of the reviews of this corpus in publications such as the *Guardian,* the *Telegraph,* and the *New York Times,* reviews that are sober and very much to the point. So the noise around *The Savage Detectives* and *2666* did not typify the reception of all of Bolaño's work in English and will probably die down in the long term.

A more serious problem would be a discrepancy between scholars working on Bolaño in Latin America or Spain and critics and reviewers writing in the United States or the U.K. It certainly happens that English-language reviewers do not always take the time to brush up on the latest Bolaño scholarship and may, in some instances, not be versed in Spanish; and that conversely Latin American scholars may be unaware of the proliferating body of Bolaño criticism being produced in the U.S. academy.[9] But by and large, scholars on both sides of the language divide tend to agree that Bolaño's signature theme is the relation between literature and evil. Bolaño himself confirms the importance of this theme when he says, for example, that in *Distant Star* he attempts "a very modest approximation of absolute evil" ("Self-Portrait," *Between Parentheses* 16), a moral failing that he describes elsewhere as the total erasure of the other: "Wieder is the incarnation of absolute evil. . . . And he is also an artist. Therefore [he represents] absolute evil and absolute art, which has room for many things but not for the presence of the Other. The absolute is a monologue, not a dialogue. All moral reason ceases to exist, every ethical consideration is put aside. The Enlightenment ceases to exist and the reign of terror begins" (Stolzmann 375). Bolaño has also speculated that crime seems to be the symbol of the twentieth century (*Between Parentheses* 222), and confirms that in *Consejos a un discípulo* he talks about violence ("Self-Portrait," *Between Parentheses* 16). We can add that in this Bonnie-and-Clyde type of novel violence forms an unholy alliance with literature. But it is in *2666* that crime, violence, and evil reach an apocalyptic dimension.

Of course, Bolaño also explores other themes: by his own admission he focuses on the theme of beauty in *The Skating Rink,* on the "pathos and grandeur of the writing career" in *Nazi Literature in the Americas,* on adventure in *The Savage Detectives,* and on narrative tone in *Amulet,* where he says he tries to give the reader "the impassioned voice of a Uruguayan woman who should have been born in ancient Greece" ("Self-Portrait," *Between Parentheses* 16). Bolaño's themes have a universal character, which helps explain the global reach of his work. But the *form* of these themes is equally far-reaching. In a

2001 interview Bolaño declared that he likes detective plots because there is nothing more profitable for an author than to track down a criminal or the victim of a disappearance (Braithwaite 118). And more than once he has repeated that if he had not been a writer, he would have liked to be a homicide detective. But Bolaño's handling of the detective genre or police thriller is idiosyncratic. Perhaps the most conventional detective novel in Bolaño's corpus—and only partially so—is *Distant Star,* to the extent that an actual detective is introduced in the later stages of the novel. A novel like *Monsieur Pain* occasionally includes elements of the noir tradition, and *Amulet* actually claims (and quickly disclaims) to be a *roman noir,* though the reader will find it difficult to make the connection between this text and conventional versions of the genre. Even the road story is subordinated to the detective model in Bolaño, as in *The Savage Detectives.* There is an evil policeman in this novel, but the detectives of the title are merely three poets who go in search of a lost poet from an earlier age. The central plot device of *2666* is also the search for an elusive writer. There are some characters in the novel that could have been featured in a police story, but as it happens the main "detectives" of the novel are four literary critics who stand as the *cultured* counterparts of the *savage* detectives of Bolaño's earlier work. In general the detective genre structures the plot in Bolaño's novels but at the cost of being stretched beyond its usual confines.

Finally the detective format is not only universal and able to cut across media (novels, films, plays, even poetry in Bolaño's case) but is a feature of popular culture as well. The post-Boom in Latin American fiction, and postmodernism in general, did involve a fusion of high art with the formats of mass culture. This is perhaps the central modification that Bolaño carried out with respect to the Boom. Without giving up certain kinds of experimentalism in his fiction or surrendering entirely to the facile formats of commercial literature, Bolaño restated the achievements and ambitions of the great Latin American novels in a more accessible language, thus reunifying a literary tradition that lost its center after the 1960s.[10]

Chapter 2

Bolaño the Poet

Bolaño's poetry has not attracted the same kind of critical attention as the author's fiction. One reason for this is that not much of it was available or accessible before the Bolaño Boom started in the late 1990s. By 1998, the year of *The Savage Detectives,* Bolaño had published three poetry collections that despite their relative merits did not enjoy a wide circulation: *Reinventar el amor* (1976)—a slim chapbook published in Mexico in a limited edition of 225 copies that has never been reprinted or translated; *Fragmentos de la universidad desconocida* (1993)—published by a provincial city hall in Talavera de la Reina, Spain; and *Los perros románticos* (1995)—issued by a foundation in Spain's Basque Country.[1] These last two publications owe their eccentric geographical locations to the fact that Bolaño successfully submitted the respective works to local literary contests.

It was not until the year 2000 that Bolaño's poetry began to assume a larger role in the context of the author's critical reception. That was the year when both a second revised edition of *Los perros románticos* and *Tres* were published in Barcelona. *Tres* is a disparate collection of three poetic works from different periods of the author's life, the last of which dates from 1994. Bolaño may have continued writing poetry after 1994 but did not publish any of it. He had spent part of the previous year preparing a major compilation of his poetic works, which was published posthumously with the title *La universidad desconocida* (2007). One wonders why that compilation had to wait a decade and a half before being published, but both *Fragmentos* and *Los perros románticos* were spin-offs of the larger work. If Bolaño's recognition as a poet was slow in developing in Spanish, in English it came even later: *The Romantic Dogs* dates from 2006, *Tres* (bilingual edition) from 2011, and *The Unknown University* from 2013. Of course with the success of *The Savage Detectives,* the novel that recreates the author's infrarealist years in Mexico, Spanish-language critics could not help but reevaluate Bolaño's Mexican poetry, though few found it compelling and the author himself chose to leave it behind.

Another reason for the critical delay in assessing Bolaño's poetry is that the author's poetic corpus does not show much coherence when taken as a whole. Its patterns are like those of a kaleidoscope. Over time poems that were once arranged under specific thematic headings (in *Fragmentos de la universidad desconocida* and *Los perros románticos,* specifically) ended up in a totally different order in *The Unknown University.* The resulting "disorder" gives the impression that Bolaño's poetic project was always provisional, which makes the appeal to the author's fiction in search of grounding an almost irresistible temptation.

The main reason for the relative neglect of Bolaño's poetry among literary critics, however, is that the author's reputation rests on his fiction. There is no question that in Spanish and in translation Bolaño is regarded primarily as the author of two exceptional long novels and some novellas and stories that changed the face of Latin American fiction in the decades after the Boom; as there is no question, furthermore—certainly not among Bolaño scholars—that the line between poetry and prose in Bolaño's writing is very thin. The consensus is that Bolaño's prose is poetic and his poetry narrative, if not prosaic. In practice this has meant that critics approach the author's poetry from the standpoint of his fiction, as sketches or rough drafts that were fully realized only in prose. This approach has its own logic since there are obvious parallels between some of Bolaño's poems and the content of his novels and stories. The poem "The Worm," for example, replicates the story "The Grub," from *Last Evenings on Earth;* the poem "Lupe"refers to an episode more fully developed in *The Savage Detectives;* the poem "The Great Pit" reappears in "Last Evenings on Earth," where it is inserted in the story of the author's holiday trip with his father; and the various poems involving detective figures evoke the hard-boiled thriller, a recurring format in the author's fiction.

Bolaño's poetry is not a supplement but rather a complement to the author's fiction. It is part of a single evolving totality, and yet it can be treated on its own, not so much on account of its intrinsic formal and thematic qualities but because Bolaño the poet occupies a different cultural frame than Bolaño the novelist. As a poet, in other words, Bolaño stands as an interlocutor in a dialogue with other poets of his generation—and their precursors—that takes place in a different and more restricted cultural field than exchanges involving his identity as a writer of prose fiction. It is not an exaggeration to say that as a poet Bolaño acquires a different identity than he has as a novelist, as he himself implies in one of the poems of *The Unknown University,* where he defines himself as a son of the middle classes and a reader of well-known poets such as Rimbaud, Ernesto Cardenal, Nicanor Parra, and Enrique Lihn (731). As a prose fiction writer, as may be imagined, Bolaño would insert himself in a different genealogy involving authors such as Borges, Cortázar, and Kafka. In any event in one of his interviews Bolaño refers to his poetry and fiction as being blood relations, even as he is careful to preserve a degree of separation between them: "My poetry and prose are first cousins who get along fine. My poetry is Platonic, my prose Aristotelian" (Braithwaite 116).

In a different interview Bolaño makes the case that the totality of his work in prose, and even some part of his poetry—as he explicitly states—make up a single whole: "Not only a stylistic but also a thematic whole: characters are constantly talking among themselves and keep appearing and disappearing" (Braithwaite 112). Yet according to this last statement, there is a part of Bolaño's poetry that does not fit in the projected totality of the author's work. Here Bolaño is implicitly referring to the poems of his Mexican phase, a stage that he overcame shortly after moving to Spain and trying his hand at a more fluid style, shorn of the trappings of the earlier neo-avant-garde poetry. In an interview on Chilean TV in the late 1990s Bolaño stated that his Mexican poems did not resist the passing of time and that his move to Spain meant a reappraisal of his poetic posture.

At the beginning of his literary career Bolaño was a neo-avant-garde ringleader who urged neophyte poets to reject social convention and revolutionize everyday life. After his move to Spain, he muted his strident calls for a poetic revolution and did not try to revive the now headless infrarealist group. His poetry became colloquial and more personal. Through different formal and stylistic means, the poems of *The Unknown University* construct a poetic subject or persona that is partially built on the facts of the author's real-life existence. This semiautobiographical subject is primarily a poetic self and should be so regarded even in those cases when the speaker of the poems refers to himself as "Roberto Bolaño." Clearly this semiautobiographical "I" lacks the authority to represent the actual author of the book. The autobiographical "pact" that demands the identity of author, narrator, and protagonist, and that in addition requires referential truth, is suspended. (The same situation obtains for "autofiction.") In the early poems, Bolaño's persona is constructed through his nostalgia for the past, through his romantic and sexual liasons, through his friends and family relations, and through the experience of being an unknown and marginal Latin American immigrant in post-Franco Spain. The self-referential discourse of the book includes everyday "scenes of writing" as well as more general reflections on the practice and meaning of poetry. In general this reflexive strategy exemplifies the fusion of art and life that Bolaño has preached and practiced since his very beginnings: "my literary project and my life are totally fused. They are one and the same" (Dés 138).

Mexican Beginnings: Infrarealism

It has been said more than once that if Bolaño had not written *The Savage Detectives*—the novel that famously recreates the author's life in Mexico in the mid 1970s—critics would have been oblivious to the poetic movement known as infrarealism. But the success of Bolaño's breakthrough novel generated a new (though small) wave of scholarly and journalistic research into a poetic and artistic movement that had little relevance in its time (see Madariaga, for example). Bolaño was the central figure of infrarealism. He not only brought the gang together but also wrote their manifesto and edited the infrarealist anthology *Muchachos desnudos bajo el arcoiris de fuego* (1979), which includes some of his own poems.[2]

The year after returning to Mexico City from his eventful trip to Chile, Bolaño met Mario Santiago at a downtown cafe and struck an immediate and enduring friendship with his wild Mexican counterpart. In an interview conducted over twenty years later, Bolaño remembers his friend as a "very strange person" and as someone who "seemed to have descended from a UFO."[3] In a different incarnation, Santiago was for Bolaño the "Ginsberg of Mexico." Other acquaintances describe the latter as the poet with the most consistent vocation for marginality among the infras and one bent on making a doomed poem out of his life, in which drugs and alcohol played a prominent role. His motto was "to live without a rudder and in a delirium," and one of his habits was to take Bolaño for long rambling walks though the streets of Mexico City after dark. In Mexican author Juan Villoro's signature novel *El testigo* ("The Witness"), Santiago appears as "Ramón Centollo," a rabid and vagrant poet who pesters his friends by recording his poems on their answering machines in the middle of the night. The real Mario Santiago was also deemed a pest by some of his adversaries. Bolaño remembers grafitti that read "Que Bolaño se vaya a Santiago y Santiago también" ("May Bolaño leave for Santiago and Santiago as well"), such a perfectly expressed text that the Chilean-born author thought it might have been composed by his Mexican "partner in crime."

At any rate Bolaño and Santiago—along with another young Chilean poet living in Mexico at the time, Bruno Montané—took it on themselves to recruit other adherents to the infrarealist group among the many aspirants who were to be found at nocturnal gatherings in cafes, or in attendance at the various poetry workshops available at the time in Mexico City. But as Bolaño implied in an interview many years later, the story of infrarealism was really the story of his friendship with Mario Santiago: "Infrarealism was a kind of Dada à la Mexicana. At one point there were many people, not only poets, but also painters and especially loafers and hangers-on. . . . Actually there were only two members, Mario Santiago and me. We both went to Europe in 1977. One night, in Rosellón, France . . . we decided that the movement, such as it was, had come to an end" (Boullosa 66). Mario Santiago died at forty-five in 1998, the year *The Savage Detectives* was published. He was run over by a bus and did not live to read the novel in which he plays such a large role as "Ulises Lima." During his lifetime he published two books of poems that failed to have any real influence on Mexican poetry. His real name was José Alfredo Zendejas.[4]

Bolaño's infrarealist manifesto pays homage to the poets of French symbolism (particularly Rimbaud) and surrealism, and to later influences such as the writers of the U.S. Beat Generation, Hollywood movies, and aspects of popular Mexican culture. Its title was "Déjenlo todo nuevamente" ("Give It All Up Again") and is a direct allusion to André Breton's "Lâchez tout," a brief proclamation to surrealist artists to drop everything and head off along the roads. Breton's text was originally published in the second issue of *Littérature* (new series) in April 1922. Bolaño's manifesto was written in 1976 and published the following year in the only issue of an infrarealist magazine called *Correspondencia Infra, revista menstrual [sic] del movimiento infrarrealista*. The label "infrarealism" may be derived from its earlier usage by Chilean surrealist painter Roberto Matta. Bolaño has stated that infrarealism was a one-man movement started by Matta when he was expelled from the surrealist ranks by Breton—the year would have been 1947—and that lasted three years.[5] In this context, infrarealism would have designated a subversion of surrealism originating from within the ranks of the surrealist movement—a rebellion within a rebellion. The rebellious connotation is important in Bolaño's adoption of the term, but in the Mexico of the 1970s, when surrealist politics had ceased to be relevant, the revolt was directed against the two great "empires" of Latin American poetry in the 1970s, those of Octavio Paz and and Pablo Neruda, as the narrator affirms near the beginning of *The Savage Detectives,* a novel where the infrarealists appear under the name "real visceralists."

In its new avatar, infrarealism designates an inversion of the surrealist vision. Just as the surrealists were searching for a point above or beyond reality where all contradictions were reconciled and the Absolute could be glimpsed, the infrarealists directed their gaze below to everyday social reality, life in the streets, and popular language and culture. One of Bolaño's criteria for recognizing the true poet was his ability to live *a la intemperie*—out in the open, exposed to the elements, with no shelter or roof over his head. Bolaño's poets were "children of the mire"—ironically the title of a seminal study of modern poetry by Octavio Paz, originally delivered as the Charles Eliot Norton lectures at Harvard. One is reminded of Baudelaire's famous parable in *Paris Spleen* about the poet's loss of halo in modernity, an age when the poet has ceased to be the "eater of ambrosia" and the "drinker of quintessences" in order to become an "ordinary mortal." His halo has slipped off his head and fallen into the mire of the macadam, which allows him to be like any other citizen adrift in the emerging urban cacophony. The infras would have liked to be descendants of Baudelaire. They came from the working classes and turned their proletarian vision of the city, society, and the literary institution into fighting words.

The infrarealist manifesto was a clarion call to "poetic action," a call that involved a revolutionary vision of society and poetry. The infras came together only a few years after the student massacre of Tlatelolco, a historical event that delegitimated the Mexican ruling party and that took place when Bolaño was fifteen and had just arrived in Mexico City. Bolaño and the infras identified with the student movement and with its demands to check government authoritarianism and corruption, a position that explains the manifesto's emphasis on sabotaging bourgeois values and on siding with revolutionary movements. The stamp of the U.S. Beat writers on the manifesto is revealed in the eagerness with which Bolaño urges poets to launch themselves on the road: "Risk is always somewhere else. The true poet is the one who's always letting go of himself. Never too much time in the same place, like guerrillas, like UFOs, like the white eyes of prisoners serving life sentences."[6] The manifesto also urges poets to explore urban space: "The death of the swan, the swan song, the last song of the black swan, IS NOT in the Bolshoi but in the intolerable pain and beauty of the streets." This exploration would not be carried out in the solitary manner of the nineteenth-century dandy (or *flâneur*) but as a group, as is fully shown in certain scenes from *Amulet* and *The Savage Detectives*.

In the end the infrarealists did not succeed in breaking into the mainstream of Mexican literature. The group was short-lived, its publications scarce and ephemeral, and its artistic legacy negligible. Infrarealism turned out to be more an ethic than an aesthetic; more about living a certain kind of literary life than bequeathing an artistic legacy to posterity. For Bolaño these were years of intellectual apprenticeship, of youthful exuberance and discovery, of passion and adventure, and of a general feeling of defiance that accorded well with the spirit of the avant-garde that informed the infrarealist approach to life and poetry and gave it its militant tone. Bolaño was the only member of the group who succeeded in fusing art and life in a lasting and meaningful way.

The infrarealist manifesto, therefore, is also a convenient snapshot of Bolaño at the beginning of his literary career, when he was a disheveled young poet looking for a place in the literary map of the strange new country where he had landed. It also serves as a general framework to place Bolaño's poetry of the period. For example one of Bolaño's poems in the *Muchachos desnudos* anthology perfectly illustrates the nonconformist drift of the manifesto and the poet's debt to Rimbaud. The poem "Notas para componer un espacio" ("Notes to Compose a Space") is almost a rewriting of a passage of Rimbaud's "The Foolish Virgin," one of the sections of *A Season in Hell*. The speaker in this passage is Rimbaud's fellow poet Verlaine, with whom Rimbaud had a dramatic affair that ended with Verlaine shooting his younger companion in the hand: "I don't love women. Love has to be reinvented, we know that. The only thing women can ultimately imagine is security. Once they get that, love, beauty, everything else goes out the window: all they have left is cold disdain, that's what marriages live on nowadays. Sometimes I see women who ought to be happy, with whom I could have found companionship, already swallowed up by brutes with as much feeling as an old log" (Schmidt 226).

In Bolaño's poem the speaker recounts in a plain narrative style how the women who arrive at the Casa del Lago (a cultural center located in Chapulte-pec Park) with their cars and kids watch him with indifference and stroll through the galleries gazing at "rotting" paintings executed by "decent young men" (from whose company the speaker implicitly excludes himself), all the while transmitting through their movements the self-assurance of a rising petite bourgeoisie. These women appear to the poet as degraded versions of their younger selves, "girls / in their first semester of Philosophy / appearing when least expected in your / room of those years and screaming I love you I love you" (142). At the end of the poem the bourgeois women stuff their things in their cars—handbags, posters, kids—and take off to pick up their husbands at the office, while the poet walks in the opposite direction sickened by the thought of those girls who not long ago had discovered sexual pleasure in his bed. Bolaño's and Rimbaud's speakers agree that love has to be reinvented.

Reinventar el amor is the most substantial work of Bolaño's Mexican pe-riod. Rimbaud's influence is obviously present in the title and perhaps too in the poem's structure. *Reinventar el amor* is a relatively long poem divided into nine sections identified by Roman numerals. It is a serial work, like Rim-baud's *Season in Hell*, though it is not written in prose. It is dedicated to Efraín Huerta, an established Mexican poet who was the mentor of the infrarealists and the cultural antagonist of Octavio Paz in the 1970s. It is not an easy poem to read, but it helps to project it against the infrarealist manifesto, which pro-vides the poem with a meaningful context. In the manifesto Bolaño states that the infrarealists have two points of departure: "the barricade and the bed," an aphorism that joins lovemaking with revolutionary fervor and that recalls the Rimbaud of the Paris Commune. The poem does emphasize these two points of departure when the speaker proclaims toward the end, "Love will come with the Class Struggle" (18), but the subversive impetus demanded of poetry in the infrarealist manifesto is tempered in the poem by Bolaño's romantic sensibil-ity. In a brief autobiographical sketch he wrote in 1979 for a poetry anthology, Bolaño confesses to have been in love with an English girl (in reality Lisa John-son, who appears as "Laura Jáuregui" in *The Savage Detectives*) and to have learned "that though the loss of love may be torrential, one must love. To love up front and sideways. Like a flying saucer. I also strongly remember that say-ing by Breton . . . : *love and poetry are both made in bed*" (Bianchi 166). Breton, of course, believed that love was an aspect of the surrealist revolution, but in *Reinventar el amor* the fusion of love and the class struggle sounds more like a statement of principle than a poetic experience. The poem does not prepare the reader for that kind of "illumination," which at any rate points toward an uncertain future and is no more than a utopian vision. The poem's closing lines are these: "From infrareality we come, where are we going?" (18).

The rest of the poem tries to impress the reader by means of a surprising juxtaposition of images (like Columbus crossing the limits of the known world in a pickup truck), by the suppression of transitions, and by the constant shift-ing of pronominal perspectives, a strategy that often creates more incoherence than the desired poetic effect. Some of the images are effective in a traditional sort of way ("Everything is born in the heart like the worm is born out of noth-ingness in the core of the apple" [7]), but those that try to sound more modern are not always as original as the avant-garde "tradition of rupture" would pre-scribe. An image such as "Rainbows like birds took off in flight" (11) evokes the poetry of Chilean avant-garde poet Vicente Huidobro—whose name is actually mentioned in the same stanza—while other passages mentioning radios and telegraphs sending mesages to "the capitals of the world" (9) recall the poetry of Mexican avant-garde poet Manuel Maples Arce, who figures largely in *The Savage Detectives*.[7]

Still, the poem has an interesting concept that illustrates one of the points made in the infrarealist manifesto: "the poem as a journey and the poet as a hero who reveals heroes." Its central structure seems to be the superimposition of three journeys or road trips: that of Rimbaud in "The Drunken Boat," that of Columbus in search of discoveries, and that of the poet through parts of Mexico handing out sodas in a delivery truck (which is actually an autobio-graphical reference). The point of the poetic trip, to quote the manifesto once again, is to reveal new sensations, a project that involves a Rimbaldian disori-entation of the senses.

The poem's structure is interesting in view of Bolaño's future development because Bolaño structures much of his later poetry and fiction as discrete blocks of text interconnected by recurring motifs that are functionally meaningful. In *2666*, for example, these motifs can be a name, a date, a place, or an anecdote mentioned in passing whose function is to hold together the five parts of the novel. The same principle applies to other novels and to semipoetic texts like "People Walking Away" and "Prose from Autumn in Gerona." In *Reinventar el amor* the links between the different sections can be the intermittent recur-rence of the Columbus figure, a repeated syntactic structure with variations ("Everything suddenly exists"), actually recurring phrases ("End of the world and waterfalls"), or single words or images ("honey" or "hips") that do not seem to have a fixed meaning in their immediate contexts. (The second section, however, is curiously isolated, as if it did not belong in the sequence.) The practice of loosely connecting different textual blocks allows for freedom of invention and composition without surrendering the notion of overall meaning.

And this practice, of course, is not confined to single works in Bolaño's corpus. The whole of Bolaño's writing is made up of discrete works that sustain implicit or explicit relations between them, relations that must often be provided by an active reader. As one critic has eloquently put it, Bolaño's expanding universe is made up of "stories and pieces and novels that evolved into sections of other stories and then novels, while sections of novels were fragmented into other novels with new names or slightly altered names but in a new relationship with other texts. Bolaño did not leave things behind but threw them back into the stew, this evolving project of a multidimensional universe turning like a grand kaleidoscope of symbols and metaphors and themes and meanings with secret passageways, wormholes back and forth in time and place, occult intentions and shadowed suggestions, placed and replaced in different orders or alongside different texts" (Miles 139).

Postinfrarealism: *The Unknown University*

The Unknown University is the most complete compilation of the author's poetry in Spanish or English to date. In this context, the term "poetry" has to be understood in a broad sense, for the compilation includes some texts in prose and in "poetic prose." On the other hand, the collection cannot be considered Bolaño's complete poetry because it excludes the infrarealist poems of the 1970s, "A Stroll through Literature" (published in *Tres*), some of the poems included in the revised edition of *Los perros románticos,* and the unpublished poetry said to be deposited in the writer's archive. (An exhibit of the archive was held in Barcelona between March and June of 2013.)[8] But it does include the bulk of the poetry that Bolaño wrote in Spain. Furthermore the book comes with notes by Bolaño himself that help to organize material that extends from the late 1970s to 1994. The notes, however, are not entirely reliable. Bolaño claims that the section "A Happy Ending" is from 1992, but it includes a poem clearly dated 1994. Because the notes are dated 1993, it is possible that this later poem was added by the book's editors and was not part of Bolaño's original design. The title of the collection is clarified in one of the poems:

> Between Friedrich von Hausen
> the minnesinger
> and strongman
> don Juanito Nazario.

> In a Barcelona full of Latin Americans
> with and without cash, legal
> and illegal trying
> to write.
> (Dear Alfred Bester, at least
> I've found one of the wings
> of the Unknown University!)
> (285)

The translation of the "strongman don Juanito Nazario" does not capture the fact that "Nazario" was in reality Nazario Luque, a cartoonist in the Barcelona of the mid-1970s, and that Don Juanito el Supermacho was one of the comic book characters he created. Alfred Bester, on the other hand, is the American science-fiction author of "The Men Who Murdered Mohammed" (1958), a story where time travel and murder intersect and where the following passage is to be found: "Nobody knows where Unknown University is or what they teach there. It has a faculty of some two hundred eccentrics, and a student body of two thousand misfits—the kind that remain anonymous until they win Nobel prizes or become the First Man on Mars." Bolaño was an avid reader of science fiction; however the significance of the title has nothing to do with that genre but rather with the fact that Bolaño was a school dropout and self-declared *autodidacta* (a self-educated person). From an early age he devoured books that his mother and friends lent him, or that he lifted from Mexico City bookstores—until later in life when he was able to afford them. Bolaño's school was the streets and cities where he lived. Referring in his notes to the first seven sections of *The Unknown University,* the author states that these are dated 1978–81 and that a "Barcelona that surprised and *instructed* me appears and disappears in all of the poems" (813; emphasis added).

The Barcelona poems, many of which were originally written down in notebooks called "Diary I," "Diary II," and "Diary III," make up the first part of *The Unknown University,* a little under three hundred pages in the bilingual edition. The second part is composed of two long fragmentary and seminarrative works dated between 1980 ("People Walking Away") and 1981 ("Prose from Autumn in Gerona"). And the third and final part is a miscellaneous series of poems dating mostly from the early 1990s and taking up about 250 pages. These divisions are only partially useful here because there is some chronological overlapping among all three sections. In addition it's hard to find a formal or thematic line separating the first from the third sections, except that the later poems are more sustained (more extensive and written in longer lines) and introduce themes that can be explained by the passing of time. Themes such as nostalgia for an increasingly distant past, the fear of death, and changes in the poet's life (illness, matrimonial separation, and the birth of a son) all find expression in the poetry. The construction of the semiautobiographical persona is thus important to examine.

The Poet's Post-Mexican Self

Bolaño lived in Mexico from the time he was fifteen until the age of twenty-three or twenty-four, with the brief but significant interruption of his trip to Chile at the end of 1973. During this time he dropped out of school, met his best friend Mario Santiago, read profusely and published some poetry, was the leader of the infrarealist poets, spent a good deal of time in the streets and cafes of Mexico City, had his first (and ultimately painful) experience of romantic love, and lived through the final separation between his parents. In the poems of *The Unknown University* the figure of the poet is partially rendered through the memories and nostalgia of these years of apprenticeship.

In the eight hundred pages of *The Unknown University* it is rare to find a poem about Mexico that does not involve a nostalgic reminiscence of the author's friends at that time. There are a couple of poems dedicated to Mexican comic movie actors ("Homage to Resortes," "Homage to Tin Tan"), one—"The Light"—inspired by daybreak in Mexico City (which made the poet cry and hide in one of "those minibuses that took you around / In circles through the suburbs of the dark city" [661]),[9] and two other poems that restate the wandering theme in oneiric terms: "Try Not to Sleep, Roberto, I Tell Myself" (574) and "Prickly Pear," written in the third person but referring once again to the speaker: "He saw the prickly pear, but so far off / it must have been just a dream" (663). The *nopal* reflects the image of a lonely teenager who stands against the threatening background of a storm brewing "on the endless Mexican horizon" (663) and vows to survive.

But most of the poems centering on Bolaño's Mexican memories are about living and dead friends, and their tone is perfectly captured by the opening line of "Mario Santiago": "What could Mario be doing in Mexico?," (227) a line that could also be rendered as "I wonder what Mario is doing in Mexico," since the original Spanish uses the conjectural future tense, "¿Qué estará haciendo Mario en México?" Bolaño's best friend appears in a few other poems including "The Donkey," the most sustained poem of this group and one that has obvious similarities with the plot of *The Savage Detectives* but, unlike its narrative counterpart, is dreamlike and not realistic: "Sometimes I dream that Mario Santiago / Comes looking for me on his black motorcycle" (695). The speaker accepts this variation of Baudelaire's invitation to the journey because the northern roads mentioned in the poem have been traveled by vagabond Mexican poets and wind their way through the desert, "the only imaginable stage / For our poetry" (695). In the third stanza the motorcycle takes on the color of night, slows down, and becomes "a black donkey dawdling / through the lands of Curiosity" (697), an unexpected transformation that expresses the mystery of the journey itself, or the uncertainty of what will be found at its end. The references to the "enigmatic signals" made by the bystanders and to the "confusing and magnetic trail / of donkeys and poets" (699) imply that the objective of this Baudelairean road trip is hidden from view and can only be revealed in its unfolding.

Some other literary friends of Bolaño's are mentioned in these "post-Mexican" poems, for example Efraín Huerta, the mentor of the infrarealists. At the outset the speaker does not know what to say to his mentor as his image comes to mind, but then he goes on to emphasize Huerta's kindness and dignity, "the ease with which / you leaned against the window of your apartment / to observe, in a t-shirt, the Mexican / sunset, while at your back the poets / drank tequila and spoke in whispers" (49). The poem successfully merges its downbeat tone with the lyricism and stillness of its imagery. There are also two poems focusing on infrarealist poet Darío Galicia, a tragic figure who at a young age underwent an operation to correct a brain aneurysm but was left unable to write and died soon thereafter (*Unknown University* 205; *The Romantic Dogs* 57). (In *The Savage Detectives* Galicia appears as "Ernesto San Epifanio.") And there is a short poem celebrating Bruno Montané's thirtieth birthday (567). Montané is the "Felipe Müller" of *The Savage Detectives* and a young Chilean expatriate who wrote poetry and lived in Mexico City between 1974 and 1976, where he became close friends with Bolaño. (Montané was born in 1957 so the poem is probably from 1987.) They both moved to Barcelona at about the same time and collaborated on some forgettable literary projects, with Montané later becoming a musician. The Montané of the poem is older than his fictional counterpart in Bolaño's novel and, unlike the latter, is represented by means of disconnected symbolic moments and not through the biographical details that characterize his later ego "Felipe Müller."

The Poet and Eros

The figure of Lisa Johnson connects these poems of friendship and nostalgia for Mexico with the discourse of love and sensuality through which the poet also represents himself in his poetry. Lisa was Bolaño's great romantic interest as a young man and lived for a few weeks with the future writer when she was sixteen or seventeen. Bolaño's mother accepted her in the family household, but Lisa's mother intervened and took her daughter away from her young lover, who was distraught after the end of the affair and may have even overdosed as a reaction to Lisa's departure (Maristain, *Bolaño: A Biography* 53). Bolaño never forgot her and remembered her in his poetry as late as 1992. In fact his memory of her seems to have intensified with the passing of time. Lisa appears in only one of the Barcelona poems: "At 4 a.m. old photographs of Lisa / / between the pages of a science fiction novel" (17). The rest of the poem has the speaker in a dreamlike reverie from which someone awakes him: "Asleep on the table I say I was a poet, / a little too late, a loved one awakes, / no one has burned the candles of friendship" (17). The translation fails to render the implicit dialogue included in the next-to-the-last line. In the original it is clear that someone addresses the half-asleep poet with a kind reminder that the lover's friendship has not died: "dear, wake up, / no one has burned the candles of friendship." The speaker within the dream may be Lisa herself.

The mood of this poem is recaptured in a later text in which the lovers' initials are carved, as it were, in the folds of memory: "Death / is R.B. and L.J.'s lips in the backseat of a minibus: now I know / no one escapes those avenues. I'll leave it as collateral: / the end of my childhood" (577). The end of childhood and the intimation of death are mixed up in this poem with the loss of the blush of first love. The fact that early experiences of sensual bliss leave lasting scars in memory is one of the lessons learned by the poet in the unknown university: "now I know."

In another of the Lisa poems it is she who now speaks about the bittersweet legacy she left to her former lover: "My gift to you will be an abyss, she said, / but it will be so subtle you'll perceive it / only after many years have passed / and you are far from Mexico and me" (633). Lisa as gift giver, however, contrasts strongly with the image of the lover projected in the most prosaic (and brutal) of these poems, which may or may not reflect the real ending of the affair. In it the poet recounts a conversation with his former lover in a phone booth, in an old Tepeyac warehouse, when she tells him that she had made love to a tall skinny guy with "long hair and a long cock who didn't wait / more than one date to penetrate her deep" (629). The female speaker rationalizes the incident by explaining to her former lover that it was the best way to get him out of her life ("Lisa"). Tepeyac is one of the Mexico City neighborhoods where the Bolaño family lived in the 1970s, a reference that endows the poem with autobiographical verisimilitude. In the second half of the poem Lisa maliciously piles on the graphic details of her escapade, including how long the sexual act took, how many times her new lover ejaculated, and what music was playing during the affair. The poet's response is straightforward: "The worst two hours of my life, / I said from the other end of the phone" (629). In one of his early Mexican poems Bolaño deplores the fact that Lisa did not choose the life of a poet but instead the inauthentic life of a conventional middle-class woman. But that poem ends with a lyrical effusion ("pudo haber sido una gran poeta / la más amorosa / amada / mía")[10] and not on the sadistic note of the later composition.

In many of the poems of *The Unknown University* romantic feelings take the form of carnal love. Bolaño once said that he owed his intellectual education to Mexico but his sentimental education to Spain: "When I came to Spain, I was twenty-three or twenty-four years old. I arrived thinking I was already a man . . . and that I knew everything there was to know about sex, and for me a sentimental education is almost synonymous with a sexual education. In reality, I knew nothing" (Álvarez 79). There is indeed a lot of sex in Bolaño's poetry, and most of it centers on another of the women he knew and who often appears in Bolaño's writing under her own name. Edna Lieberman was an intense Mexican Jewish lover with whom the poet lived for a short while in Barcelona in 1979 and who much later wrote a tasteless and opportunistic book about her time with the writer and about her own fantasies of love following his death.

The most graphic of the Edna poems is "You'll Walk Away," whose blunt beginning is indicative of the rest of the poem: "You'll walk away from that bleeding cunt / who first laughs and then plagiarizes / your poems" (147). Two other traits used to describe the female figure—her sexual smell and freckled legs—reappear in "Go to Hell, Roberto" (101) and in "El Greco" (97), but in other poems concerning the same person it is the eyes that draw the speaker's attention. The poem that begins "I don't feel safe" (279) recalls a later composition called "The Ghost of Edna Lieberman" (711) where the same woman's eyes shine once more for the poet. But there is a great difference between the two poems in the poet's attitude toward his lover. In the earlier poem, the searching gaze belongs to a lover whose erotic intensity overwhelms and threatens the speaker, much like the character of the "Mexican woman" living with the narrator in "Enrique Martín" (*Last Evenings on Earth*), whose temper threatens to make the relationship between him and her "the death of her, and me, and the neighbors, and sometimes even the people who ventured to pay us a visit" (29). In the later poem "The dirt path that led to the madhouse / unfolds itself again like the eyes / of Edna Lieberman" (711), but the poem ends on a note of reconciliation, the former lover's eyes no longer seeking out the poet wherever he hides: "In the dream you go back / to shaking her hands / and no longer ask for anything" (713).[11]

In the poems tracing the speaker's sexual education other women occasionally show up: Lola Paniagua, whom Bolaño remembers making love to in a tent "full of wind and green leaves" in a text from 1979 (Bianchi 167); an Irishwoman named Molly; some other anonymous lovers—but it is Edna who defines the poet's sexual apprenticeship in his early years in Barcelona. In one of the more memorable poems in the collection ("The Acrobat on the Ramblas Says" 151), Bolaño merges the memory of his former lover with the advent of poetry and locates the production of poetry and the lovers' farewell on the Ramblas, Barcelona's main thoroughfare. The crowded boulevard, however, becomes a desert after love is over, and the poet is transformed into a mere street performer, writing poetry for no one. Bolaño's desert is not David Jasper's sacred desert or the messianic territory of Chilean poet Raúl Zurita, but rather a metaphor for the poet's abandoned condition.[12] Finally in "Hope" the poet thanks "heaven for having made love / to the women I've cared about" (179), a statement that seems to encapsulate the lessons learned by the poet in the battlefields of love. These women—Lisa, Edna, Carolina, and others—are serially remembered in "The Sunset," a poem written in the early 1990s.

The Nomadic Proletarian

When Bolaño arrived in Barcelona in 1977, he was an undocumented immigrant in search of work whose brief experience of imprisonment in Pinochet's Chile extended him a passport, as it were, to frequent many other exiles from Latin American dictatorships. To be sure, Barcelona was not the only Spanish city to receive an influx of refugees in the late 1970s. Figures show that between 1976 and 1986 twenty thousand Argentines, for example, migrated to Spain for political and economic reasons (Actis 149). It is not surprising, therefore, that many of Bolaño's Barcelona poems portray the writer as a recently arrived outsider reduced to wandering the streets and docks of the city by himself or frequenting bohemian groups made up of local residents and displaced foreigners. In the poem beginning "In District 5 with the Latin Americans" (275), the speaker addresses himself as part of a group, but in the Spanish original the "Latin Americans" of the opening line are *sudacas,* a pejorative term applied in Spain at the time to South American exiles.

The poems in the Barcelona section of *The Unknown University* tend to be brief—sometimes composed of no more than two lines—and are not backed by any sort of manifesto, like the author's Mexican efforts. They don't evince, as a critic points out, a "persistent poetic project" (Ayala 92) but strike the reader as a series of occasional insights drawn from everyday reality and from the experience of life in a new city where the poet is a marginal denizen. As stated earlier many of them were written down in notebooks that functioned as a diary for the author. Bolaño's notebooks, as one scholar writes, are interesting because they give clues about the writer and his context and because they "offer a glimpse of Roberto Bolaño's time as a *flaneur* [*sic*] in Barcelona, where his exercises in voice, point of view and style render a fly-eyed reality of life in District V during the late 1970s" (Miles 138). Indeed, the poem as journal entry may be read as a testimony of an external reality but only if one takes into account the predominance of a subjective point of view. The term "flâneur," however, seems less appropriate than that of "nomadic proletarian" that the poet applies to himself as he meditates on his itinerant existence in his new urban environment (181).

There is an interesting reference in the District 5 poem to the troubadours because a short section of the Barcelona poems is dedicated to the medieval Provenzal poet Guiraut de Bornelh; the troubadour serves as a projection of Bolaño the urban nomad. Guiraut, furthermore, is known for having given up the hermetic style of some Provenzal poetry (*trobar clus*) in order to cultivate the more popular style known as *trobar leu*. It is possible to find in Bolaño's poetry the same oscillation between cryptic and demotic poems. The latter are more prosaic and less elliptical and tend to be narrative in form, like the poem that begins "It's nightime and I'm in the Zona Alta / in Barcelona and I've drunk / more than three cafés con leche / with some people I don't know" (245). The best ones, however, fall somewhere in between, like the last poem in the section (287), in which the reader does not know who is being addressed in the final tercet but understands that the message to that mysterious "you" is a response to the poet's isolation, which here takes the form of a quarantine. This is the only poem in Bolaño's work in which the speaker represents himself as a leper.

There are many other poems in the Barcelona section of *The Unknown University* in which Bolaño portrays himself as a lonely outsider suffering from anxiety (5), reflecting on his marginal condition (43), reading by himself improbable books in a bar (123), or working as a night watchman in a campground (249). At times this solitary figure is specifically Chilean, as in the poem that begins "The day will come when they'll call you from the street" (117).[13] At other times, the poet's self-portrait is more ironic than confessional: "In the reading room of Hell . . . / With cigarette in mouth and with fear / Sometimes / green eyes / And 26 years / Yours truly" (135).

But Bolaño also presents himself as a poet either in the act of writing or reflecting on the meaning and status of poetry. The theme of poetry, for example, is highlighted in the two "Trojan" poems of this section. "With the Flies" is as brief as it is intense:

> Poets of Troy
> Nothing that could have been yours
> Exists anymore
>
> Not temples not gardens
> Not poetry
>
> You are free
> Admirable poets of Troy.
> (187)

In Bolaño's work poets and writers in general are often located in the middle of historical upheavals, as may be seen in a story like "Henri Simon Leprince" and in *Distant Star* and the last part of *2666*. In these texts writers and poets have a role to play in conflicts such as the Second World War or the Pinochet coup in Chile. This location of writing brings out pointed issues concerning literary politics and ethics and endows literature with an epic dimension that Bolaño seems to be giving up in the poem above, where the Trojan War appears as a remote occurrence from the past (and a new *Illiad* seems impossible) and poets are relieved from the responsibility to take on grandiose themes and have to forge new poetic myths. In the Latin American tradition, Neruda was the epic poet par excellence. Bolaño could never fully shake Neruda's influence (see "Dance Card" in *Last Evenings on Earth*), but in this poem—where flies replace traditional poetic symbols like the swallow, nightingale, or swan—he is attesting to some kind of poetic failure that may have to do as much with his own limitations as with the nature of the times he is living through or the status of poetry in the postmodern world. As in the other "Trojan" poem (188), poets continue to be admirable survivors, but poetry is affected by "plague and leprosy" and linked once again to the desert.

There is no coherent poetic project in *The Unknown University* and no unified manifesto that might function as a poetics of the book. There is a section called "Manifestos and Positions" with only three poems in it and a prose text that might have been included in any of the author's story collections. But the poems belong to different periods and none of them embodies anything like a theory of poetry. The one from 1979—"Chilean Poetry Is a Gas," a title that alludes to the Rolling Stones' "Jumpin' Jack Flash"—is too anguished and bitter even to serve as a theory of antipoetry.[14] In it Bolaño admits that only he cares about what he writes and that what he writes has ruined him. The later "manifesto" poems are invectives against Spanish and Latin American poets who found a place in the system but sold out in the process: "And I saw / their satisfied little faces, solemn cultural attachés and rosy / Editors in chief, manuscript readers and poor / Copy editors, poets of the Spanish language, who go by the / name of Horde" ("Horde" 523). Obviously the speaker in these poems is situated outside a cultural establishment that rejects him. At this point in his career Bolaño was still a little-known writer whose chief claim to fame were the provincial prizes he had won in Spain.

The Poetic Self in "People Walking Away" and "Prose from Autumn in Gerona"

In formal terms many of the poems included in *The Unknown University* are characterized by pronominal shifts that displace the figure of the speaker from the conventional "I" to the second- and third-person pronouns, or to symbolic projections like the mysterious "Gaspar" of some of the poems. (Quezada—a family friend who knew Bolaño as a teen—refers to Bolaño as "Kaspar Hauser" on account of his lone-wolf habits at the time, 22.)[15] In fact one of the Barcelona poems opens with the question, "Does it amuse you that I write in third person?" (98), where all three personal pronouns refer to the poet himself. These shifts and projections are particularly marked in the long seminarrative works that make up the central section of *The Unknown University,* and contribute to making these aborted narratives, more than enigmatic, almost illegible.

In both these texts poetic space is "deconstructed" even more radically than in a Cubist painting or Cubist poetry, partially because the use of cinematographic techniques means that transitions are faster and whatever action there is, moves dizzyingly in and out of the frame. Montage, juxtaposition of images taken from "real life" and from what appears to be a movie screen, ellipsis, and the puzzling use of quotation marks (as if coming from random movie scripts) are some of the techniques displayed by "People Walking Away" and "Prose from Autumn in Gerona." In the latter the image of the kaleidoscope functions as a master trope for the whole composition. Both these works are long and fragmentary. They generate large gaps between (and within) the fragments for the implied reader to operate what is ultimately an improbable synthesis. They are baroque narrative experiments for an author who had yet to publish his first novel or story. And if they illustrate the fusion of poetry and prose in the author's work, they do so less effectively than many of the more manageable narrative poems included in the same volume. Understanding these two works is a challenge that can be only partially met.

"People Walking Away" is from 1980, but it was not published until it was issued as a novel in 2002 (with the title *Amberes*), probably to the consternation of Bolaño's readers, who had become acquainted with the author through the novels he had published since *Nazi Literature in the Americas* and for whom this new Bolaño installment must have seemed dissonant, to say the least. Amberes (Antwerp) is not just the name of a Belgian city (and therefore linked to the figure of Sophie Podolski) and the title of one of the poem's fragments. It is also a street in Mexico City's "Zona Rosa," which used to be fashionable but that began its downward slide in the 1980s. There are some differences between the original version of "People Walking Away" and *Amberes* that to some degree enhance the narrativity and intelligibility of the text (Moíño Sánchez). In English, however, these few changes are enriched by the fact that two different translators were involved in rendering these two versions in a second language, though the different translations neither add nor take away from the work's complications. Both "People Walking Away" and *Antwerp* preserve the same structure, according to which the narrative fragments are introduced by thematically relevant titles. Each of these fragments could be considered a prose poem, and each poses the question of its relative autonomy. The threads or links between the fragments are equally problematic, but so is the whole referential system of language, since time, space, and the speaker's identity—as well as the constant ambiguity between dream and reality, and between movie scenes and "real" occurrences—are quite fluid.

An important critic (quoted on the back cover of *Antwerp*) described the novel as the Big Bang of Bolaño's fictional universe, but that claim is hard to sustain. Bolaño himself is less sanguine about the novel's achievement, admitting in more than one interview that it was mauled by the critics and is practically illegible. In his notes to *The Unknown University,* he calls "People Walking Away" a *poem* that owes much to his reading of William Burroughs and says that he wrote it while he worked as a night watchman in a campground in Castelldefels (a beach community half an hour by train from Barcelona). But he calls the same work a *novel* in his prologue to *Antwerp,* significantly titled "Total Anarchy." He adds that he wrote it for himself or for his ghosts, and that in those days he lived exposed to the elements and without papers. He implies that he was aware of the work's difficulty when he says, "I never brought this novel to any publishing house. . . . They would've slammed the door in my face and I'd have lost the copy" (ix). But of course by 2002 Bolaño was getting on with publishers and editors like a house on fire. Despite the work's hermeticism, it is possible to follow a semiautobiographical thread that grounds the text on familiar territory and gives the reader some interpretive parameters. But even here there is ambiguity because the speaking "I" can easily become a "you" or a "he," or take on other identities.

"People Walking Away" opens with a "kid" (*muchacho*) approaching the Tara mansion in a Hollywood lot and with the implicit declaration that the whole poem—like a movie set—is nothing but appearance. The initial fragment is focalized through three pronominal perspectives (I, you, he) all of which refer to the protagonist approaching the dismantled mansion. The dismantled mansion is a metaphor for the "self-deconstructed" work that the reader has in his hands. The speaker of the fragment is a South American whose accent is mocked by his Spanish acquaintances. This character is replaced in the next fragment by a "man" who "writes postcards because breathing prevents him from writing the poems he'd like to write" ("People" 305). This foreign subject who is described as a frustrated poet is given the name "Roberto Bolaño" in the fourth fragment and located in the same neighborhood and street where the author lived when he moved to Barcelona. It is significant that as he lies in bed he repeats "meaningless words" to himself, words "that drift away from one another" (311).[16] In Spanish the verb translated as "to drift" is *alejarse,* which connects the fragment with the work's title ("Gente que se aleja").[17] One final note about this chapter is that the speaker is haunted by ghosts that in the poem arise indistinctly from his memories and from images seen on a movie screen.

In a later fragment the Bolaño character is given the correct age that the author had in 1980 when he wrote the poem, twenty-seven (317). In this same text (and elsewhere in the poem) the speaker identifies with the Belgian poet Sophie Podolski, dead by her own hand at an early age. He also concedes that he is alone and that all the "literary shit"—presumably the author's literary life and works of the previous years—fell by the wayside: "poetry journals, limited editions, the whole dreary joke behind me now" (317). This means that "People Walking Away" was a turning point for Bolaño, both an endpoint to what at the time seemed like a frustrated career but also the possibility of a break with the past and a new beginning. In one of the Barcelona poems the speaker wonders why he cannot write something that will interest readers (8). The loosely handled crime elements of the story (the poem is full of references to one or several murders, stretcher bearers, policemen, and detectives) have led critics to assert that in this poem Bolaño was experimenting with the techniques of detective fiction that would later prove useful in his better-known novels. The crime-thriller plot in "People Walking Away," however, is truncated and never jells. But the detective and police figures are avatars of Bolaño himself, one of whose often repeated statements is that he would have preferred to be a homicide detective to being a writer.

The autobiographical references continue throughout the text, and the author (dramatized as such in one of the fragments) portrays himself in a manner similar to the poems of *The Unknown University* analyzed earlier, namely through his memories of Mexico, his romantic and erotic relations, and his identity as both an immigrant and a writer. The two women mentioned earlier—Lisa and Edna—reappear in certain fragments, and the local police are described as being on the lookout for illegal immigrants. The section entitled "Summer" synthesizes some of these motifs:

> There's a secret sickness called Lisa. Like all sicknesses it's miserable
> and it comes on at night. In the weave of a mysterious language whose
> words signify without exception that the foreigner "isn't well." And
> somehow I would like her to know that the foreigner is "having a hard
> time," "in strange lands," "without much chance of writing epic
> poetry" (419).

The text goes on to describe the writer—who works as a night watchman in a campground—as a "dirty man . . . hauling barrels of garbage" and as a "waiter who sees himself being filmed as he walks along a deserted beach" (419). Lisa, then, functions as a perspective from which the author looks at himself in these years of desperation and frustration, but so do movie images that multiply the author's imaginary identities. One of the recurring and more puzzling characters in the work is the hunchback, who may or not be a deformed projection of the author. The narrator says that "Bolaño" may have met him in Mexico but there is no record of such a personage in the author's Mexican experience. The hunchback may be a reflection of a story by Roberto Arlt (an important early twentieth-century Argentina writer whom Bolaño mentions in "The Vagaries of the Literature of Doom," *Between Parentheses*) called, precisely, "El jorobadito" ("The Hunchback").

In the last analysis, "People Walking Away" is not the truncated story of a crime (as some critics argue) but the story of the difficult birth of a personal literary style. The final fragment states the following: "Of what is lost, irretrievably lost, all I wish to recover is the daily availability of my writing, lines capable of grasping me by the hair and lifting me up when I'm at the end of my strength" (433).

The companion piece of "People Walking Away" in *The Unknown University* is "Prose from Autumn in Gerona," another fragmentary and dislocated prose poem (or poetic narrative) written a year after the earlier work when Bolaño had already moved to his sister's empty house on the outskirts of that provincial Spanish capital. "Prose from Autumn" is considerably shorter than "People Walking Away" and does not use subtitles to identify the various fragments that compose it, some of which are only one or two lines long. The poem appears to be an unhappy love story involving an unnamed female figure and the same autobiographical subject who recurs in the Barcelona poems. ("People Walking Away" can also be considered a Barcelona poem in terms of its date and some thematic characteristics.) Once again the influence of the movies and cinematographic techniques (panning shots, dissolves, montage) are paramount in structuring the text, but the master trope of this image-centered work is the kaleidoscope.

The text begins by introducing the general narrative situation from the perspective of a narrator who refers to himself as a second and third person and who is inside a kaleidoscope catching sight of an eye that watches him. The function of the kaleidoscope is to mediate the relation between the text and external reality and to "authorize" the constant shifts in perspective that typify the narration. At times the constant pronominal displacements create the impression that the poem is a movie script or the action of a movie in the process of being filmed, as when a movie camera is mentioned or the female lead screams something to the effect that the script is rubbish. Textual self-consciousness is also displayed by the narrator when he demands to get out of his own text.

There are some moments in the text when Bolaño's kaleidoscopic writing finds an anchor in autobiographical reality, as when the narrator alludes to

R.B.'s passport, issued in October 1981 and authorizing the bearer to live—but not work—in Spain for three months. But more generally this narrator, plainly recognizable as Bolaño, projects himself as the "author" of the work in question or as one of his characters. The female protagonist of the poem is also viewed from different perspectives but seems to be the same person throughout. She is seen in the narrator's apartment and also on her way to a train station when the brief affair is over. The romantic nature of the story is encapsulated by the phrase "Crack, his heart" (471), an utterance belonging to the narrator as he watches his presumed lover asleep but remote from his concerns.[18]

Self-Portraits

Bolaño exemplifies his belief in the fusion of art and life by projecting a semi-autobiographical persona in his poems, a poetic self grounded on aspects of the author's life in Mexico and on his apprenticeship in the "unknown university" of an alien city in which he is a marginal stranger. Bolaño also wrote poems focused on his mother and father in which he presents himself as a filial figure (for example "A Happy Ending" 803). In other poems he himself becomes the father and talks affectionately about his newborn son. The final section of *The Unknown University* is called "A Happy Ending" and is subtitled "the poet as child and the child of the poet." It includes several poems addressed to the poet's son, Lautaro, as well as two self-portraits referring to the time when the author was a child in his native Chile. In a third poem "Roberto Bolaño's self-portraits" give way to "Lautaro Bolaño's self-portraits," as the father's youthful dreams—shattered by the weight of reality—are reborn in the son's illusions (801).

In other poems of this type, in which the poet comes close to autobiographical writing, Bolaño reviews key moments of his life. In "Self-Portrait at Twenty Years" he remembers the fear experienced during his trip to Chile at the time of Pinochet's coup and his brief incarceration: "I put my cheek against Death's cheek" (621). But in this experience he also finds a peculiarly Latin American kind of solidarity: "thousands of guys like me, baby-faced / or bearded, but Latin American, all of us, / brushing cheeks with Death" (621). In "The Romantic Dogs" the poet is again twenty years of age and returns to the memory of his lost native country, but he emphasizes the dream he gained as compensation: "I'd lost a country / but won a dream. / As long as I had that dream / nothing else mattered, / not working, not praying, / not studying in morning light / alongside the romantic dogs" (673). The romantic dog is an image of the infrarealist poet, orphaned, nomadic, and marginal.[19] And maturing back then, he adds, would have been a crime: "I'm here, I said, with the romantic dogs / and here I'm going to stay" (673). But time caught up with the poet and the romantic and poetic dreams of youth were eventually tested by the hostile realities of middle age. "Roberto Bolaño's Devotion" is a poem written in the third person detailing the author's illness and his separation from his wife but reaffirming his faith in the poetic dream: "Dreams took him to that magical country / he and no one else called Mexico City / and Lisa and the voice of Mario Santiago / reading a poem" (723). And in another self-portrait written in the third person Bolaño gives a full account of himself, emphasizing his personal qualities (a brave and beautiful boy unconcerned with money), his poetic upbringing (a reader of Rimbaud, Lihn, and Parra among others), and his identity as a vagabond Latin American poet full of dreams and a foreigner in Europe (731).

The last poem of *The Unknown University* is not strictly speaking a self-portrait (though Bolaño refers to himself by name) but a homage to the poetic muse that echoes Dante's line about the love that moves the sun and the other stars: "She was more beautiful than the sun / and I wasn't even 16 years old. / 24 have passed / and she's still at my side" ("Muse" 805). The muse is like an amulet from which the poet seeks protection for himself and his son: "Take care of my steps and the steps / of my son Lautaro" (805) It is also the spirit that guides the poet through the upheavals of his life and his wanderings in the desert: "I saw you in the hospitals / and in the line / of political prisoners. / I saw you in the terrible eyes / of Edna Lieberman. . . . Because with you I can cross / the great desolate spaces" (807–11) The last stanza is fully Dantean: "Muse, / more beautiful than the sun, / more beautiful / than the stars" (811).

Postscript: "The Neochileans" and "A Stroll through Literature"

"The Neochileans" (dated 1993) is the last poem that Bolaño wrote for *The Unknown University,* but it was first published, along with "Prose from Autumn in Gerona" and "A Stroll through Literature," in *Tres* (2000). It is a narrative poem written in short and broken lines whose theme is the road trip of a Chilean rock band through the Chilean desert and into Peru and Ecuador. As such the poem anticipates the final section of *The Savage Detectives,* but its time frame is that of the Pinochet dictatorship in Chile and the terrorism of Shining Path in Peru, which was at its peak in the 1980s. The poem is more visionary than realistic and does not focus on the autobiographical subject but on a third person, namely the vocalist of the band, who is seized by fever and dies after having hallucinations about lost friends and the ravages of history, and after attempting to recount a novel read many years earlier. The novel is not named, but it can be identified as Jorge Délano's *Kundalini, el caballo fatídico* ("Kundalini, the Fateful Horse"). The Bolaño who portrays himself in his own poetry is recognizable in this poem as the narrator who is possessed by a nomadic impulse and acquainted with two "South American pilgrims" who end up in Barcelona. The poem's title is ambiguous but seems to refer to both the new Chile under Pinochet and to the imperative to break with it. The poem is dedicated to Rodrigo Lira, a young Chilean poet much admired by Bolaño who committed suicide during the military dictatorship.

"A Stroll through Literature" (1994) is a sequence of fifty-four numbered fragments that read like an oneiric diary of the author's literary preferences. All but a few of the fragments begin with the clause "I dreamt." The text invokes a number of different Latin American and world writers who do or say improbable things and who appear to the author as if in a vision. In some of the fragments the poet represents himself as "Bolaño," as when the poet dreams he is a sick and old detective who looks in the mirror and recognizes in it the image of Roberto Bolaño (17). In two of the other fragments, the poet dreams that he is fifteen and is about to abandon the Southern Hemisphere. In one of them (26) he stops at the house of Nicanor Parra to say goodbye, and in the other (27) he puts César Vallejo's *Trilce* in his backpack, and the backpack catches fire.[20] The first and last fragments focus on Georges Perec, the author of *W or the Memory of Childhood,* where Perec writes, "I have no childhood memories" (6).[21]

It is ironic that Bolaño's first dream in "A Stroll through Literature" is about Perec at three years of age. Perec visits the poet's house, and the poet embraces and kisses him and tells him he is an adorable child. In the final fragment Perec is once again a three-year-old child, but this time he's crying disconsolately, and the speaker dreams that he offers him candy and takes him to the park. It begins to rain, and they both walk calmly home. The text ends by asking where home is. There is some autobiographical detail in this sequence of numbered fragments, but the whole sequence articulates a literary biography of the author. Borges constructs the protagonist of his well-known story "Pierre Menard, Author of the Quixote" by means of an *active* bibliography, that is, by meticulously listing all the works authored by his character. Bolaño, for his part, portrays himself in "A Stroll through Literature" through a *passive* bibliography, by enumerating the works he has read.

Chapter 3

The Turn to Fiction

Bolaño's Early Novels (1981–93)

When Bolaño arrived in Barcelona in January 1977, he brought with him a poetic reputation that did not extend beyond a small circle of friends—most of whom had been left behind in Mexico City—but he sought to build on that reputation by writing a more direct and colloquial kind of poetry than he had written in his Mexican years and by remaining involved in editorial projects that still bore the infrarealist stamp. For example as late as 1983 he was collaborating with friend and former infrarealist poet Bruno Montané in the publication of a literary review called *Berthe Trépat* (after one of the characters in Cortázar's *Hopscotch*), whose only two issues (corresponding to the months of July and November) included material from poets within the infrarealist movement or close to it in spirit. These poems are dated variously from 1979 to 1983, and their authors range from Enrique Lihn and Diego Maquieira to Mario Santiago, Montané, and Bolaño himself.[1] (A few years earlier, in 1979, Bolaño had edited the *Muchachos desnudos* anthology of infrarealist poetry, but the contract for this publication had been signed by Bolaño before his departure from Mexico.) These editorial projects did not do a great deal to increase Bolaño's visibility, and the poems that the transplanted Chilean author had been writing since 1977 were not published until 1993—in fact, many of them were published only posthumously, and many others have yet to be published at all. It must have become gradually clear to Bolaño that if he wanted to achieve recognition, he would have to give his poetic muse a rest and try his hand at a new genre, one that he had been dabbling in inconclusively since he was a teenager in Mexico City.

In one of the Barcelona poems Bolaño challenges himself to write "stuff" that will amuse and interest readers (*The Unknown University* 9). And in a notebook dated 1978 he writes, "I want to write a novel but it's so hard for me to get started." In the same notebook he adds, "I write verses, dream of a novel" (Miles 137). During his first year in Barcelona, Bolaño met an aspiring Spanish writer of about the same age—A. G. Porta—who helped him realize his dreams of becoming a novelist. The two friends soon engaged in a series of common projects only one of which came to fruition, the novel *Consejos de un discípulo de Morrison a un fanático de Joyce,* published in 1984. Other stories and movie scripts fell by the wayside, though an early story by Bolaño ("Diario de bar"; "Bar Diary") survived and was published with the second edition of *Consejos de un discípulo* (2006). This story, dated 1979 and written in the form of a diary, marks the beginning of Bolaño's career as a fiction writer. By 1993 Bolaño had written or cowritten a total of four novels, none of which was an immediate success and one of which was published only posthumously. *Monsieur Pain* (1999), written in 1981 or 1982, is the earliest of the four and was originally published in 1993 as "La senda de los elefantes" ("The Elephant Path"). With that title it won a prize awarded by the Toledo city council and was printed by that same organization. *Consejos de un discípulo* is reputed to have sold no more than five hundred copies when it first came out. *The Third Reich* was written in 1989 but published only in 2010, seven years after its author's death. And *The Skating Rink* was published in 1993 by the city council of Talavera de la Reina (Toledo, Spain) after winning yet another literary competition. Of interest is that the second edition of this work (published in 1998, the year of *The Savage Detectives*) was the first Bolaño novel to be published in Chile, the author's native country.

Since these four novels are often read as prefigurations of the author's later work, it is fruitful to identify continuities between Bolaño's earlier and later phases. As a group, and on account of their setting, they may be considered the author's "Spanish" novels. (*Monsieur Pain* is set in Paris, but some of the characters are Spaniards who are supposed to be part of an international conspiracy.) They were certainly meant to be published in Spain. The author's identity as a transplanted Latin American writer living in Spain is reflected in the Latin American characters that populate all four novels. Understanding an author's work is often a matter of contextualizing it properly, but this is hard to do in Bolaño's case. It is not easy to find parallels between Bolaño's early novels and the fiction being produced by other Latin American writers of the period, not even those who published in Spain.

Categorizing novels such as *Consejos de un discípulo* and *The Third Reich* as exile literature is not particularly helpful, though it is true that the novels of this period set in contemporary times implicitly allude to the migration flows that characterized the relationship between certain Latin American countries and Spain in the 1970s and 1980s. It is also difficult to locate Bolaño's early work in the context of Spanish fiction. Bolaño has stated that the starting point of his generation was marked by two early novels by Spanish authors Javier

Marías and Enrique Vila-Matas: *Los dominios del lobo* (1971) and *La asesina ilustrada* (1977), respectively (*Between Parentheses* 153). In a later prologue to *Los dominios del lobo* Marías says that at the beginning of his career he wanted to locate himself outside the main tendencies of 1960s Spanish fiction, preoccupied as it was with stylistic experimentation and anti-Franco politics. He set his first novel in the United States—where he had never been—and inspired himself on American movies of the 1930s, 1940s, and 1950s, which he was able to see during a six-week stay in Paris. Vila-Matas's inspiration for his *Asesina ilustrada,* on the other hand, came from Nabokov's *Pale Fire,* and its theme had little to do with the transformations that Spanish politics and society underwent in the decade of Franco's death. Bolaño's early fiction too has an eccentric relationship to the mainstream of Spanish literature. His later works, beginning with *Nazi Literature in the Americas,* have a distinctive Latin American feel to them, a development of crucial importance in Bolaño's canonization as the central reference point of post-Boom Latin American fiction.

Bolaño's early novels will be discussed in their order of composition. All four, except for *The Third Reich*—first published after Bolaño's death, when he was already a major author, and a posthumous one at that—reached a wider audience when they were reprinted, but there are no significant variations between the original and later editions, not even in the case of *Monsieur Pain,* which was first published—as stated before—with a different title.

Monsieur Pain: Poe, Poetry, and the Death of the Avant-Garde

Bolaño began writing his first novel a year or two after moving from Barcelona to Gerona, a small provincial capital about an hour northeast of the Catalan metropolis, where he would live for five years in relative obscurity despite his continuing efforts to write poetry and fiction. Spanish author Javier Cercas recalls meeting Bolaño at that time and records a conversation between a friend and the struggling Chilean writer in which the former asks the latter how his novel is going, and the latter replies, "It's going, it's going but it's hard to tell where it's going" (Cercas, "Bolaño in Girona" 150). This novel could be *Monsieur Pain,* whose plot Bolaño himself has elsewhere characterized as "undecipherable" ("Preface: Self-Portrait," *Between Parentheses* 16). Had Bolaño been referring in the conversation to the other novel he might have been working on at the time—*Consejos de un discípulo de Morrison a un fanático de Joyce*— he would presumably have mentioned that he was collaborating with another writer in its composition. Actually it's harder to tell where this latter novel "is going" than is the case with *Monsieur Pain,* which does have some structural defects regarding character and plot development but that shows more authorial control than its counterpart: it is shorter (130 pages in the English translation), it was written by only one author, and it does without the metafictional device (the novel within the novel) that is only partially successful in *Consejos de un discípulo.*

Monsieur Pain is divided into two parts of unequal length: the main narrative (told in the first person by the eponymous character and set between April 6 and April 20, 1938), and an epilogue of obituaries in which different testimonial voices provide supplementary information on several of the characters' lives following the chronological end of the main plot.[2] But even though the narrator and protagonist is Monsieur Pain, the plot centers on the death of Peruvian poet César Vallejo, who died in a Parisian hospital on April 15, 1938, and who remains one of the towering figures of twentieth-century Latin American poetry, along with other giants like Pablo Neruda and Octavio Paz. The novel is set in Paris at the time of Vallejo's death, which coincided with the Spanish Civil War (1936–39) concurrently going on across the Pyrenees. Vallejo, a member of the Spanish Communist Party since 1931, was a strong supporter of the Republican side in that conflict, and one of his most famous works is *España, aparta de mí este cáliz* ("Spain, Take This Cup from Me," 1939), a series of fifteen poems inspired by the suffering of the common people in that fratricidal war.

Given Vallejo's political inclinations it is not surprising that in the poems the Spanish "salt of the earth" are identified with the Republican militias. Bolaño's novel includes significant references to the historical context of Vallejo's death. One of its characters is a French fascist who returns to Paris after spending a year in Spain collaborating with Franco's forces and is in cahoots with two sinister Spaniards—presumably Franco loyalists—who keep lurking around the city and try to stop Monsieur Pain from practicing his healing arts on the dying Vallejo. Monsieur Pain himself is deeply concerned with the news coming out of Spain because he realizes that the Luftwaffe is trying out new weapons of war that could later be deployed against France itself. (According to historians, the newly developed Stukas were first employed by the Germans in the Spanish Civil War. German dive-bombers escorted by Italian planes wiped out the town of Guernica in the Basque region of Spain on April 26, 1937, an episode that gave rise to Picasso's masterpiece of the same name.) Pain, who is a veteran of the First World War and of the battle of Verdun, is disheartened by the new war technologies available to the Nazis. Bolaño's novel does a creditable job of indirectly suggesting the coming European apocalypse by means of symbolism, its somewhat Gothic ambience, and the recounting of the protagonist's nightmares. It should be noted that when the novel was written Spain was undergoing a transition to democracy after decades of dictatorship. A progressive constitution was enacted in 1978, and in 1982 the socialist party, under the leadership of the charismatic Felipe González, began an uninterrupted fourteen-year rule.

As Bolaño points out in the preface to the novel, *Monsieur Pain* is partially based on documentary evidence, namely the memoirs of Vallejo's widow, Georgette, who watched over her husband's agony and took care of editing his unpublished poetry the year after the poet's death. She tells how around the middle of March Vallejo contracted a fever and was interned in the Arago Clinic thanks to the efforts of an important Peruvian diplomat, who also offered the services of his private physician, Dr. Lejard. Lejard is described in the novel in the same way Georgette portrays him in her memoirs: incompetent, indifferent, and hostile to both herself and Vallejo. On April 7 the eminent Dr. Lemiére joins Vallejo's medical team, but all he can do is ascertain the patient is dying without being able to identify the cause or prescribe a course of treatment. The diagnosis he makes on his visit is quoted literally in the novel. By now Vallejo has begun to suffer from uncontrollable hiccuping.

As a last resort and at the prompting of a friend (who in the novel is Madame Reynaud), Madame Vallejo calls on a certain Pierre Pain, a middle-aged bachelor who is a student of the occult sciences and has a modest reputation as a mesmerist and acupuncturist. Pain is considered a charlatan by the medical authorities and is kept away from the clinic, but he does manage to visit Vallejo on one occasion and cures him of the hiccups by holding his hand above the dying man's head (for two hours, adds the widow, who was present to observe the treatment). Georgette notes that on his way out Pain affirms that there is hope for the patient. Bolaño borrows this sentence for the novel. In the end, though, neither physicians nor mesmerists could save Vallejo, who died poor and forgotten in that Parisian hospital and was buried in the cemetery of Montrouge. In 1970 his remains were moved to Montparnasse, to join the graves of other famous writers. Vallejo's mysterious disease was officially diagnosed as an intestinal infection, but doubts remain as to its actual nature.[3]

Monsieur Pain is preceded by an epigraph taken from Poe's "Mesmeric Revelation," a story cast as a dialogue between the narrator and a hypnotized patient on the immortality of the soul and on the possibility of life after death. Poe's narrator is a mesmerist, and his interlocutor is described as a "sleep-waker" who may be speaking from "the region of the shadows." Poe's narrator is identified as "P," the same initial replicated in Pierre Pain's name. Bolaño also makes the mesmerist his narrator, but the reader sees him only once practicing his healing arts—though he is shown to be quite an authority on animal magnetism and on the lore of the occult sciences. Pain, however, can also be described as the "sleep-waker" of Poe's story. He has recurring dreams and nightmares that contribute to the phantasmagoric ambience of the novel, along with some uncanny descriptions of Paris and weird juxtapositions of events and characters. The French capital, of course, is where Poe set his Auguste Dupin stories. Some critics have read *Monsieur Pain* as an off-beat detective story in which, admittedly, it is not clear that a crime has been committed (unless one speaks of medical negligence) or who the detective is.

One critic points out the phonetic resemblance between Poe's detective *Dupin* and Bolaño's mesmerist *Pain* and suggests that these two characters embody opposite approaches to the solution of mysteries, the rational versus the magical. According to this logic, furthermore, Bolaño's subversion of the detective genre would go hand in hand with his questioning of modern reason (Sepúlveda 105). At one point in the novel, Monsieur Pain denies he is a detective, and at any rate he is as mystified as the reader by the meaning of certain events. The only formal detective to appear in the novel is a character in a movie watched by Pain and recounted by the narrator. The novel works better as a mystery thriller than a detective story. Vallejo's undiagnosed disease sets the tone for the appearance of mysterious characters in mysterious circumstances doing mysterious things. But the only mystery revealed at the end is that Vallejo was a poet, a fact unknown to Pierre Pain but not necessarily to the readers of the novel.

Monsieur Pain begins with the protagonist receiving an invitation from the woman he loves (the widow Madame Reynaud) to meet her at a café, where she asks him to help the sick husband of a friend of hers who is no other than Madame Vallejo. In the novel, but not in Georgette's memoirs, Pain had failed to cure Madame Reynaud's own dying husband six months earlier but had obtained the widow's gratitude for his efforts. On the way to the meeting Pain runs into two sinister figures lurking in the stairwell of his apartment building that seem to come straight out of a noir 1940s film. These are the two Spaniards who haunt Monsieur Pain throughout the novel and who later bribe him so that he will not help with Vallejo's recovery. The mesmerist consents to the widow's request and visits his new patient in the Arago Clinic, where he is mocked by the doctors and prevented from seeing Vallejo. He comes back a second time and temporarily stops the patient's hiccups. He makes further attempts to see Vallejo but is frustrated at every turn. He accepts the Spaniards' bribe and vents his guilt to a Monsieur Rivette, an old mentor who in bygone days had gathered a small group of scientists interested in the occult and having some relation with the Curies. One of the members of this circle is Pleumeur-Bodou, the Franco supporter who has a violent political dispute with Pain late in the novel. (This character calls himself an intelligence officer who uses his mesmeric powers to interrogate prisoners and spies.) Pain spends most of his time wandering the streets of Paris, meeting acquaintances and strangers at cafés and the movies, and wondering where Madame Reynaud has disappeared to. She had left Paris for a week and returns with a new lover. At the end of the novel he runs into her (and her lover), and she informs him that Monsieur Vallejo is dead and that he was a poet. In the epilogue the reader finds out that Madame Reynaud lived to the ripe old age of seventy and that Monsieur Pain got through the war by reading palms in cabarets and circuses.

Although death (variously inflicted by illness, war, and suicide) is the preeminent theme of the novel, love, politics, and poetry also play a role in the novel's thematic structure. The protagonist gets involved in the Vallejo affair out of his unspoken and unrequited love for Madame Reynaud but is ultimately disappointed and dies a lonely and broken man. Terzeff, a character who appears only in other characters' conversations and in the movie that Pain fortuitously watches with Pleumeur-Bodou and one of the plotting Spaniards, is also a victim of love. He hangs himself from a bridge when his love for Madame Curie's daughter is unrequited. (This incident takes place many years before the action of the novel begins.) But the love between Vallejo and Georgette is strong and survives death both in real life and in Bolaño's fiction. Politically the novel is set toward the end of the Spanish Civil War and before the outbreak of the Second World War, and many of its characters are divided between the ideals of socialism and fascism. Vallejo, furthermore, was an avant-garde poet whose death coincided with the eclipse of the historical avant-gardes. A very important part of his work—the *Poemas humanos* and *España, aparta de mí este cáliz*—was published posthumously in 1939, only as a result of his widow's efforts. His later poetry abounds in intimations of an early death, and while he did not live to see the collapse of the Spanish Republic, he knew at the end of his life that the days of Spanish socialism were numbered.[4]

Through Vallejo, Bolaño joins historical to artistic crisis. It is eerie to ascertain to what extent the life of Vallejo prefigured that of Bolaño: both were committed to avant-garde poetry, but their faith in the viability of poetry wavered; both died prematurely; both were aware that they would die an early death; both endured long periods of literary obscurity; both were disappointed in their political expectations; and the widows of both were responsible for the posthumous publication of some of their key works. When Bolaño wrote *Monsieur Pain* he was unaware that his life would be cut short by illness; but when the second edition of the novel came out in 1999—the first with its current title—its author had already been diagnosed with a terminal liver disease.

The death theme in the novel is sounded from beginning to end, as the plot is framed by Vallejo's agony in the Arago Clinic and culminates with the revelation of his death and some details concerning his funeral.[5] But there are two episodes that deserve special mention because of the way Bolaño restates the theme of death in a dream-like register. The first comes when Monsieur Pain is driven to an unfamiliar neighborhood of Paris and enters a cafe with nothing in particular in mind. He is surprised by how odd the place looks and even more surprised by the absence of a waiter and by meeting twin brothers who point him in the direction of a fish tank in the back of the establishment, set against satin curtains as if the cafe were a theater stage where a magic show is about to unfold. The tank contains "miniature boats, trains and planes arranged to depict calamities" (47) and displays metal figures of the dead and mangled all around the bottom and half buried in the sand. This weird installation is a materialization of Paul Valéry's famous poem *Cimetière Marin* and restates the relationship between death and poetry in a surrealist way. (Duchamp's installations are not too far removed from the brothers' underwater apocalypse.) According to the obituaries in the epilogue, one of the brothers commits suicide when the Germans occupy Paris while the other goes off to Buenos Aires where his fish tanks are ignored just as they were in Paris. Put together the twins add up to the recurring figure in Bolaño's work of the poète maudit, a category that comprises failed artists, suicides, and obscure geniuses living on the margins of society. The miniature apocalypse and the connection between art and war prefigure later Bolaño novels such as *Distant Star* and *2666*.

The feeling of the uncanny that Bolaño elaborates in this episode is even more pronounced in a later passage of the novel where Pain loses his way in one of the many labyrinths that make up the symbolic space of the novel and experiences the kind of terror that afflicts many of Poe's characters.[6] After a night of drinking with occasional companions he is trapped in a kind of warehouse occupied by an assortment of farming implements and machines, a place cold and dark that is described both as a labyrinth ("I discovered that all the passages led to the centre," 73) and as a "singular cemetery" (73) where he has to spend the night curled up in a bathtub that reminds him of a coffin. In the middle of the night he hears sounds that might be coming from the hereafter and that replicate Vallejo's hiccups in the clinic. Is it the poet's ghost, he wonders, that is approaching him in the shadows, or someone playing a trick on him? This Gothic episode may be read as a figurative descent into the underworld (such as that of Orpheus in search of Eurydice), as a reconfiguration of the "live burial" topic of horror fiction, or as one more of the protagonist's recurring nightmares taking place on a different fictional level because it is "real." But mostly it reaffirms the connection between death and haunting.

Monsieur Pain has been read as Bolaño's farewell letter to poetry on account of its central motif (the death of a poet) and because Bolaño had put his faith in poetry on hold in the early 1980s in order to experiment with fiction (Valenzuela). But poetry was not dead and buried in Bolaño; it had simply been displaced to the language of fiction and the genres of the novel and short story. *Monsieur Pain,* in fact, is a *novela-cementerio* (a fictional mausoleum) that speculates on the posthumous life of poetry. Vallejo's poetic text is implied and complicit in Bolaño's narrative discourse. One obvious example of this is the (surrealist?) coincidence between the name of the protagonist—Pierre— and Vallejo's most famous poem on the intimation of his own death, "Black

Stone Lying on a White Stone," a coincidence particularly marked in Spanish because the poem's original title is "Piedra negra sobre piedra blanca," "piedra" and "Pierre" being the same word in Spanish and French. In that poem Vallejo writes, "I will die in Paris, on a rainy day, / on some day I already remember."[7] Predictably it is always raining in the Paris of Bolaño's novel. Vallejo also wrote poems on hope (or hopelessness), on the pain of being human in an alien world, and on his experiences in prison cells and hospitals. Could it also be a coincidence that Tristan Cabral, a French poet much quoted by Bolaño, published a book in 1977 called *Du Pain et des pierres*? At any rate the novel as a poetic cemetery, and haunted by the spirit of poetry, sets the tone for much of Bolaño's later fiction where the lives and deaths of poets play such a large role.

Consejos de un discípulo de Morrison a un fanático de Joyce: Four-Handed Writing

Bolaño's first published novel was written in tandem with coauthor A. G. Porta. Critics have to rely on Porta's recollections, many years after the event, in order to sort out Bolaño's contribution to the novel, though it seems clear that the narrator's diary appended to the main body of the narrative is fully Bolaño's doing. This inference is justified because that kind of "paratextual" strategy is common in Bolaño: the diary of *Consejos de un discípulo* functions as an epilogue, much like the polyphonic obituaries at the end of *Monsieur Pain;* and *The Third Reich,* another novel of the author's early period, is written entirely in the form of a journal, as are the first and third sections of *The Savage Detectives.*

In his introduction to the 2006 reprint of *Consejos de un discípulo,* coauthor A. G. Porta reveals some interesting facts about the novel and engages in speculation about its method of composition, by then half-forgotten since the novel's original date of publication in 1984. *Consejos de un discípulo* was written when Porta lived in Barcelona and Bolaño in Gerona. The earliest draft of the novel dates back to 1979, when it was called "Flowers for Morrison." The manuscript was finished in 1983 and sent to various literary contests and publishing houses. It failed to win most prizes and was rejected by important publishers like Planeta and Argos Vergara, but it did emerge the winner of the Premio Ámbito Literario de Narrativa in 1984. Its eventual title was adapted from a poem by Mario Santiago, who makes a fleeting appearance in the novel's appendix. It may be assumed that since Porta was a fan of Joyce, then Bolaño would have to be Morrison's disciple ("A. G. Porta," *Between Parentheses* 135). By his own admission, Bolaño was in the habit of giving advice "right and left" but would never take advice from anybody else, not even from his physician (*Between Parentheses* 368).

If the first pages of the novel were drafted in 1979, the earliest written record of Bolaño's involvement in the project is a letter from December 1981, where he suggests to his friend and collaborator that they should "deepen the Joycean vein of the protagonist." (In *Consejos de un discípulo*, the protagonist and narrator Ángel Ros is working on a novel called—in Catalan—*Cant de Dèdalus Anunciant Fi*. The protagonist of this fictional novel is a James Joyce devotee who is also a bank robber. Chapter 12 of *Consejos de un discípulo* contains the most explicit description of the *Cant*, but in the appended diary the would-be author admits that he has given up on the idea of writing his "Song of Daedalus Announcing the End.") In late 1981 Bolaño's vision of the novel that he and Porta were working on was to do with Joyce what Joyce had done with Homer's *Odyssey*, in a modest way—Bolaño is quoted as saying[8]—and in the style of a police thriller. The final version, however, reads more like a Bonnie-and-Clyde type of story than a Joycean police procedural.

As to how the novel was written and the creative work distributed between two amateur novelists from different literary backgrounds, Porta cannot remember who wrote what but offers three theories as to the actual method of composition, always implying that the work in progress was being passed back and forth between both collaborators until the final draft was completed. It could have been, as Bolaño is quoted as remarking, that each of the authors wrote alternate chapters, either with a clear and previously agreed ending in sight or in a more improvised manner that reminds Porta of the surrealist "exquisite corpse" method.[9] The third theory—that Porta wrote the basic draft and Bolaño took it to its final conclusion—is the one that receives the most credit. In practice, though, it must have been difficult to separate any one of these methods from the other two. At one point in the novel, for example, some characters play the game of the exquisite corpse, a passage that may be read as a self-reflexive commentary on the novel itself, specifically on its production. In a more general way, the reader may assign to Porta the passages showing the greatest insight on Barcelona life in the late 1970s and early 1980s, and other sections of the novel, like the appendix, to Bolaño. Or the "accent" of the narrator may give away the authorial identity of selected passages. Bolaño's influence is also perceived in the choice of a *sudaca* (Ana) to play the role of Bonnie Parker.[10] There are hints that she is either Argentine or Chilean, and it is made clear that she is in cahoots with other South Americans living in Barcelona at the time—immigrants and exiles from military dictatorships—to commit her crimes. She is the killer in the novel, and Ángel, her passive lover and wannabe writer, falls into a life of crime only to follow her. Chapters 16 and 17 feature a "South American" who gives Ángel shelter when he is running away from the police. This "South American"—called Claudio in the novel—is none other than Bolaño himself living in his small apartment in Tallers Street. It is intriguing, though useless, to speculate on who—Porta or Bolaño—wrote these chapters in which Bolaño portrays himself or is portrayed by a friend who knew him well and had visited him often at that very apartment.[11]

The novel is told in the first person by a narrator who was Bolaño's (and Porta's) age at the time of composition and whose curriculum vitae includes several half-written novels, several "half-published" volumes of poetry, two Super 8 shorts directed and financed by himself, and occasional stints as a bass player in a band. He meets Ana at a discotheque two years before the main action of the novel (that takes place in the span of a summer) and falls in love with her. Ana's mother arrives in Spain and lives with them in a boarding house after they both lose their jobs. Much is made in the novel of the unemployment and criminal violence affecting Barcelona at the time of the story, a crisis made worse by the arrival of great numbers of immigrants and exiles from Latin America. Ana becomes a coldhearted criminal and drags Ángel with her to her new life. They stage several bloody robberies, in which Ángel plays a secondary role, and live a clandestine life, always haunted by the police and by the specter of their photos in the newspapers. Ana is killed in their last job, and Ángel manages to escape to Paris, where he lives under an assumed name. The last scene of the narrative has him taking flowers to Jim Morrison's grave in the Père Lachaise cemetery. The diary appended to the main narrative is also narrated by Ángel and reviews some of the scenes with Ana in Barcelona but adds scenes written in Paris after Ana's death. In the final scene the protagonist is looking at books through the shop window of a bookstore when he sees the image of several policemen closing in behind him. But the agents run past him on the way to apprehend somebody else.

Despite winning the 1984 Anthropos Literary Fiction prize *Consejos de un discípulo* is not a particularly successful novel: it is disjointed, its plot lacks tension, and the Dedalus character of the novel within the novel is only a sketch. But two aspects of the novel deserve special mention: the link between literature and crime—visually enacted in the final scene of the diary, when a police chase is superimposed on the cover of several books on offer—and the attempt to blend high art and popular culture. This last point is a staple of early postmodernism and to a large extent defines Bolaño's stylistic signature from *Monsieur Pain* all the way to *2666*. Bolaño's penchant for popular fiction also defines his relationship to the canon, which he transforms into a more accessible language without giving up the achievement of the great canonical figures of Latin American and world literature.

As to the first point, the narrator muses on the relationship between literature and crime when he sees himself as a deluded twenty-something who once believed that literature would have the same drawing power as rock music and that writers could reach the status of rock stars. But it seems that the age of the poet as rock star had passed. "What was literature for me," he wonders. "The Form through which life would have to be, if not clear, at least legible, stable. But the Form gradually took on the face of crime" (51). And in later passage the narrator ironically rationalizes his situation—or criminal status—as the typical predicament of young artists everywhere, "cornered between poverty and silence," and then proceeds to list some of the *poètes maudits* with whom he identifies—Sophie Podolski, Tristan Cabral, Philippe Abou (89).[12] From this comment it would seem that the various episodes of extreme violence in the novel deliberately convey an antisocial attitude on the part of writers excluded from the power centers of the cultural field. But, however ambiguously, Ana's criminal activities are linked to political terrorism in the novel, which offers another way to explain, if not justify, the killing of innocent victims. The 1970s were the decade of revolutionary organizations in Europe and Latin America— ETA in Spain, the Red Brigades in Italy, the Baader-Meinhof Gang in Germany, the Tupamaros in Uruguay, the Montoneros in Argentina, the MIR in Chile, and so on—that used violence as a means to advance their agenda. In the late 1970s and early 1980s, furthermore, the military were in power in both Argentina and Chile, and Spain was undergoing a transition between the Franco dictatorship and a new democratic order.

These issues indirectly permeate the novel. The Franco regime, for example, had repressed the Catalan language, which explains the significance of the narrator's projected novel, whose title is always given in Catalan. Given this context, Ana's viciousness could then be seen as a misplaced response to dictatorship. The fact that at the end she dies as a result of the violence she herself instigates says something about the novel's stance in relation to the perennial conflict between civilization and barbarism. But the line separating the citizen from the criminal is indeed thin; thin enough, at any rate, to always demand from writers a renewed commitment to accepted cultural norms or a constantly evolving legitimation of their transgression. It is important to remember that much of the novel's violence is directed against banks and other capitalist institutions, a fact that evokes the epigraph from Brecht that Argentine author Ricardo Piglia used in his hard-boiled novel *Burnt Money:* "What is the robbing of a bank compared to the opening of a bank?" The justification of violence in political and social terms is a problem that dogs Bolaño's fiction and has much to do with the justification of writing itself. In later works Bolaño will expand the connection between literature and crime to embrace war, fascism, and state terror, a connection that implies the ethical questioning of the literary enterprise.

The Third Reich: The Sorrows of Young Udo

A year after the 1984 publication of *Consejos de un discípulo* Bolaño married Carolina López and settled in Blanes, a working-class resort in the Spanish Costa Brava popular with British and German tourists and less than two hours by train from Barcelona. While his wife took a position with the local city council, Bolaño continued working on his fiction—some of it still unpublished—and by 1989 had completed the manuscript of *The Third Reich,* a fully achieved novel that for reasons unknown was not published during the author's lifetime. (The English translation came out in 2011, the same year that the novel was serialized in four issues of the *Paris Review.*) In his free time the writer would help his mother run her small costume jewelry business. His social circle included local fishermen, waiters, and young drug addicts—according to the testimony quoted in chapter 1 above—but also the owner of a video store that the writer visited regularly to check out westerns and Fassbinder films, as well as the owner of Jocker Jocs, a store that sold board games both in their table version and in their later PC formats.[13] The Third Reich is, in fact, the name of a hex-and-counter war game that made its debut in 1974 and has since gone through several editions and been distributed by more than one publisher. It simulates the European and African theaters of World War II. According to the game's most recent publisher, the Third Reich has a "deep grounding in the historical background of the Second World War," and "interweaves not only the land, naval and air struggles, but also the equally important economic and political battles. Players must guide their nation to victory by capturing key objectives while making sure no one else—in particular their allies—gets there first."[14] Bolaño's fascination with the history of the Second World War is obvious not only in *The Third Reich* but also in some of his later stories and in *2666.*

The game is the central "counter" in the plot and characterization of the novel, which is narrated in the form of a diary by Udo Berger, a German tourist in his midtwenties who after a ten-year absence returns with a new girlfriend (Ingeborg) to a hotel located in a Mediterranean resort (very much like Blanes) where he used to come with his family in summers gone by. When he was a teen Udo had become infatuated with Frau Else, the hotel's manager and owner's wife, who still runs the facility and continues to attract the young man's attention. Udo is a fanatic of board games and writes for specialized magazines with names like *Front Line, Jeux de Simulation, Stockade, Casus Belli,* and others. Therefore he is also a writer and one trying to make a name for himself by reaching broader audiences. His justification for keeping a diary is to improve the mechanics of his writing as well as his grammar, whose solecisms have at times kept him from being published. (The novel, of course, is in Spanish, but the reader must suspend disbelief and assume that the original language of the journal is German.) Upon arrival at the Del Mar, Udo asks for a large table to set up the Third Reich board and finish an article on new strategies for winning the game. He plans to stay in Spain for only two weeks, but for reasons having to do with his own internal turmoil, he overstays his welcome by almost a month, a development that his friend and game mentor Conrad back in Germany does not approve of. Ingeborg returns home after the planned two-week vacation and leaves Udo plenty of time and freedom to exorcize his inner demons.

The most important character in Udo's self-exploration is El Quemado ("The Burnt One"), a mysterious beach dweller who rents pedal boats to tourists and whose upper body is horribly deformed by burns that "covered most of his face, neck, and chest, and that he displayed openly, dark and corrugated, like grilled meat or the crumpled metal of a downed plane" (19).[15] He is said to be of South American origin. The informant, a local bar owner, adds that his burns were not accidental. He describes El Quemado as a fighter who had to fight tooth and nail against the "real Nazi soldiers on the loose around the world" (174). It is difficult not to think in this context of the young Chilean photographer Rodrigo Rojas who was burned alive in July 1986 following a street demonstration against the Pinochet regime in Santiago. Rojas died of his injuries whereas El Quemado is implicitly portrayed as a political exile with an explicit grudge against Germans. Udo seeks him out, befriends him, teaches him how to play the Third Reich, and engages him in a match lasting days that has everyone around them worried for its obsessiveness. Frau Else's dying husband is not the only character who warns Udo to pack and leave immediately. He cautions Udo that if he does not heed his advice, he will have to suffer the consequences of losing the match, which are not limited to the actual rules of the game: "It's in all the history books," he clarifies: "let the trial of the war criminals begin" (250).

Unfinished sentimental business with Frau Else and the death by drowning of another German vacationer with whom Udo and Ingeborg develop a relationship are other reasons why the narrator extends his stay in Spain and becomes an unwelcome guest and an object of collective derision. Karl ("Charly") and girlfriend Hanna bring unresolved issues with them to the Costa Brava and lean heavily on Udo and his partner for beach siestas, nighttime outings, and drinking sprees. Two local blue-collar characters of uncertain background— the Wolf and the Lamb—are always hovering around the German quartet. The group made up of these six characters plus El Quemado often gives the impression of being a powder keg about to explode. And Charly and Hanna do in fact enact a violent episode, sometime after which Charly suddenly grabs his wind-surfing board—while the two tourist couples are relaxing on the beach—and swims into the ocean never to be heard from again. His body washes out on the shore after a few days, and Udo identifies it, though he expresses some doubt later that the decomposed body is actually that of his friend.

Charly's accidental or suicidal death is a major plot development that occurs less than halfway through the novel. The rest of the plot concerns Udo's advances on Frau Else and his Third Reich match against El Quemado. In the background there are recurring references to a gamers' convention in Paris, on which occasion Udo is expected to give a lecture on a strategic variant of the game. This convention functions as the anticlimactic ending of the novel—or a kind of epilogue, like the last encounter in Germany between Udo and Ingeborg, in which the former couple give up notions of marriage and decide to be just friends. What interests Bolaño is the inner life of his narrator, a troubled young man who does not mind losing his regular job back home, who cannot keep his commitment to "sweet" and "charming" Ingeborg and start a conventional married life with her, and who in the last analysis is to some extent a freak, less spectacular than the disfigured Quemado but not too different either. It is not difficult to find parallels between Udo and Ángel Ros, the narrator of *Consejos de un discípulo,* or between Udo and the protagonist of many of Bolaño's poems in *The Unknown University.* All these characters are drifters and wanderers, urban nomads not unlike the protagonist of the more settled *Monsieur Pain,* who spends most of his time in that novel going from one place to another in Paris and getting increasingly lost as the story progresses. Three aspects of Bolaño's writing come together in these and other cases: character "psychology" (such as it is in a postrealist author like Bolaño), urban exploration, and a narrative strategy that depends on mapping a space that will then be traversed by the characters, and either remain the same for purposes of identification or become uncanny.

Charly's premature death is only one of the experiences that put an end to Udo's carefree existence. The novel's central theme is the end of adolescence and the beginning of a new phase of life, uncertain but reconciled. Udo's frustrating "affair" with Frau Else and his stressful match with El Quemado are two other such experiences. The first teaches the narrator that youthful infatuations are unrealistic, and the second that there can be much more at stake in a game than seems obvious at first sight. Part of the novel's merit is how well it transposes the game from its conventional setting—two players sitting across a board and obeying previously established rules—to a much broader reality that calls into question the players' subjectivities and life experiences.

As they get to know each other better and become each other's nemesis in the game, Udo and El Quemado play out the dialectic between self and other. For Udo, El Quemado is already an "other" to himself: "To lose an arm or a leg is to lose a part of oneself, but to be burned like that is to be transformed, to become someone else" (20). The story is consistently told from Udo's point of view, which means that readers never gain access to El Quemado's consciousness or unconscious, as they do to the workings of the narrator's mind and to his dreams and nightmares. Therefore knowing what Udo means to his opponent is a matter of speculation in which the characters willingly engage. The character stonewalls the reader, but it does not take long for Udo to realize that he has lost the contest: "It's the end of summer and the end of the game. The Oder front and the Rhine front collapse at the first onslaught. . . . My final circle of defense is Berlin-Stettin-Bremen-Berlin; everything else, including my armies in Bavaria and the north of Italy, is cut off from supply lines. . . . Tomorrow there is no doubt I'll be defeated" (263–64). After the defeat the winner takes the loser to his hut on the beach—which is variously described through the novel as a fortress, a barbarian's burial mound, a Third World shack, and a child's hideout—picks him up like a "rag doll" (268), and pitches him inside through the small hole that serves as a door. The gesture is supposed to emulate the act of birth but in reverse. But it also puts the carefree tourist concerned only with strategy games and summer romance in the place of the other, the "eternal mourner" (268), the survivor of an unspecified holocaust that is nevertheless part and parcel of modernity. To no avail, Udo discharges himself: "I whispered that I was no Nazi, that none of it was my fault" (268). The scene is punctuated by a quotation from Goethe to the effect that until one experiences dying and rebirth, one is nothing but a "sullen guest on the gloomy earth."[16]

In his *Anatomy of Criticism* Northrop Frye identified the mythos of summer with romance and the mythos of autumn with tragedy. Udo, however, is aware of living in an "amnesiac" Europe with "no sense of the epic or heroic" (83). Fall does indeed descend on the increasingly empty seaside resort where the novel is set, but Udo only plays at being a tragic hero, perhaps in imitation of the real-life protagonists of World War II listed in the chapter "My Favorite Generals." El Quemado, on the other hand, comes straight out of the conflagration and bears the stigma of historical violence. He is Udo's monstruous double, a mirror in which Udo sees a new image of himself: "I commenced my trip inside. Then I did close my eyes and I saw myself inhabiting another day, less black but still not bright" (268), a half-glimpsed epiphany followed by the return home.

Unlike Goethe's young Werther, Udo does not kill himself. (Suicide is plausibly displaced onto the figure of his friend Charly.) But he is a sentimental hero (or antihero) like his illustrious predecessor. Goethe's novel, of course, is written in the form of letters, but the letters are never answered, so that the narrator's correspondence takes on the form of a diary. Werther's addressee, as a critic points out, is merely a rhetorical device: "Even Wilhelm, the supposed addressee, serves a more rhetorical function as a placeholder in the novel. Details, such as his exact location, the frequency with which he writes, and his overall investment in Werther's life and missives, are never known. As a result Werther writes himself into suicidal despair because he has no writing partner who is present, and no reliable postal service to transmit his effusions." (Schiffman 422). Udo has Conrad, who in a sense is also a rhetorical addressee (he is supposed to read the diary but never does); but Conrad's phone calls substitute for the letters that in Goethe's text end up in the dead letter office, if they are ever sent. It would be too much to say that Conrad's friendship saves Udo, but much is made of male bonding in the novel, which makes the isolated figure of El Quemado stand out in even sharper contrast.

On a different level, the bond between colleagues relates *The Third Reich* to *Consejos de un discípulo,* a collaboration between two writers that also involves a third, Bolaño's friend Mario Santiago, one of whose poems gives the earlier novel its title and who is mentioned in passing in the epilogue, also written in the form of a diary. A further connection between these two novels, and between them and the bulk of Bolaño's fiction, is the recourse to the detective fiction format. In *The Third Reich* Ingeborg is often seen reading a detective novel by a certain "Florian Linden," pages of which Udo reads before falling asleep and having nightmares that Linden is at the door of his hotel room with a warning to leave the premises. The novel's content is undisclosed, but in the frame novel (Bolaño's) Udo plays the role of detective when he confronts the mystery of El Quemado's identity, the facts of Charly's death, and the mysterious identity of Frau Else's husband, a recluse in one of the hotel's rooms who seems to control the other characters. In the end Udo's investigation leads him back to his own troubled self. And just as in his previous novel Bolaño tried to bring together an elite writer and a rock musician, and in *Monsieur Pain* popular fiction coexists with Vallejo's hermetic poetry, in *The Third Reich* the roman noir is juxtaposed with canonical German literature: "Conrad knows our national literature. One night in his room he reeled off the names of two hundred German writers. . . . He especially loved Goethe" (30).

The Skating Rink: Bolaño's Whodunit

According to the information contained in the catalog of the Bolaño archive exhibit, Bolaño worked on *The Skating Rink* between 1986 and 1990 (*Archivo Bolaño* 28–29). Yet there are details in the novel suggesting that its composition was not completed until sometime in 1992 when Bolaño was separated from his wife, had a two-year-old son, and had been diagnosed with the liver disease that would eventually kill him. Remo Morán, one of the three narrators of the novel, is an obvious projection of the author himself: he is a transplanted Chilean poet and novelist who lived in Mexico when he was young and hung out with a group of marginal poets; he was briefly imprisoned in a detention center when he returned to Chile the very same month in which Pinochet's coup took place; and he runs a campground with the same name as the one where Bolaño worked in his early years in Spain. More to the point, he meets a woman who works for the local city council, marries her, has a son with her, but agrees to a separation when the son is two years old. Marriage, fatherhood, separation, and illness are all elements of Bolaño's biography, and they appear as such in the poem "Roberto Bolaño's Devotion," whose opening lines are: "Toward the end of 1992 he was very sick / and had separated from his wife" (*The Unknown University* 723). Furthermore, in one of the novel's scenes Remo looks "critically ill" from the perspective of one of the other narrators (52),[17] an impression that makes more sense in the context of the later date and that is not developed in the rest of the novel, which makes it seem like an extraneous, perhaps autobiographical detail. Finally one of the novel's central characters is a figure skater who is trying out for the Spanish Olympic team. The summer Olympic Games were held in Barcelona in 1992, which makes that date all the more plausible for the novel's composition or at least its final touches, though it's hard to see how *The Skating Rink* could have been conceived *without* the character of the figure skater.

This is not to say that the drafting of *The Third Reich* and *The Skating Rink* do not overlap. The similarities between the two novels are obvious: the setting is the same (with the same Del Mar hotel and the same Paseo Marítimo), the German widow and El Quemado of the earlier novel reappear briefly in the later one, and the action of both takes place in the span of a summer. In addition they are both narrated in the first person, but whereas the narrative format of *The Third Reich* is a diary, that of *The Skating Rink* is a polyphonic monologue that is not bound to any specific written format within the fiction. The novel has three narrators, and they all write, but as narrators they are merely voices addressing specific narratees or, more generally, the reader.[18] As characters each of these narrators is provided with a substantial biographical background. The convergence of these biographies on certain female characters and around the space of the skating rink forms the plot of the novel. There is a love triangle and a narrative triangle in the novel, but they are not symmetrical. Nuria, the figure skater and nodal point of the love triangle, is not involved in the narrative scheme and is perceived only externally, from the point of view of other characters, not just her admirers and lovers but also the two members of her immediate family. Something similar is true of Caridad, the other love object in the novel. What the reader knows of her is heavily influenced by how her older companion Carmen and her eventual partner Gaspar see her.

The narrative monologues alternate regularly through the novel, always following the same order and always ending with *puntos suspensivos* (ellipses). Some of the endings deliberately seek to create suspense, as if the novel were written in installments. The most dramatic instance comes at the end of one of

Remo's monologues and at a point in the novel when the reader is not aware that a dead body is involved: "The way I see it now, all those years of minding my own business in Z were just a preparation for finding the body" (37). The monologues crisscross each other and form a pattern of correspondences that endows the novel with its particular dynamism and keeps readers on their toes. Some scenes are viewed from different perspectives, and some characters are invisible to others. Enric, the third narrator, never mentions Gaspar, the second narrator and an important character in the story. Gaspar, on the other hand, is never quite aware of what Enric and Nuria have going on at the skating rink even though he spies on them more than once when he goes looking for Caridad. For him Nuria is "the skater" and Enric "the fat guy."

The novel is about an embezzlement scandal in a small tourist town (probably Blanes) involving a murder, a love triangle, and local politics. The characters are a combination of civil servants and elected officials, Latin American immigrants with and without papers, homeless and transient types from the town's surroundings, and a beautiful figure skater who is trying to work her way back to the Spanish Olympic team after losing a grant that allowed her to train with her peers. One of the main characters is Enric Rosquelles, a powerful local bureaucrat who becomes infatuated with the beautiful figure skater—Nuria—and secretly builds her a skating rink with diverted public funds in an abandoned mansion. Another of the main characters is Remo Morán, a Chilean expatriate who succeeds as a businessman in the local community and quickly earns Enric's displeasure on account of his origin and the friends he keeps, and because he has an affair with Nuria. One day Remo finds out that an acquaintance from his Mexican days (Gaspar Heredia) has arrived in town and needs a job. Remo puts him to work as a night watchman in the campground he manages, where the new arrival meets an older transient woman called Carmen and her young protégée Caridad. Gaspar is intrigued by Caridad—a kind of anorexic and Gothic femme fatale—and successfully pursues her. The rink is the central space of the novel. The mansion (or palace) where it is sited is a ruin from earlier decades that had been built by a local businessman whose fortune was made in America—Cuba, Mexico, and the United States. (The Chilean Morán and the Mexican Heredia thus exemplify the topic of the "return of the galleons.")[19] The grounds evoke imaginary and real buildings like the Xanadu mansion of *Citizen Kane* (and therefore William Randolph Hearst's castle in California), the Vizcaya palace in Miami, and the hotel in Kubrick's movie version of Stephen King's *The Shining,* explicitly referenced by the text. The avuncular Enric spends most of his working hours supervising his protégée's training, but his secret project is discovered by Carmen, who blackmails him in return for an apartment of her own. When Carmen is found dead in the middle of the skating rink, Enric is charged with the murder and thrown into prison.

The real culprit, however, is a homeless friend of Carmen's—the Rookie—who kills her in a senseless act of desperation. Enric is eventually released, though the police never find out who the real criminal is. The Rookie confesses his crime to Remo, who mostly keeps the secret to himself. Not even Enric, the presumed murderer, finds out whodunit.

Remo is a reader of detective fiction, but Bolaño's novel does not follow the rules of the genre. As a critic points out, if the hard-boiled thriller typically tells two stories—that of the crime and that of its investigation—*The Skating Rink* does without the latter. There is no detective in the novel, no real interest in solving the enigma, and no justice done, since the murderer is never punished. Furthermore neither the murderer nor the victim is a central character in the story, which is more concerned with existential issues and the relationships tying the characters together (Solotorevsky 112–13). It should be added, though, that Bolaño touches on social issues involving the tense relations between the settled local characters and the transient population of a town like Blanes and of other towns and cities in the Catalan country of Spain. For Enric, Remo is no more than a disreputable "South American dealer" whom he cannot stomach (79), an undesirable outsider who boasts of "flouting the current regulations forbidding the employment of foreigners without work permits" (80). Remo acknowledges this point of view and the underlying tensions between the local population and outsiders when he learns—after the visit of a social worker to his place of work—"that South Americans are regarded with a certain degree of suspicion" (35) in the region. He toys with the idea of decamping from Z at summer's end and gives Gaspar and Caridad a generous bonus to buy two plane tickets back to Mexico after the affair of the skating rink is over.

According to Bolaño, as mentioned in chapter 1 above, *The Skating Rink* talks about beauty, "which is fleeting and usually meets a disastrous end" ("Self-Portrait," *Between Parentheses* 16). The beautiful Nuria is touched by the scandal and has to leave town. She ends up working in Barcelona as a secretary for a Dutch firm and achieves fame not as a figure skater but as a pinup. Her "artistic nude shots" (176) circulate in a well-known magazine with a wide circulation and disturb Enric's dreams, though he can never lay hands on the relevant publication.

The Skating Rink is the most successful of Bolaño's early novels in terms of achievement and critical reception. The narrative monologues anticipate a technique abundantly displayed in *The Savage Detectives,* and the serial murders recounted halfway through the novel (99) prefigure the most famous section of *2666*, "The Part about the Crimes." Also of interest is the disappointment of Bolaño's alter ego with the social status of poetry, which—in his own words—is a waste of time "on the planet of happy eunuchs and zombies" (101). Remo and Gaspar were poets once in Mexico but are reluctant to discuss poetry when they run into each other again in Spain. Remo becomes a novelist, and in jail Enric has a chance to read Remo's bizarre novel *Saint Bernard*. But one should not read too much into this note of despair concerning the social relevance of poetry. In the same year that Bolaño published *The Skating Rink*, he finished preparing the manuscript of *The Unknown University* for publication. Novelist and poet were still talking to one another, a dialogue that would prove extremely fruitful for the author in the years to come.

Siamese Twins

Nazi Literature in the Americas and *Distant Star*

In 1993 Bolaño was forty years old, had a three-year-old son, was separated from his wife, and had been diagnosed with an incurable liver condition. He was still a largely unknown writer despite having won some literary prizes and having published not only two novels but also a poetry collection that same year. He had been living in Blanes for almost a decade, on the fringes of Barcelona, the publishing capital of Latin American fiction since the 1960s. He occasionally entertained writers and friends who had business in the city—to the extent allowed by his meager means—and had physical access to local editors and publishing houses. He kept working on his poetry and on a perennially unfinished novel that would eventually be published as *The Woes of the True Policeman*. Finally in 1996 he got a break and had a manuscript accepted by Seix Barral, the publisher that had been instrumental in the international success of the Latin American novel three decades earlier. This work was *Nazi Literature in the Americas,* which he had also sent to rival publisher Anagrama as an entry in an annual competition sponsored by that entity since 1983. There it met with its chief editor's enthusiastic approval, but Bolaño withdrew the manuscript before it could be entered into the contest so he could honor the Seix Barral contract. Jorge Herralde, the Anagrama editor who was destined to play such a key role in Bolaño's career, was unaware that Bolaño had submitted *Nazi Literature in the Americas* to other publishers but was intrigued enough by the work's quality to ask its author for more unpublished material. Bolaño gave him the manuscript of *Distant Star,* which was issued toward the end of 1996, certainly a banner year for a struggling author who until then had mostly been published by local presses attached to city councils and town halls in different parts of Spain.

Herralde and Anagrama would subsequently bring out the vast majority of Bolaño's fiction—including the posthumous works—at a rate of one book a year while the author was alive. The only exception was 2002, when Bolaño published a minor work—eventually translated as *A Little Lumpen Novelita*—that had been contracted earlier with Italian publisher Mondadori for its Year Zero project, which consisted of a series of works by Hispanic authors set in different world cities and synchronized with the advent of the millennium. Bolaño's publishing breakthrough of 1996, however, did not immediately translate into commercial success. Most of the Seix Barral edition of *Nazi Literature in the Americas* had to be remaindered because of poor sales, and *Distant Star* sold less than a thousand copies in the first year (Herralde 40). The favorable critical reception of both publications, however, set the stage for the Bolaño boom that was soon to follow.

These two works demand to be treated in conjunction not only because they were published the same year but because *Distant Star* is a revised and expanded version of the final "entry" of *Nazi Literature*. In the author's own words, *Distant Star* is the "quick and lethal Siamese twin" of *Nazi Literature,* which is its fat, slow, and clumsy counterpart, "a massive encyclopedia of beastly stillness" (Braithwaite 113). Furthermore, and in an ironic turn of events, one of the characters in *Distant Star* conceives a project to write a book on Nazi literature in the Americas. The final chapter of *Nazi Literature in the Americas,* "The Infamous Ramírez Hoffman," is the longest in the book and stands apart from the others because it is narrated in the first person by a character named "Bolaño," while the other twenty-nine entries of Bolaño's fictitious encyclopedia are presented in a detached tone by an impersonal narrator. The final chapter, therefore, is Bolaño's earliest experiment with "autofiction," a mode or genre that may be broadly defined as a mix of autobiographical fact and fiction, and—more concretely—as the projection of the author onto imaginary situations under the aegis of a fictive reading contract (Toro et al. 11). The protagonist of the story is a fascist aviator who draws artistic inspiration from the murders he commits during the military regime in Chile, which thematically links the chapter to the rest of the book. The Pinochet dictatorship is only one of the authoritarian or totalitarian regimes mentioned in the book, which also alludes to the military dictatorships in Brazil (1964–85) and Argentina (1976–83) and to Castro's communist regime in Cuba, in addition to Spanish and Italian fascism and to the Nazi regime in Germany. A historical link between Nazi totalitarianism and the South American dictatorships is presumed in the relevant cases.

It must be remembered that several South American countries harbored Nazi fugitives after the war. Some of the leading Nazis who ended up in the continent were Adolf Eichmann (captured in Buenos Aires in 1960 by the Mossad and convicted in Jerusalem of crimes against humanity), Josef Mengele (a foreign resident of Argentina since at least the early 1950s, who died on a Brazilian beach), Josef Schwammberger (extradited from Argentina to West Germany in 1987), Ante Pavelic (who arrived in Buenos Aires in 1948 but had to leave shortly after Perón's overthrow in 1955), Klaus Barbie (the "butcher of Lyon," extradited from Bolivia in 1983), Gustav Wagner (who together with Franz Stangl escaped to Brazil), Paul Schäffer (founder of the infamous Colonia Dignidad in Chile, called "Colonia Renacer" in *Nazi Literature in the Americas*), and Walter Rauff (who managed a crab cannery in the south of Chile in the late 1950s and died in Santiago in 1984). Nazis also found refuge in the United States, a country that in 1945 was about to switch enemies from Hitler's Germany to the Soviet Union. (The case of Michael Karkoc—a top Nazi commander with a shady past who had been secretly living in Minnesota for decades—made the headlines in 2013.) This twisted history of hospitality does not mean that there was a specifically Nazi literature in Latin America, which is perhaps why Bolaño felt compelled to make one up. There were writers like Leopoldo Lugones in Argentina and Braulio Arenas in Chile who caved in to the fascist temptation, but in both Chile and Argentina the predominant literary traditions have been either liberal or affiliated to one degree or another with the left.

While the political context of these works is inescapable, it should not be taken for granted that Bolaño's approach to what the French call *la grande politique* is immediate and direct. Instead it is mediated by *literary politics*. Like the aviator of *Distant Star*, all the protagonists of *Nazi Literature in the Americas* are writers and poets, a choice that allows Bolaño to filter history and politics through literature. Bolaño himself was a personal victim of repression in the early days of the Pinochet regime, an event that shaped his political perspective for life. But he also made statements condemning the intransigence of the left and the betrayal of young Latin American revolutionaries at the hands of the apparatchik. One of the characters in *Nazi Literature in the Americas* ("Harry Sibelius") writes a voluminous novel modeled on Arnold J. Toynbee's *Hitler's Europe* because he wants to question and update the historian's original purpose to "testify against crime and ignominy" (121). Sibelius believes that "the crime in question has definitively triumphed" and proceeds to catalogue it in his novel's multitudinous pages. Sibelius's novel is a "dark mirror" of history, a statement that also applies to Bolano's *Nazi Literature in the Americas* and *Distant Star*. But again the mediation is literary. The main question is not what happened or why it happened but what role writers played in what happened. In the interview quoted above, Bolaño states that *Nazi Literature in the Americas* is primarily a work about literature, and that the characters who appear in it are "deformed reflections of the writer's trade," which he goes on to describe as "contemptible, sad, and mediocre" but possessed of a certain dignity even at its worst (Braithwaite 112). To be sure, literary politics play a role in both *Nazi Literature in the Americas* and *Distant Star*. Literary friendships, mentoring, and acceptance or rejection of new voices by the powers that rule the cultural field receive a large measure of attention in both texts. This is the arena where the writer's relation to history and politics is played out in Bolaño's work, in which it is difficult to find politicians or other public actors unrelated to the literary enterprise. Bolaño was in the habit of excoriating "official" writers, those closest to the bureaucracy and state apparatus. It is interesting that most of the protagonists of *Nazi Literature in the Americas*—but not Ramírez Hoffman or his avatar in *Distant Star,* who are supported by the regime—are marginal writers lost in their own literary and political delusions, which endows the work with a sympathetic tone that easily turns into black humor or caricature.

Nazi Literature in the Americas: Context and Sources

Nazi Literature in the Americas is a mock encyclopedia or literary dictionary—it is difficult to call it a novel, like Bolaño sometimes does—comprising thirty imaginary biographies of writers with right-wing sympathies from a variety of American countries, supplemented by an abundant bibliography of the authors, works, reviews, and publishers that make up the bulk of the book. Some of the bibliographical information in this "Epilogue for Monsters" expands on the content of the relevant entries, showing their potentially infinite capacity for expansion, as the Ramírez Hoffman chapter demonstrates. Not all the writers included in the collection deserve literally to be called Nazis, but they generally display political, national, social, or racial prejudices that align them with the radical worldview of fascist totalitarianism. As Michael Wood states in his review of the book, the work "looks like a single gag—the brief deadpan biography of an imaginary Fascist or near Fascist writer—multiplied by 30-odd cases over 200 pages. . . . This book is not a satirical attack on the right-wing imagination in North and South America: it is a darkly comic celebration of the wilder horizons of writing, good, plodding, lunatic and terrible. . . . Here are socialites, adventurers, psychopaths, thugs and dreamers, united in a single obsession: literature."[1] The strain of literature that unites most of these characters is the tradition of the avant-garde. In the opening chapter there is a reference to Breton's second surrealist manifesto (14), but Marinetti's futurism is also implicated in Bolaño's sketches of fascist literature.

The ideological tendencies of the historical avant-gardes were predominantly left-wing, with the exception of futurism, which became the official art of Mussolini's fascist regime in Italy. Futurism is known for its cult of the machine and of modern technology as much as for its exaltation of war and militarism. Despite ideological differences, there is some coincidence between Breton and Marinetti on the subject of violence. In his second manifesto (1929) Breton writes that the "simplest Surrealist act consists of dashing down into the street, pistol in hand, and firing blindly, as fast as you can pull the trigger, into the crowd," an appeal to revolutionary violence that has been used as justification to forge a link between art and crime. In his own Futurist manifesto (1909), on the other hand, Marinetti calls for the destruction of museums, libraries, and academies, and asserts that "art can be nothing but violence, cruelty, and injustice." In addition Marinetti strikes an explicitly misogynous note in his manifesto that becomes particularly relevant in the context of Bolaño's works when one remembers that both Ramírez Hoffman and the protagonist of *Distant Star* torture and murder women. A few years after proclaiming his Futurist ideas Marinetti became a friend and active supporter of Mussolini and remained one until his death in 1944. By then other notable American and European artists (Ezra Pound and Nobel Prize laureate Knut Hamsun among them) had declared their allegiance to fascism and Nazism. It is of interest that both Pound and Hamsun—like some of Bolaño's characters in *Nazi Literature*—spent time in mental hospitals.

Presumably no conventional history of Latin American or U.S. literature includes a chapter on Nazi literature as a significant part of the cultural tradition. Bolaño begins by inventing a tradition and "documenting" it with exemplary zeal. Not that there is not an actually existing Nazi or fascist literature: Goebbels's novel *Michael* (1929) is an example of the former, and Marinetti's manifesto illustrates the latter.[2] (Furthermore Louis-Ferdinand Céline's works attest to an anti-Semitic strain in European modernism.) This is a literature of "bad intentions," which does not mean that communist literature or social realism is necessarily a literature of good intentions. But when Sartre affirms in *What's Literature* that good intentions produce bad literature, he is referring to a liberal literary tradition in which literature is not fundamentally perceived as ideological or militant but as a humanitarian and progressive endeavor, one grounded on ethical principles and moral idealism, and one that has the potential to bring readers together in a consensual and civilized debate. Bolaño's project can only shock readers embedded in this tradition or maybe feeds on them by choosing such a noisy title for his book. The adjective "Nazi" has a shock value denied to most other terms and is constantly used and abused by public figures and in the media as a way to discredit domestic and foreign opponents. Overused as the term is, though, its semantic charge cannot be discarded; and because it is overused, "Nazi" can refer to a number of different aberrations, many of which find their expression in Bolaño's menagerie. Bolaño counts on the shock value of the term to expose his readers, if not to the actual existence of fascist and Nazi writers, then certainly to the underside of the writer's métier, which he finds contemptible and dignified at the same time. Would Bolaño's editors have been equally interested, say, in a book on the humanitarian literature of the Americas as they were in American Nazi literature?

This is not to say that Bolaño's use of the term is exclusively driven by a marketing imperative, far from it. Bolaño's conception of literature as a "ticking time bomb" relates the shock value of his title to a deeper level of meaning that justifies the writer's vocation and the existence of literature.[3] Literature is not something to be toyed with but rather the name given to verbal artifacts that can explode at a moment's notice in readers' hands. Of course there is also a historical and political basis for Bolaño's use of the term in a Latin American (and indeed Panamerican) context, given the uncounted number of Nazis and Nazi collaborators who found shelter in the Americas.

But missing from the list of leading Nazis who fled to the American continent is Hitler himself, who, according to official history, committed suicide in his Berlin bunker on April 30, 1945. This historical fact, though, was only the beginning of an alternative story about his death that still keeps the presses rolling. *Tras los pasos de Hitler* ("On Hitler's Footsteps") is only the latest in a string of books by Argentine journalist Abel Basti that seek to prove that the Nazi leader did not commit suicide during the fall of Berlin but escaped to Argentina with Eva Braun and settled in Bariloche—a beautiful ski resort in Argentine Patagonia originally settled by German-speaking immigrants— where he lived under an alias for many years. Basti is also the author of "Hitler in Argentina," "Hitler's Exile," and "Hitler's Secrets," all of them books based on highly speculative readings of documents and testimonies. British authors Simon Dunstan and Gerrard Williams made their own contributions to this revisionist narrative in *Grey Wolf: The Escape of Adolph Hitler*, a book that became a documentary film soon after being published in 2011 and a central claim of which was that Hitler died in 1962 in Argentina. The authors were accused of plagiarism by none other than Abel Basti.

If it is hard to distinguish between fact and fiction in this line of research, it is impossible to separate fiction from delirious fantasy in the works of Chilean author Miguel Serrano, a writer so improbable that he would not have had trouble fitting in Bolaño's gallery of authors in *Nazi Literature in the Americas*. Serrano was a convinced Nazi to the end of his life and a self-described specialist in esoteric Hitlerism. One of his books is *El cordón dorado: Hitlerismo esotérico* ("The Golden Thread: Esoteric Hitlerism"), in which he claims—or at least does not dispute—that Hitler was an initiate into cosmic mysteries whose mission in this world was to "transmute Fate" and that his body was the vehicle through which the light of the spirit shone through. He also quotes "evidence" (in reality, someone else's delusions) that flying saucers do not come from outer space but from inside the "hollow Earth," and that their appearances have increased since the end of the war—particularly around Antarctica—to warn mankind of the danger of atomic destruction. Not content with divulging this bit of occult lore, Serrano quotes another specialist in flying saucers who in a book called "The Twelve Triangles of Death" (which may or may not exist) claims that extraterrestrials are in reality Nazis based in Antarctica who are just pretending to be from outer space in order to "confuse witnesses."

Serrano is also the author of the six-hundred-page *Hitler: El último avatãra* ("Hitler: The Last Avatar"), where he discloses further bits of mystical wisdom. He actually states not only that the Aryan race has an extraterrestrial origin but that he himself comes from another planet and from an earlier time when he was privileged enough to speak to the gods. In almost every page of this monstrosity the reader is exposed to hermetic "revelations" linking the most disparate realities, periods, and events in a way that surpasses even the most fertile literary imagination. Hitler, for example, is linked to the Hyperborean gods, who no longer live in the northern regions of the Earth—as their name implies—but have moved to Antarctica following a natural catastrophe that reversed the location of the North and South Poles. There, in an underground base, they presumably huddle together awaiting the coming of the Fourth Reich. (For decades there was a persistent rumor that the German navy had a secret base in Antarctica, but that allegation has convincingly been put to rest by scholarly research.) It is ironic that in *Nazi Literature in the Americas* the "Fourth Reich" is "one of the most peculiar, outlandish and stubborn publishing ventures spawned by the Americas, ever fecund in enterprises verging on insanity, illegality, and idiocy" (214), the kind of publisher that might specialize in books like Serrano's—or, indeed, Bolaño's.[4] In actual fact *Hitler: El último avatãra* was appropriately published by a press called Ediciones la Nueva Edad (or New Age Editions).

All this goes to show that the Nazi mystique has proven harder to dislodge from the popular imagination than Hitler's regime from the pages of history. Its consequences can be brutal—as in the violence inflicted by neo-Nazi gangs on immigrants—or preposterous, as in the books mentioned above—or in movies like Steven Spielberg's *Raiders of the Lost Ark,* in which Hitler sends a team of Nazi archeologists to find the lost Ark of the Covenant before the U.S. government does. Bolaño's "Nazism" feeds on both legacies, the brutal and the bizarre, thus creating a grotesque tapestry of cruelty, excess, and lunacy. Actually existing Nazi literature may count as a source of Bolaño's fiction, but the connection between a literature of hate and a fictional work that delights in lunacy and pseudepigraphy (false authorial attributions) is tenuous. Borges's *Universal History of Infamy* and Rodolfo Wilcock's *Temple of the Iconoclasts* are closer in form and spirit to *Nazi Literature in the Americas.*[5]

Nazi Literature in the Americas explicitly references Borges's *Universal History of Infamy* in the "Infamous Ramírez Hoffman" chapter. Borges's *Universal History of Infamy* was published in book form in 1935 by Tor, a popular Buenos Aires publishing house that, as a critic points out, specialized in "cheap editions with graphic, color-saturated covers." Tor, the critic adds, "was a natural choice for this motley collection of capsule biographies of tricksters, assassins, and thugs from different parts of the globe" (Wells 425). The stories, however, had originally appeared in *Crítica,* a leading Buenos Aires daily in the 1930s, whose weekly cultural supplement—the *Revista Multicolor de los Sábados,* which was coedited by Borges himself and where the stories actually appeared—was not averse to using garish colors, sensationalist illustrations, and cartoons to appeal to a mass audience.[6] These stories are important because they were Borges's first attempts at fiction and allowed the future author of *Ficciones* and *El Aleph* to experiment with a Baroque style that in later years would produce the masterpieces that garnered him universal renown. They were not original, though, but "the irresponsible game of a shy young man who dared not write stories and so amused himself by falsifying and distorting . . . the tales of others," as Borges himself explains in his prologue to the 1954 edition of the book. In apparent unison with this statement, the sources are duly listed at the end of the book in a way that would convince the credulous reader, but at least one of them is bogus—the translation from the Arabic attributed to a certain Alexander Schulz and presumably published in German in 1927 that is supposed to be one of the sources of "The Masked Dyer, Hakim of Merv." "Alexander Schulz" was in reality Alejandro Schulz or Xul Solar, a friend of Borges and a writer and painter in his own right, but not the translator of a nebulous Arabic original called "The Annihilation of the Rose." Literary hoaxes are a well-known Borgesian device. Bolaño's *Nazi Literature in the Americas,* it goes without saying, is one massive hoax that uses a scholarly apparatus to render plausible the historical existence of thirty apocryphal authors and their works.

Another device that brings both works together is their external form: "capsule biographies" in the case of Borges; encyclopedia or dictionary entries in Bolaño's case. They are not that different, since in a very real sense Bolaño's work is (or pretends to be) a biographical dictionary. Furthermore encyclopedias and dictionaries—even whole libraries—figure prominently in Borges's writing, and one of his most famous—or infamous—characters (albeit from the later *Ficciones*) is the apocryphal Pierre Menard, "author" of the Quixote, who is described in the story by that name solely in terms of his bibliography. Bolaño characterizes his authors in terms of their bibliography but usually pads this bookish approach with plenty of biographical and historical detail.[7]

Both works also share an obvious tendency toward morally dubious characters, probably in keeping with the idea that lawbreakers and other characters beyond the pale are more interesting from a literary point of view than the average disciplined citizen who might actually be the reader. It could be argued that on this level there is a difference between Borges, whose characters are gangsters, pirates, and hustlers, and Bolaño, whose protagonists are all writers.

But it must be remembered that in Bolaño's fiction poets and other writers are interwined with conspirators, criminals, terrorists, gang leaders, pimps, serial murderers, policemen, and detectives. The real difference between the Borges of *Universal History of Infamy* and the Bolaño of *Nazi Literature in the Americas* and *Distant Star* is that in the former aesthetics takes precedence over ethics, while in the latter ethics and aesthetics are typically in conflict. Moral turpitude is not really an important theme in Borges's collection, in which narrative experimentation (combining avant-garde writing with exoticism and mass appeal) is a priority. In Bolaño moral transgression is rendered as literary foible.

Two additional points regarding the affinity between Borges's *Universal History of Infamy* and Bolaño's *Nazi Literature in the Americas* should be made. One has to do with the explosive nature of the respective titles. Critic Gene Bell-Villada points out that in the prologue to the 1954 edition of his work, Borges "termed the book's sonorous title 'excessive,' though some years later, on a French radio interview, he admitted having wished to shock readers with a 'bombastic word'" (63). Bolaño inherited this desire to "make noise" with his own choice for a title, but again such a design cannot be reduced to a marketing strategy. Furthermore both Borges and Bolaño have recognized their debt to Marcel Schwob, the author of *Imaginary Lives* (1896) and of *The Children's Crusade* (1896). In a 1946 review Borges remarked that around 1935 he wrote "a naïve book called *A Universal History of Infamy*. One of its many sources, still ignored by the critics, was this book [*Imaginary Lives*] by Schwob. . . . For his writing, he invented a curious method. His characters are real but the events are mostly fictitious. . . . This vacillation results in the volume's peculiar zest" (*On Writing* 108). The same zest is evident in *Nazi Literature in the Americas*, but it is not produced by the vacillation between the characters' reality and the fictitious events they experience. It is the tension between history and fiction that provides the spark for Bolaño's enterprise, even when history becomes a record of the future.

Another important influence on *Nazi Literature in the Americas* is Rodolfo Wilcock's *The Temple of the Iconoclasts,* a mock encyclopedia of eccentric authors, philosophers, inventors, and scientists translated from the Italian into Spanish in 1981 (and years later into English).[8] Wilcock was born in Argentina and was part of Borges's intellectual circle in the early 1950s but left the country for political reasons and settled in Italy, the country where his mother was born. He wrote most of his work in Italian. *La sinagoga de los iconoclastas,* as the book is known in Spanish, contains thirty-five short biographical sketches of real and imaginary characters whose common denominator is their extravagant rebellion against accepted beliefs and common sense. Among them the reader finds a mystic who plays chess by telepathy with opponents located in different cities, an author who writes a combination of spy and pornographic novels based on the entries of a French-language dictionary, a utopian thinker who wants to return the contemporary world to the days of Elizabethan England by suppressing all the progress made since 1580, an inventor who designs dozens of useless devices such as elastic underwear for dogs in heat and a grooved plate for eating asparagus, and so on. Unreal as these crackpots seem to be, many of them were actual historical figures, as documented by Martin Gardner in *Fads and Fallacies in the Name of Science,* one of the sources of Wilcock's book. Here Wilcock's reader will find Roger Babson, who spent his life looking for a substance that would neutralize gravity; Charles Littlefield, who by sheer willpower made salt crystallize in the shape of small animals; Charles Piazzi-Smyth, founder of popular pyramidology; Benedict Lust, inventor of "zone therapy" (which consisted of squeezing the appropriate fingers or toes to cure all manner of diseases); and Hans Hörbiger, a Viennese engineer who believed that the Earth had had six previous moons before the present one and that these had crashed into the planet causing great catastrophes such as the biblical Flood and giving rise to legends involving dragons and other flying monsters. Hörbiger had disciples and formed a kind of astronomical cult with millions of followers. In photographs he appeared in the guise of a Knight of the Teutonic Order. His doctrines found favor among the Nazis, who compared the astronomer's intelligence with that of Hitler. Franz Zwickau, one of Bolaño's characters in *Nazi Literature in the Americas,* is described as "a talented, iconoclastic boy who refused to grow up" (89).

The Cast

The thirty biographies of *Nazi Literature in the Americas* are distributed in thirteen subtitled sections that provide readers with a fairly accurate description of their general types. The above-mentioned Franz Zwickau, for example, is one of two writers covered in "Germans at the Ends of the Earth." The incorrigible plagiarist Max Mirebalais is the sole occupant of the section entitled "The Many Masks of Max Mirebalais," just as the infamous Ramírez Hoffman occupies all by himself the section of a similar name. There are also self-explanatory sections called "Speculative and Science Fiction," "North American Poets," "The Aryan Brotherhood," and "The Fabulous Schiaffino Boys." Other section headings are more arbitrary: "Forerunners and Figures of the Anti-Enlightenment," for example; or "Magicians, Mercenaries, and Miserable Creatures." The reason they are relatively arbitrary is that none of the authors appearing in the collection can be said to be particularly enlightened, and many of them can claim to have miserable lives, not just the three characters represented in that section. In general, though, the section headings are one of the structural principles operating in the book because they organize a large number of otherwise disparate biographical sketches. Another such principle is the recurrence of certain characters (Edelmira de Mendiluce, Segundo José Heredia, and the infamous Ramírez Hoffman) and of the publisher *The Fourth Reich*, which endows the book with a degree of formal autonomy. And the epilogue, by collecting in alphabetical order the numerous secondary characters of the main entries (and being obviously located at the end of the book), contributes to the work's structural coherence by sealing it with a kind of summary.

Nazi Literature in the Americas is composed exclusively of writers (poets, novelists, playwrights, and the occasional pseudophilosopher or pseudoscientist), but this cast of characters is remarkably varied in terms of nationalities and other features. In terms of nationality, Bolaño's history of Nazi literature in the Americas stands as a regional version of Borges's *Universal History of Infamy*. There are writers from twelve different American countries, eight of whom are from Argentina and seven from the United States. Only three hail from Chile—Bolaño's native country—and one from Mexico, the country where the author spent his adolescent years and became a writer. Four of Bolaño's featured writers are women, and the remaining twenty-four men, but many of the secondary characters listed in the bibliography are women and some of them are writers. All but two of the characters are white—not a surprising count in a book about Nazi literature. The Guatemalan Gustavo Borda is short and swarthy but prefers blondes. Furthermore his characters are tall, fair-haired, and blue-eyed, an imaginary compensation for the indignities he has to endure in Hollywood, where he keeps falling in love and being rejected by the blondes of his dreams. The other nonwhite character is the Haitian Max Mirebalais, who "was excited by the idea of being a Nazi poet while continuing to espouse a certain kind of *négritude*" (130). This oxymoronic or hybrid Nazi mulatto is an ironic counterpoint to the members of the Aryan brotherhood featured in another of the book's sections.[9] Finally a number of Bolaño's characters live well beyond 1996, the date of the book's publication, though none lives as long as the year 2666: Schürholz dies in 2029, Soderstern in 2021, Borda in 2016, Heredia in 2004, Ramírez Hoffman in 1998, and so on. This peculiar device, which turns *Nazi Literature in the Americas* into a history of the future, attests to Bolaño's interest in the science-fiction genre. Harry Sibelius, for example, is an avid reader of Norman Spinrad and Philip K. Dick and writes a novel in which the Axis powers win the war and the United States is divided into German and Japanese possessions. (This fictional novel closely echoes Philip K. Dick's *Man in the High Castle*, a well-known representative of the "alternate history" or "counterfactual" mode.)

Not all the authors assigned late death notices are science-fiction writers or write alternate history, but to the extent that they are all creatures of the imagination, their proper domains are the alternative realities best exemplified in science-fiction novels. Rory Long, for example, is not a novelist but a poet, and yet he concocts a poem in which Leni Riefenstahl—the famous director of Nazi propaganda films like *Triumph of the Will* and *Olympia*—makes love with Ernst Jünger, a conservative German modernist, a "hundred-year-old man and a ninety-year-old woman," as the narrator states after doing some math (145). Prophetic glances into the future—the future being merely one form of alternate reality—are scattered throughout Bolaño's work, and they may be extravagant (as in chapter 13 of *Amulet*) or apocalyptic, as in *2666*.

Counterfactual history is not the only approach to the past essayed in *Nazi Literature in the Americas*. Factual history is a dynamic background for many of the authors whose lives and works overlap with right-wing regimes in Brazil, Argentina, and Chile between the mid-1960s and 1980s; for Pérez Masón, the Cuban crypto-Nazi subjected to the repression of the island's communist regime; and for a number of other characters who find themselves in Spain during that country's Civil War or who travel to Germany during Hitler's ascent to power. Thus the Brazilian Amado Couto joins a government death squad after his stories are rejected by every publisher and participates in kidnappings, torture of political prisoners, and extrajudicial killings. He even concocts a plan to use his paramilitary influences to kidnap Brazil's great novelist Rubem Fonseca, the (real) author of novels like *High Art*—made into a movie starring Peter Coyote and a recent TV series called *Mandrake*—and *Vast Emotions and Imperfect Thoughts*. Couto's novels are full of skeletons, and his criminal past and lack of artistic success lead him to hang himself in a Parisian hotel. He dies in 1989, four years after democracy had returned to Brazil. The military were in power for twenty-one years and were responsible for hundreds of deaths and thousands of torture cases, including that of current president Dilma Roussef, who was imprisoned and tortured for three years in the early 1970s. Brazil's violent political past is currently being investigated by a human rights commission.

The Brazilian dictatorship began in 1964 and was the result of the Cold War. The military government seized power just a few years after Castro overthrew Batista in Cuba and sponsored guerrilla activity throughout Latin America. The government justified its actions in the name of national security, a doctrine developed by the U.S. government and the Pentagon and imparted to the large numbers of Latin American officers trained in the United States. (In the movie *Four Days in September* guerrillas kidnap the American ambassador to Brazil.) State repression was directed against left-wing militants, but abuses were committed against a broad spectrum of dissidents. The Chilean and Argentine dictatorships of the 1970s were also a result of the Cold War and of the collusion between local military authorities and U.S. interests. With the implantation of the national security doctrine, Latin American armies deemphasized their traditional role as protectors of national borders and concentrated their efforts on fighting internal subversion. Counterinsurgency measures thus became notoriously prominent. The internal enemy was defined in broad terms and included actual left-wing militants as well as anyone suspected of espousing left-wing ideology or endorsing social change. Many of the victims of dictatorships were idealistic lower- or middle-class youths who believed in a more just society, which is why Bolaño tended to refer to these political struggles as the Latin American guerras floridas, stressing their romantic inspiration. The military in countries like Argentina, Brazil, and Chile coordinated their actions, and those of their intelligence branches, through the secret "Plan Condor," which came to light only many years after the event. This agreement ensured that guerrillas or guerrilla sympathizers, left-wing intellectuals, trade union leaders, and social activists who crossed national borders in an attempt to escape repression in their countries of origin would be hunted down by the appropriate security apparatus in the country of destination.

The Argentine Dirty War is reflected in several of the sketches of *Nazi Literature in the Americas*. The political background of these sections of the book, which on one or two occasions involve events dating back to the mid-twentieth century, can be briefly summarized as follows. Juan Domingo Perón, the dominant personality of modern Argentine history, was elected to power in 1946 and reelected in 1952, the year his second wife (Eva Perón) died of cancer. Although Argentina was neutral during the conflict and ended up supporting the Allies, Perón's sympathies were with the Axis powers. When the war was over he welcomed many fugitive Nazis and Nazi collaborators into the country, some of whom had committed crimes against humanity. There was talk during this period of a Fourth Reich preparing its emergence in the Southern Hemisphere. Perón was overthrown in 1955 and after a prolonged exile in Franco's Spain returned to power in 1973, when Argentina was experiencing high levels of political violence. He died the next year and left his third wife, Isabel Martínez de Perón, in power. "Isabelita," as she was called, was unable to stop the violence between the left-wing Montonero guerrillas and the army (and paramilitary death squads that had prospered under her protection) and was overthrown by a military junta in March 1976. This marks the beginning of the Dirty War, which the military officially called the Process of National Reorganization. The dictatorship soon became infamous throughout the world for its repressive methods.

Imprisonment of political enemies, exile, torture, extrajudicial killings, and disappearances became the order of the day. The government's record of human rights abuses and its failure to make economic progress forced it to relegitimate its authority. Thus in April 1982 the members of the ruling junta chose to invade the Malvinas (or Falkland Islands), which were under British jurisdiction but that Argentina had been claiming since the nineteenth century. The Argentine army was poorly prepared for the British response to the invasion and was forced to surrender in June of that year. The war, though, did bring an end to military rule. The members of the last junta stepped down, elections took place in December 1983, and the new president quickly formed a human rights commission to investigate the fate of the disappeared. The officers of the four different juntas that had ruled since 1976 were tried in 1985 and condemned to prison terms ranging from life sentences to only a few years.

The sense of history frames many of Bolaño's portraits in *Nazi Literature in the Americas*. The lives and works of several of his Argentine writers, for example, are tightly woven with these historical events. Edelmira Thompson de Mendiluce, whose life span covers most of the twentieth century and includes a trip to Germany—where she has a picture of herself and her daughter taken with the Führer—and an improbable friendship with Eva Perón, returns from Europe to Argentina in 1955 after the fall of Perón and decades later subsidizes a memoir of the Falklands War that catapults an ex-soldier to literary prominence. This patroness of the arts is widowed but has a son and a daughter. Her son, Juan, writes a successful early novel featuring a French neoroyalist and a young German Nazi, occupies important posts during the first two Perónist governments, and is eventually appointed ambassador to Franco's Spain. In 1975, the year Franco died, Juan gives up literature and serves "the Peronist and military governments with equal loyalty" (17), an ironic statement showing the character's opportunistic streak since Perón's third wife and successor was exiled by the military junta that came to power in 1976. The widow Mendiluce's daughter, on the other hand, exploits the dubious fame granted to her by her baby photograph with Hitler and eventually becomes seriously infatuated with a promising female poet who is kidnapped by a group of strangers and whose body is found two months later in a garbage dump. The strangers are undoubtedly members of one of the many death squads that operated during the Dirty War and roamed the streets of Argentine cities in unmarked Ford Falcons kidnapping and disappearing presumed subversives.

The two portraits of the Schiaffino brothers that make up the section called "The Fabulous Schiaffino Boys" mix references to the Dirty War with allusions to the *barras bravas* of Argentine soccer (organized groups of hooligans responsible for much of the violence in and around stadiums) and to a mishmash of pseudoliterary endeavors that endow the characters in question with cultural prestige among their followers. The older brother's two passions in life are soccer and literature. When he is twenty, he takes over the leadership of the Boca Juniors gang (Boca being one of the two traditional Buenos Aires clubs) and publishes a manifesto accusing Jews and communists of ruining Argentine soccer. He also publishes a magazine that serves as a mouthpiece for his ideas. In one of the issues he pretends to be a fan of Boca's traditional rivals River Plate and pokes fun at its players and supporters. He dies while listening to "one of the last reports on the Falklands war" (160). (Boca Juniors was founded by Italian immigrants in the ethnic neighborhood of La Boca, a district located at the mouth of the Riachuelo, a small tributary of the Río de la Plata. River Plate was founded in the same location at the turn of the twentieth century by dock workers but lacks a distinctive ethnic identity. The Schiaffino brothers are obviously of Italian descent. The older one's first name is Italo.)

The younger Schiaffino lives until the year 2015 and follows in his brother's footsteps. He becomes a fanatic member and eventual leader of his brother's Boca gang and in his early years writes poetry, plays, stories, and manifestos in the worst possible taste, published at his own expense and in small mimeographed editions: "a series of thirty epigrams entitled *Anthology of the Best Argentinean Jokes*" (162); a story imagining a bloody war with neighboring Chile; a manifesto attacking "the league's umpires, whom he accused of bias, lack of physical fitness, and, in some cases, drug use" (162); and an extravagant play (influenced by Copi)[10] featuring a summit of several Latin American presidents who meet in order to end the supremacy of European "total football," a concept popularized in the early 1970s by the Dutch national team. The general consensus among the leaders is a kind of final solution: to physically eliminate the finest exponents of European football. At the beginning of the Dirty War, Schiaffino is said to have participated in the activities of a death squad. In 1978, when the World Cup was held in Argentina and the generals used it to project a sanitized image of the country around the world, he writes a long chaotic poem in praise of the national team that won the tournament, possibly forgetting the fact that in order to win its group of four and move on to the final against Holland, Argentina had to defeat Peru by four goals. The final score was 6–0 in favor of the local side, and to this day rumors persist that bribes were involved and that there was collusion between the military leaders of Peru and Argentina. At the time of the Falklands War he tries and fails to enlist as a volunteer to fight the British, but he does attend the 1982 World Cup in Spain, where Argentina was eliminated by Italy. He and his group of die-hard fans create serious disturbances after the game, and Schiaffino spends three months in a Spanish prison. On his return to Argentina he is hailed as the leader of the Boca gang, in which capacity he is involved in an ambush of River Plate fans that ends with the death of two of them. Schiaffino becomes a fugitive but still manages to attend several other World Cup tournaments. Before leaving Argentina for the United States, where he is presumed to have links with the Ku Klux Klan and is ultimately murdered outside a gambling den in New Orleans, Schiaffino regales his fans with *The Best of Argentino Schiaffino*, a book that appears without a publisher's imprint or date of publication: "the cognoscenti were quick to surmise that the book had been produced by the Fourth Reich in Argentina, a mystagogically inspired venture, which kept popping up and then vanishing again in Buenos Aires publishing between 1965 and 2000" (169).

It is worth noting one of Schiaffino's works is a thinly disguised memoir that contains historical inaccuracies that may, however, "be deranged metaphors for truths of another kind" (175–76). While a deranged reading of history cannot be discounted as a literary approach in Bolaño's fiction, the section on Willy Schürholz contains historically accurate information that reads like a distorted metaphor for something else. Willy is (presumably) a Chilean born in a German enclave—the Colonia Renacer (or "Rebirth Colony")—who learns Spanish at only ten years of age and who is allowed to leave the colony in order to study agricultural science in Santiago. The description of the colony seems fantastic but is all too real, or at least it is based on rumors that many people in Chile believed for years to be true: the commune is located twenty-five miles from Temuco, in the south of Chile; all the colonists are German; no outsiders are allowed in; the settlers bury their own dead; they work communally from sunrise to sunset; the site served as a refuge for fugitive Nazis; sexual slavery is accepted; inbreeding produced albinos, "idiot children and freaks" (93); and after 1973 it disappeared from the news. In September of that year the military staged a coup against Marxist president Salvador Allende that interrupted the long tradition of Chilean democracy. Pinochet's regime was brutally repressive and set up detention camps throughout the territory where political prisoners were held and tortured, and could easily disappear. One of these was the Colonia Dignidad, the historical version of Bolaño's Colonia Renacer. (Its name was later changed to Villa Baviera.) The actual founder of this commune was Paul Schäffer, a former Nazi pedophile and cult leader who became a fugitive in 1997 and was eventually arrested in Buenos Aires, returned to Chile, and sentenced in 2006 to a twenty-year prison term for child abuse. He died in prison in 2010. Much of what went on for decades inside the colony's perimeter is now a matter of public knowledge, but further investigations are still going on. The colony is now a tourist destination, and Schäffer's former residence has been turned into a guesthouse to entertain visitors (see Falconer).

Bolaño could not resist the kind of material provided by Colonia Dignidad in a book like *Nazi Literature in the Americas.* Not only was the commune the site of a pedophilic Nazi cult, but it also lent itself to a rich mix of fact and fiction. Willy Schürholz, the writer in the story, is obsessed by the experiences of his early years in the colony and uses his artistic talent to work through the trauma of growing up in what was basically a concentration camp, surrounded by barbed wire and guarded by imposing towers. When democracy returns to Chile in 1990, Willy publishes a book of children's stories under the pseudonym "Kaspar Hauser," the name of the German wild child who one day appeared in the streets of Nuremberg and claimed to have grown up in the confinement of a homestead with little or no contact with the outside world: "Hauser-Schürholz idealized a childhood that was suspiciously aphasic, amnesic, obedient and silent. Invisibility seemed to be his aim" (97). But during Pinochet's regime Willy's artistic work was characterized by compulsive references to Nazi concentration camps and their Chilean versions: "His first poems combined disconnected sentences and topographic maps of Colonia Renacer" (94). They were unintelligible to most critics, but some suggested that they showed the locations of secret graves. His second series of poetic experiments was an installation of huge cryptic maps that, according to one interpretation, were inspired by the maps of concentration camps in Nazi Europe. Then Willy publishes a series of books entitled *Geometry I, II, and III* that "set out countless variations on the theme of a barbed-wire fence crossing an almost empty space" (96). His culminating work is digging a map of an ideal concentration camp in Chile's Atacama desert and inscribing on it the five vowels with a hoe and a mattock, which may be a schizophrenic reference to the Soviet Union's hammer and sickle. The Atacama desert has actually been the site of artistic experiments, such as the giant hand sculpture emerging from its surface and executed by Chilean artist Mario Irarrázabal. Poet Raúl Zurita also used the same desolate space for artistic purposes. In 1993 he inscribed the line "Ni pena ni miedo" ("Without pain or fear")—a one-mile-long geoglyph—in the sands of the desert, a work of land art that must be seen from the air. Willy's concentration camp map had also to be viewed from the air.

As a result of his poetic and artistic experiments Willy Schürholz was "considered the only disciple of the enigmatic, vanished Ramírez Hoffman, although the young man from Colonia Renacer lacked the master's excess" (95). The story of the infamous Ramírez Hoffman, the master of avant-garde fascist poetics, appears again in *Distant Star,* the novel that expands on the aviator's poetic and murderous antics. Suffice it to say for now that *Nazi Literature in the Americas* is populated with avant-garde authors closely linked to totalitarian political projects like Italian and Spanish fascism or German Nazism. Ernesto Pérez Masón stands out among them because his fascist bent is played out in the context of a different kind of totalitarian project, namely Cuban Communism, which makes him resort to certain forms of cryptic writing in order to get his anticommunist message across. Pérez Masón is "a rather atypical member of the group that formed around the magazine *Orígenes*" (54), in reality one of the most important journals in Latin American cultural history. (The magazine lasted from 1944 to 1956 and published work by important writers like José Lezama Lima, Cintio Vitier, Eliseo Diego and Virgilio Piñera, all of whom are referred to by name in this chapter. Adding to the ambiguity between fact and fiction in Bolaño's book, Pérez Masón's feud with Lezama Lima—reported by the narrator at the beginning of the section—makes Bolaño's character appear as a shadow version of Virgilio Piñera, who challenged Lezama three times to a fight, exactly as recounted in the text.) Pérez Masón's first novel is a coded affront to Castro's regime: "The censor quickly smelled a rat. The first letters of each chapter made up the acrostic *Long Live Hitler*" (55–56), while the first letters of each chapter's second paragraphs formed other offensive tirades: *This Place Sucks, USA Where Are You,* and *Kiss My Cuban Ass.* Clearly this is Nazism with a drop of Caribbean spice. Later in life Pérez Masón forms an association that may exist only in his mind: its acronym is AWC, Aryan Writers of Cuba. And a few years before he dies he manages to flee the island and settle in New York: "Surprisingly, his name figures in the *Dictionary of Cuban Authors* (Havana, 1978), which omits Guillermo Cabrera Infante" (58). (Cabrera Infante was one of the Cuban writers associated with the Latin American Boom of the 1960s. In his *Vidas para leerlas* he includes a chapter on the parallel lives of Lezama and Piñera and gives details of their feud. This book was published two years after *Nazi Literature in the Americas.*)

Distant Star: Wings of Infamy

The last story of *Nazi Literature in the Americas*—"The Infamous Ramírez Hoffman"—is the source of *Distant Star,* one of Bolaño's most highly regarded novels on account of its powerful mix of art, horror, and politics. The novel came out in Spanish when Bolaño was beginning to be noticed by the literary establishment in Latin America and Spain, and in English before *The Savage Detectives* and *2666,* the author's major works. It was Bolaño's second novel to appear in English, immediately after *By Night in Chile,* a one-two punch that led critics and reviewers to notice the appearance of a new major talent from the Hispanic world, and one that seemed to endow Latin American literature with a new identity beyond the clichés of magic realism. The title of the novel refers to the star in the Chilean flag, the *estrella solitaria* or "lone star" whose similarity with the lone star of the Texas flag is mere coincidence. The novel's protagonist draws a star under the Chilean sky as part of his poetic sky writing. When *Distant Star* was published in 1996 Chile was undergoing the final phases of a transition between dictatorship and democracy. The military regime had come to an end through constitutional means in a 1988 referendum and in a subsequent presidential election, but Pinochet was still a powerful man with a high approval rating among the middle classes and business circles. The human rights issue lay dormant, after the failure of the Rettig human rights commission to bring perpetrators to justice.

Narrating dictatorship has always been a staple of Latin American literature, a task that has been undertaken in a critical spirit by liberal writers like José Marmol and Domingo Faustino Sarmiento in the nineteenth century and Mario Vargas Llosa in modern novels like *Conversation in the Cathedral* and

The Feast of the Goat, but a task that other authors concerned with issues of cultural identity and neocolonialism (like Alejo Carpentier and García Márquez) have approached more ambiguously. Bolaño's perspective on dictatorial politics is decidedly unambiguous and critical, as befits a member of a revolutionary generation. But Bolaño does not focus on the traditional concerns of the dictatorship novel—articulating a liberal project for a nation gripped by *caudillismo,* denouncing the corrupting effects of dictatorship on a whole generation, portraying the personality cult of a paradigmatic Latin American leader, or revealing the links between dictatorship and certain cultural traits deeply rooted in Latin American society. Instead, he memorializes the victims of the *guerras floridas*—the idealistic struggle against tyranny and social injustice that took the lives of so many of his generational peers—and keeps coming back to the question of art's role in the historical process.

In·addition *Distant Star* is also a postdictatorial novel but one that steers away from the usual treatment of this genre in Latin American literary criticism, a treatment characterized by framing this type of novel in terms of trauma and mourning for a lost socialist project. In *Distant Star* the loss of the revolutionary ideal is not an occasion for political soul-searching. Neither does time stand still in the novel inflicting the same historical wound over and over again. As is the case throughout Bolaño's work, history and politics are inextricably bound up with literature, so that the loss of the future—which is what the failure of the Chilean socialist experiment meant for its adherents—is "transcoded" in Bolaño in terms of the literary style most concerned with the future, namely the avant-garde. All the poets in the novel are concerned with revolutionizing Chilean poetry, though the more naive ones among them can conceive only of leftist poets as qualified to carry out such a task. The novel's protagonist, of course, is a different species and uses different means "to show the world that the new regime and avant-garde art were not at odds" (77). Ultimately *Distant Star* stages a literal and allegorical search for truth. On the literal level, the detective hires the idle poet and narrator to browse a pile of trashy literary journals in order to help him locate the vanished protagonist of the novel, the perpetrator of various criminal acts during and after the dictatorship. Allegorically this detective ploy brings out literature's redeeming power in the face of its own complicity with evil. (One could even relate the violence typical of avant-garde gestures—pointing toward an explosive break with the past—to the foundational violence of military regimes such as the ones that ruled in Argentina and Chile in the 1970s.) Guilt and redemption are bonded together to the extent that the poet and the criminal are twin figures or figures superimposed on one another. In this sense there is a significant passage toward the end of *Distant Star* where the narrator encounters the criminal he and the detective are looking for and has a disturbing epiphany: "For a nauseating moment I could see myself almost joined to him, like a vile Siamese twin" (144).[11] This passage is missing from the original nucleus of the story, in which the narrator is only tangentially related to the criminal and devoid of any symbolic identification with him.

The plot of "The Infamous Ramírez Hoffman" remains structurally intact in *Distant Star* but the novel changes many of the characters' names, expands details in many different directions (twenty-five pages become 150), and adds an authorial prologue and several important characters to the mix. The Latin text written in the sky also suffers some alterations but without losing its reference to the biblical Genesis, which correlates with the political project of the military regime, namely to reestablish the national community along authoritarian and neoliberal lines and propitiate a new historical beginning. The *Nazi Literature in the Americas* version of *Distant Star* is simply the germ of the larger story. There is nothing in it that is not also—and more fully treated—in the expanded version. But it should be noted that the narrator of "Ramírez Hoffman" is no longer called "Bolaño" in *Distant Star,* and that in the novel Ramírez Hoffman (alias Emilio Stevens) becomes Carlos Wieder (alias Alberto Ruiz-Tagle), the two poets who run poetry workshops in Concepción (Juan Cherniakovski and Martín García) become Juan Stein and Diego Soto respectively, and the Venegas *sisters* become the Garmendia *twins*. Some of the new characters are the narrator's friend Bibiano, the twins' maid Amalia Maluenda, the literary critic Ibacache (a character who also appears in *By Night in Chile*), and—in one of the novel's digressions—the bisexual artist and amputee Lorenzo/Petra, one of the many examples of dual identity in the novel.

The plot of both versions of the story is based on a character with no past (and sporting one or more aliases) that at the beginning of Allende's socialist regime in Chile (1970–73) shows up at a poetry workshop and seduces a pair of sisters who the other apprentice poets in the workshop all long for. A few weeks after the 1973 coup, this character reappears in the sisters' lives. He visits them at their remote country estate, spends an evening with them reading poetry, accepts their hospitality, and in the middle of the night kidnaps them with the help of hired goons after slashing their aunt's throat. The sisters become two of the hundreds of people disappeared under Pinochet's rule. (One of the bodies will appear years later in a mass grave.) The narrator does not disappear in the violence that follows the coup but is imprisoned instead in a makeshift detention camp on the outskirts of the city—an autobiographical detail that Bolaño has mentioned on many occasions. As a prisoner in that camp, one day he witnesses the strange spectacle of a vintage World War II plane doing acrobatics and writing oracular poetry in the sky.

The author of this aerial writing turns out to be the narrator's former acquaintance from the poetry workshop, but he now reappears in the guise of a lieutenant with the Chilean air force. The aviator next performs his sky writing in downtown Santiago for a multitude of spectators officially invited to the show, mostly young army officers, journalists, and civilian artists—plus one society belle and the performer's father. The second act of that day involves a secretive photographic exhibition at a late party in a friend's apartment attended by some of the same people who had witnessed the air show. Playing host for the night, the now famous or infamous airman invites the guests to enter one by one into the veritable chamber of horrors he has secretly prepared for them in the apartment's spare bedroom, which is decorated with hundreds of photos of tortured, mutilated, and dead bodies posted on the walls and ceiling. These are the victims of the dictatorship—the dead, the tortured, and the disappeared—whose photographic archive has become a shocking artistic installation. This time the perpetrator (of both art and crime) has gone too far and is outcast by his peers, going underground for the next twenty years. He is rumored to be hiding under various aliases, moving through different countries, and scratching a living in the porno industry. Finally the narrator—who by this time is living in Barcelona—receives the visit of a Chilean detective closely connected to the Allende regime who hires him to help find the former poet, aviator, and serial killer. The detective argues that it takes a poet to find another poet. Despite his protestations to the effect that the suspect is not a poet but a criminal, the narrator does help the detective solve the case. It is ironic that the former airman is found to be living in Lloret, a destination just a bus ride away from Blanes, the town where Bolaño was living in the mid-1990s. The narrator points him out to the detective, and the latter takes care of business, quietly executing the culprit.

In many police stories the detective who becomes obsessed with the criminal sees something of himself reflected in the object of his search. It would not be fair to say that either Bolaño's detective or narrator are obsessed with the criminal they are after, but this standard detective fiction motif is not totally inoperative in *Distant Star.* It is, however, transcoded in literary terms. The contiguity between the narrator and the criminal—two poets, after all, though only one is criminally transgressive—lends itself to a metaphorical reading, to a relation of resemblance. Both criminal and poet are practitioners of literature, an activity that can be used for either good or evil and that demands continued ethical vigilance especially when the evil is being exorcized through the good (as in stories that denounce violence but run the risk of replicating the very violence they denounce).[12] The narrator and the protagonist, as expressed earlier, are "Siamese twins." Precisely because of this uncomfortable consanguinity the narrator reacts with disgust to his reading of the trashy magazines that the detective puts at his disposal in the search for the criminal artist: "This is my last communiqué from the planet of the monsters. Never again will I immerse myself in literature's bottomless cesspools. I will go back to writing my poems, such as they are, find a job to keep body and soul together, and make no attempt to be published" (130). After immersing himself in the *mar de mierda* of literature (as the original reads), the narrator has to come up for air and to separate the wheat from the chaff. The magazines to which he was exposed "were not the usual sort of right-wing literary magazines: four were the work of original skinhead groups, two were brought out irregularly by football fans, at least seven were mainly given over to science fiction, three were offshoots of war games clubs, four . . . were devoted to the occult and one of these . . . openly advocated devil worship" (120). The narrator's reaction to the seamy side of literature is similar to that of the spectators of the photographic display earlier in the novel. This display, furthermore, cannot be attributed to the "usual sort" of right-wing imagination but rather to a mind oriented toward the exploration of absolute evil, a quest in Bolaño's novel that is more literary than political.

Both versions of the story end with the detective saying farewell to the narrator, but the formulation of the ending differs. In *Nazi Literature in the Americas* the text reads: "Look after yourself, Bolaño, he said, and off he went." And in *Distant Star* the last words are: "Look after yourself, my friend, he said, and off he went" (149). In the first of these two quotes, the English "yourself" translates the informal "tú" pronoun in Spanish ("Cuídate, Bolaño"), while in the second one the "yourself" does duty for the more formal "usted" ("Cuídese, mi amigo"). Clearly Bolaño decided to downplay the familiarity between his narrator and the detective in the transition from *Nazi Literature in the Americas* to *Distant Star,* probably in order to preserve the tough guy image of the classic detective of hard-boiled fiction. But he is also being consistent with the play between fact and fiction in the prologue to the novel, where not Bolaño but his alter ego Arturo B. is put forth as the original narrator of the story.

The autofictional and metafictional prologue is an important element for understanding the novel. It is a mixture of fact and fiction and a refelction of the story within the story, but it is grounded in Bolaño's authorial voice. The author comments on the conception of the novel by casting a backward glance at *Nazi Literature in the Americas* that is both factual and revisionary. He confirms that in the final chapter of *Nazi Literature in the Americas* he recounted the story of lieutenant Ramírez Hoffman of the Chilean air force but adds that he heard this story from a fellow Chilean, "Arturo B., a veteran of Latin America's doomed revolutions" (*guerras floridas,* in the original). The introduction of this fictitious storyteller is the first indication in the novel of the prominence of the theme of the double, which is restated at the end of the prologue when the author invokes the "increasingly animated ghost of Pierre Menard," the character who rewrites the *Quixote* in Borges's famous story ("Pierre Menard,

Author of the *Quixote*") by duplicating certain paragraphs originally written by Cervantes but endowing them with a different interpretation. *Distant Star* is an expanded duplication of "The Infamous Ramírez Hoffman": its protagonist is Carlos Wieder (a last name that in German means "again," as the elaborate philological dissertation that begins on page 40 makes clear), both Wieder and Ramírez Hoffman have at least one alias, they both attend two simultaneous poetry workshops whose directors mirror one another, there are two "Juan Steins," and the Venegas sisters in the original story become the Garmendia twins in the novel.

As Bolaño considers these works to be Siamese twins of one another—not only because they are formal duplicates of one another but also on account of their monstruous content—it is no surprise that Wieder, writing under one of his aliases, is the author of a one-act play whose main subject is torture and "whose action unfolds in a world inhabited exclusively by Siamese twins, where sadism and masochism are children's games" (94–95). Art and crime may be considered to be another pair of Siamese twins but so could the Janus-like face of literature, a practice that has the power to instigate evil or keep it in check. The passage quoted near the beginning of this section regarding the uncomfortable identification between the narrator and the serial killer when they are both sitting in the café is not the only one of its kind. Another similar passage is the narrator's shipwreck dream in which the complicity between good and evil is revealed. In the dream the narrator is crossing the ocean in a boat, and when a tornado sinks it he sees Wieder clinging to a barrel of brandy in the water while he himself clings to a spar: "And only then, as the waves pushed us apart, did I understand that Wieder and I had been travelling in the same boat; he may have conspired to sink it, but I had done little or nothing to stop it going down" (122). The sinking boat is the Ship of State, a metaphor also alluded to at the very beginning of chapter 2.

It should be noted that the introduction of the author's alter ego in the prologue complicates the identification of the novel's narrator: is it Bolaño or Arturo B.? The latter is the original bearer of the story, but the story, in its written form, results from the collaboration between both "authors": "we took that final chapter [of *Nazi Literature in the Americas*] and shut ourselves up for a month and a half in my house in Blanes, where, guided by his dreams and nightmares, we composed the present novel." This ambiguity is responsible for the disappearance of the name Bolaño as the narrator's name in *Distant Star*. In addition Arturo B., being a veteran of the Latin American revolutions, stresses the political aspect of Bolaño's identity. Arturo B. is the incarnation of the Bolaño who spent a few days after the coup in a detention camp on the outskirts of Concepción, from where (in *Distant Star*) he—or his alter ego—has witnessed Carlos Wieder's first poetic action in the sky. No attention is paid to life in the camp, which is significant because prison narratives became an important subgenre of testimonial literature throughout Latin America in the wake of dictatorial regimes. Bolaño moves beyond these concerns in *Distant Star,* but he does touch, however lightly, on the pursuit of justice that characterized the postdictatorship period in countries like Argentina and Chile: "Finally, a courageous and pessimistic judge indicted Wieder in a case that would never get very far. The defendant, of course, did not appear for the trial. Another judge, in Concepción this time, named him as the prime suspect in the murder of Angélica Garmendia and the disappearance of her sister and aunt" (110). Chilean justice was unable to deal effectively with the crimes perpetrated under the dictatorship until 1998 when Pinochet was detained in London at the request of a Spanish judge who wanted the general extradited to Spain to be tried for crimes against humanity. Pinochet was ultimately sent back to Chile by the British authorities, but the way to further indictments of the former strongman was open.[13]

It is important to note that Bolaño's justification for rewriting the last chapter of *Nazi Literature in the Americas* was that it was not sufficiently powerful in its original formulation. The original version was part of a series and had a particular function within the series of portraits that make up the book. It "was meant to counterbalance the preceding excursions into the literary grotesque, or perhaps to come as an anticlimax, and Arturo would have preferred a longer story that, rather than mirroring or exploding others, was, in itself, a mirror and an explosion." According to this critique, "The Infamous Ramírez Hoffman" was well placed to set off the other stories of *Nazi Literature in the Americas* but was too sketchy to function in and by itself as a self-contained narrative explosion. It cannot escape the reader that in this passage Bolaño once again invokes the metaphor of the literary artifact as a ticking time bomb, a metaphor that amounts to a whole poetics of writing (and reading) in the work of the Chilean author, as has been pointed out more than once in this book. In *Distant Star* the transformation of the apprentice poet Alberto Ruiz-Tagle into Carlos Wieder is an explosion unto itself, whose external manifestations are the poetic actions in the sky and the photographic exhibit of tortured and mutilated bodies. Only in retrospect can the narrator and his surviving friends fully understand the mystery of Wieder's earliest avatar, who in the days of the poetry workshops (and of Chile's socialist experiment) was mostly viewed as a decent poet and well-dressed seducer from a good family but not as the serial killer and mass murderer that he would eventually become. His associates did, however, notice the uncanny aura that separated him from the rest. Only one of the narrator's friends had some true insight into the character at that early stage: "Fat Marta was the only one who glimpsed a part of what was lurking behind the façade" (12). Fat Marta's words are prophetic: "Marta looked me in the eye . . . and said, Alberto is a good poet, but he still hasn't made his breakthrough" (14). (The original Spanish says "he still hasn't exploded.") Not only that but Marta perceives as well that when Alberto talks about revolutionizing Chilean poetry, he is not referring to the poetry that he is going to write but that he will *perform* (15; in italics in the original). And what Wieder will perform is not just aerial writing but the murder of the victims whose lifeless bodies will make up his artistic installation.

Within the fiction, these two explosive actions are meant to set the tone for the new Chilean art at a time of a radical break with the past, when the new military authorities were intent on doing away not only with the remnants of Allende's socialist government but with all manner of democratic institutions and with politics as a whole. To what extent does this fictional representation of art correspond to the reality of the Chilean art and cultural scene in the months and years following the coup? This question is relevant because readers unacquainted with this period would understandably think that the performances described in Bolaño's novel are the over-the-top inventions of a highly imaginative author. They would be right but only up to a point, because both photography and urban performance were integral elements of the artistic avant-garde that emerged in Chile at the end of the 1970s.

To state it briefly, two avant-garde groups developed in the country toward the end of that decade: the *avanzada,* theorized by cultural critic Nelly Richard and composed of conceptual and visual artists like Eugenio Dittborn, Carlos Leppe, and Carlos Altamirano, and CADA (Colectivo de Acciones de Arte), which included writers Diamela Eltit and Raúl Zurita, visual artists Juan Castillo and Lotty Rosenfeld, and sociologist Fernando Balcells. (Their differences matter less for the present purposes than their common location in the margins of officially sanctioned art, their disconnection with popular art groups that produced "posters and graphics mainly informed by the aesthetics of commitment," and their common aim to challenge the regime's attempts to "keep the production of meaning under surveillance" [Richard 23].) While CADA is remembered for a number of its street performances, the emergence of the avanzada coincided with and was enabled by a discussion of the role of photography in the work of art. According to Richard, avanzada works "recontextualize the photograph starting from a repertoire of graphical operations (cropping, juxtapositions or superimpositions, transfers, reproductions or enlarged details) which subject its image to new types of critical readings" (37). Naturally none of these works involves the display of tortured and disappeared bodies as in Wieder's exhibit, whose pornographic nature is highlighted by the proximity, in the space of the novel, between the sadomasochistic images of the photographs and the pornographic images that the same Wieder—now under the pseudonym R. P. English—takes as he shoots pornographic films "showing real criminal acts" (125). (Both photographs and films suggest connections with snuff movies.) But photography remains a common medium in the artistic perversion practiced by Bolaño's fictional character and the work of the avanzada visual artists, which grounds *Distant Star* in a realistic cultural and political context.[14]

The poet aviator's aerial performances recall the Futurist *aeropittura* of the 1920s as well as the skywriting performance of poet Raúl Zurita in the skies over New York in June 1982. Airpainting was a renewed effort by Futurism to become the official art of fascist Italy it "posited the quintessentially modernist perspective offered from the air and depended on biomorphic and geometric forms to represent aerial views" (Stone 136). On this level the connection between Wieder's aerial antics and the military regime on the ground is quite direct, but it is more convoluted when the lieutenant's skywriting is projected against Zurita's poetic text, whose main subject is God, while Bolaño's character replaces God by Death. Both Zurita's and Wieder's texts are enumerative repetitions having a single subject governing a variety of complementary clauses. The subject of Zurita's text is God, and some of its complements are hunger, snow, disillusionment, carrion, paradise, pampa, Chicano, cancer, emptiness, wound, ghetto, and pain. The subject of Wieder's text is Death, and some of its complements are friendship, Chile, responsibility, love, growth, communion, cleansing, and "my Heart."[15] Both texts are in their own way sacred, liturgical, and devotional, but the meaning of God has been radically displaced in the second. Perhaps it is significant that Zurita's words were written in white smoke against a perfectly blue sky, while those of his fictional counterpart were composed in grey and in the middle of a storm. Bolaño has shown great appreciation for Zurita's poetry but has also disparaged the poet's messianic posture. In *Distant Star* he expropiates these messianic traits and ascribes them to his fictional creation.

The place of *Distant Star* in Bolaño's fiction is pivotal. The author's interest in Nazi history and in the Second World War was already evident in *The Third Reich*, but until the creation of Carlos Wieder (or of his prematurely born twin Ramírez Hoffman), none of Bolaño's characters had a mythical stature. Wieder, who is also a designer of war games,[16] is explicitly described in larger-than-life terms: "In spite of the rumors of his death and the lack of evidence to the contrary, rather than sinking into oblivion with the passing years Wieder became a mythic figure and his alleged ideas found a following" (107). Wieder is thus the forerunner of later Bolaño characters who share his mythic stature: Cesárea Tinajero in *The Savage Detectives* and Benno von Archimboldi in *2666*, both of whom are writers who disappear as a result of historical circumstance and are tracked down by "savage" or scholarly detectives. The very idea of tracking lost figures by following literary clues—an idea that structures the author's major novels and that has a remote antecedent in Borges's "Approach to Al-Mu'tasim"—is firmly established in this novel. *Distant Star* only barely suggests a cult following for the messianic aviator-poet, but in *The Savage Detectives* and *2666*, the figure of the (missing) writer is in fact accompanied by a narrow circle of devotees. Did Bolaño imagine himself as a cult writer in the mid-1990s? It is possible since this status is an intermediate stage between anonymity and massive acclaim. This is the stage where Bolaño was before the publication of *The Savage Detectives*, the novel that launched him on his way to being the central reference of the Latin American post-Boom generation.

Chapter 5

Bolaño's Breakthrough

The Savage Detectives

In the 1960s and 1970s the Rómulo Gallegos prize was the high road to canonization for Spanish American novelists. It was instituted in 1964 in honor of Venezuelan novelist Rómulo Gallegos, author of *Doña Bárbara* (1929)—one of the classic Latin American novels of the era before the Boom—and awarded for the first time in 1967 to Mario Vargas Llosa for *The Green House.* At the beginning of its history, the prize was awarded every five years. The next two winners were Gabriel García Márquez for *One Hundred Years of Solitude* and Carlos Fuentes for *Terra Nostra.* In its first ten years, therefore, the Rómulo Gallegos award was closely tied to the Boom of Latin American fiction. Beginning in 1987 the prize was awarded every two years to the best novel published in the previous biannual span. In 1995 the competition was opened to any novelist writing in Spanish, regardless of his or her nationality. In 1999 Roberto Bolaño won that year's prize for *The Savage Detectives,* a novel whose reputation very quickly surpassed that of some of the other prizewinners of previous years.

In his acceptance speech Bolaño did not refer explicitly to the novel that canonized him but did make comments of general relevance to it. After rambling on about his soccer years when he could not figure out left from right (being left-footed but right-handed), about Rómulo Gallegos's novels, about his own mixed-up nationality, and about literature being a dangerous game, Bolaño hones in on Cervantes and *Don Quixote,* a book "in which the relative merits of military service and poetry are argued" ("Caracas Address," *Between Parentheses* 34). Bolaño updates the Renaissance debate between arms and letters and places it in the context of his own generation, which he defines as those born in the 1950s, many of whose members chose the path of active or passive resistance against the dictatorial and oligarchic governments of the region. He concludes that everything he has written is "a love letter or a farewell letter" to a generation that sacrificed itself for the cause of the revolution and that was betrayed by the forces of history and by its own leadership: "we fought for parties that if they had won would have sent us straight to labor camps" (35), he says, indirectly alluding to the treatment meted out to Cuban dissidents after the triumph of the revolution.

These comments bring into focus the political dimension of Bolaño's fiction. *The Savage Detectives* alludes to well-known political events like the repression of the student movement in Mexico in 1968, the Pinochet coup in Chile (1973), and the triumph of the Sandinistas in Nicaragua (1979). But even though the discourse of politics cannot be ignored when analyzing the author's major works, politics in *The Savage Detectives* frequently becomes a literary matter, as the novel dramatizes the tug-of-war among various writers and groups vying for recognition, and literary preferences are a mark of inclusion and exclusion. Political affiliation, furthermore, can be a superficial labeling game—a mere pose—as when the narrator classifies his friends as past or present Trotskyites, anarchists, communist homosexuals, failed guerrilla recruits, or radical feminists (66–67). This lighthearted catalog serves as a reminder that *The Savage Detectives* was written in a decade when Latin American literature had lost the political authority it could claim in the 1960s and the illusion that it had a key role to play in advancing the region's social progress. Bolaño's novel is "post" in several related senses: postmodern, post-avant-garde, and post-Boom.

Books, sexual rites of initiation, romantic liasons, the lure of the nightlife, and the exploration of the city provide a stronger bond than politics for the members of Bolaño's generation, as these characters are portrayed in the novel. *The Savage Detectives* features the comings and goings of the "real visceralists," a band of young bohemian poets who come together at poetry workshops and cafes in nighttime Mexico City and struggle to make a dent in the literary establishment. When these poets, male and female, are not busy writing poetry or planning to launch their own literary magazine, they behave like cultural guerrillas and interrupt readings and other cultural events staged by establishment figures. The real visceralists are a fictional version of the infrarealists of the 1970s, just as their leaders Belano and Lima are the alter egos of Bolaño and close friend Mario Santiago, respectively (see chapter 2 for a discussion of infrarealism). *The Savage Detectives* is a generational novel in which individual experience has a collective value. If the novel is a "farewell letter" to a whole generation, it is because it was composed some two decades after the fact and because most of the individual members of the group did not live up to expectations. Infrarealism itself failed to make a mark on the Mexican cultural landscape and would have been forgotten if it had not been revived in Bolaño's novel.

Bolaño did pronounce himself explicitly on *The Savage Detectives* in a blurb published as part of the program for the Rómulo Gallegos award ceremony. In this text he views the novel as a response to *Huckleberry Finn* and adds that the Mississipi of *The Savage Detectives* is "the flow of voices in the second part of the novel" (*Between Parentheses* 353). This interpretation of the novel highlights its adventurous spirit and its affiliation with the genres of the bildungsroman (or growing-up novel) and the *roman-fleuve* (or "river novel"). The latter term refers to a story of several generations of a family, community, or social group that is usually told in a series of novels, as in works by Balzac, Zola, and Proust. Despite being a one-volume novel, *The Savage Detectives* can lay claim to belonging to such a genre all by itself. Thematically it does follow the lives of a cohesive social group. In terms of form, a plurality of narrators takes over the middle section of the novel, and each story or monologue is like a rivulet feeding into a mainstream. Stories proliferate and branch out in a centrifugal motion; time moves forward but also returns to its source; the protagonists disappear and reappear in different places and are viewed from different perspectives. Yet the structural frame remains firm. The first and third parts of the novel act as bookends to its extensive middle section.

In the same blurb Bolaño makes other comments about the novel that reveal his personal interpretation of it. It is strange that he does not write that the novel is a more or less faithful transcription of his life between, say, 1973 and 1996, but that it is a "more or less faithful transcription of a segment of the life of the Mexican poet Mario Santiago." To be sure, Mario Santiago, in the guise of his alter ego Ulises Lima, is a constant presence in the first and third parts of the novel, whereas in the middle he becomes more elusive and somewhat legendary. But the same can be said about Bolaño's alter ego in the novel, Arturo Belano, a character that is always at Ulises Lima's side at the beginning and at the end of the novel but that comes and goes in the middle. The point, however, is not to confuse autobiography with autofiction, a confusion that would lead to an evaluation of the Belano and Lima characters in terms of their mimetic qualities, in other words, and—to quote Bolaño—as more or less accomplished transcriptions of their real life models. The characters' names, which evoke Arthur Rimbaud and Ulysses, already suggest that Belano and Lima exist in a symbolic as well as a realist dimension.

In this same text Bolaño takes up one of the themes sounded in his Caracas address when he states that "the novel tries to reflect a kind of generational defeat and also the happiness of a generation" (353). Happiness is fleeting, as in any romantic scenario, but defeat is lasting. Bolaño's protagonists have to transcend the collapse of their literary ambitions and political sympathies, though their only answer seems to be to keep moving on "without a rudder," to quote the often-repeated statement by Mario Santiago. Belano and Lima are countercultural revolutionaries and do not directly represent the armed militants who engaged in guerrilla warfare in the 1960s and later. Their defeat is the defeat of ideals and not of ideologies, which is why Bolaño's melancholy approach to the path of his generation has an important poetic component. In fact the larger defeat inscribed in the novel is the failure of the Latin American avant-garde to bring modernity to the region. This failure is ironically captured by the last real visceralist scholar in Mexico—a provincial critic from Pachuca—when he states that researching visceral realism, a movement in which no one else is interested, at least has the merit of "bringing Pachuca into the modern age" (520). Experience shows that cultural schemes have a better chance to succeed when they have the the support of the state or of other powerful interests. Given its inherently unofficial stance, avant-garde art is at a disadvantage on this point. Avant-garde poetry, and perhaps poetry as a whole, is particularly vulnerable to the material conditions imposed by the global publishing industry. One of the characters in the novel claims to be satisfied with writing poetry but warns that any day now he might commit the vulgarity of writing stories (46). *The Savage Detectives* may be a farewell letter to poetry, but it is still a novel about poets, which in itself makes it into a countercultural "intervention."

And finally Bolaño contends that the novel can be read in as many ways as there are narrative voices in it, though he singles out two ways of reading it: as a "deathbed lament" or as a game. The novel certainly has playful aspects, such as the interplay between real and fictional characters, riddles, the collage form of its central section—which makes a puzzle out of the text and calls on the reader to put voices, dates, and plot events together—and humorous passages. Reading the novel as a "deathbed lament," on the other hand, foregrounds the theme of loss but also turns the novel into a personal testimony of its author's struggle against death. In the original Spanish, "deathbed lament" is *agonía*, a word that connotes the struggle that precedes death. Bolaño had been diagnosed with an incurable liver condition years before he wrote the novel and was aware, in his own understated and often ironic way, that he was condemned to an early death. The author's "race against death" is one of the topics that reviewers seized on in the early phases of Bolaño's reception outside his native language.

The Savage Detectives came out in English in 2007, on the heels of two short novels and a collection of stories by Bolaño published by New Directions in the previous four years. In contrast with the much shorter *By Night in Chile* and *Distant Star,* the author's breakthrough novel is six hundred pages long in the original Anagrama edition. Reviewers for the *New Yorker,* the *New York Times,* the *London Review of Books, Bookforum,* and the *Guardian* were quick to point out its virtues. One writes approvingly of Bolaño's use of the detective format in a story that might otherwise "seem leadenly preoccupied with literary matters" (and adds that novelists "have been smashing high and low together for a century, but [that] Bolaño does it with the force of a super-collider"); another that the novel is "wildly enjoyable"; a third that "a large part of its distinction is its virtually unprecedented achievement in multiply-voiced narration"; and yet another that at its best the novel "is dark, funny, thrilling, tender, and erotic at one and the same time, in a way few novels before it have been."[1] Even the *Guardian* reviewer, the least generous of the group quoted here, admits that Bolaño writes with elegance, verve, and style and that he is immensely readable. If there is a cultural gap between the world of the novel and its U.S. readership, Natasha Wimmer's colloquial translation eases the passage across the cultural divide.

Narrative Structure and Plot

The Savage Detectives is divided into three parts of unequal length. The first part, about 120 pages long, is called "Mexicans Lost in Mexico" and is the diary of Juan García Madero, a seventeen-year-old student who joins a poetry workshop and is inducted into the "visceral realist" movement. Madero meets the gang leaders—Belano and Lima—at the outset of the workshop and bonds with them for the few months of the journal entries. Madero's diary covers the four months between November 1975 and February 1976, but only the first two months of this chronology are detailed in the first part of the novel. The earliest entry is from November 2, the Day of the Dead, an ominous introduction to the diary and the novel that foreshadows the violence of the ending.

The second part of the novel is about four hundred pages long and is a compendium of fifty-three narrative voices that attest to the lives, times, and travels of Arturo Belano and Ulises Lima. Madero does not speak in this section. Neither is he the addressee of the various testimonies making up the novel's central section. There is a passing comment about him that disqualifies him for this role (520), and occasionally Belano, or Belano and Lima together, or an unidentified you (in the plural) take the place of the narratee. Belano and Lima do not speak either but are always viewed from an external perspective, a narrative strategy that gives rise to different kinds of value judgments regarding their character. This section is entitled "The Savage Detectives," and its dates range from January 1976 to December 1996. It consists of twenty-six chapters subdivided into several subchapters, each one headed by an indication of the speaker, time, and place of the narrative monologue. (The Spanish original includes a useful table of contents that the English translation dispenses with.) Time flows progressively in these chapters except for the monologues attributed to Amadeo Salvatierra, a (fictitious) survivor of the Mexican avant-garde scene of the 1920s. The central part of the novel begins and ends with these monologues, all thirteen of which are dated January 1976 and all of which refer to a conversation between the speaker and the visiting Belano and Lima, who come to his apartment in search of information about a forgotten avant-garde poet of the 1920s. Some of the "interviews" or "testimonies" of this part of the novel are fictional statements uttered by well-known writers, artists, and intellectuals like Carlos Monsiváis (the eminent chronicler of contemporary Mexican life), Michel Bulteau (the neo-avant-garde French poet), Manuel Maples Arce (the premier Mexican poet of the avant-garde), Luscious Skin (the real-life pseudonym of performance artist Jorge Hernández), and Veronica Volkow (Mexican poet, translator, and great-granddaughter of Leon Trotsky).

Other narrators of this part of the novel are thinly disguised friends, lovers, and acquaintances of the author: Laura Jáuregui is Lisa Johnson (Bolaño's first romantic liason); Edith Oster is Edna Lieberman (the author of a book on Bolaño, as mentioned in chapter 1); Felipe Müller is Bruno Montané (the Chilean poet and jazz musician whom Bolaño met in Mexico City); Auxilio Lacouture is Alcira Soust Scaffo (a Uruguayan teacher and resident in Mexico who was friends with Bolaño's mother); Iñaki Echevarne is Spanish literary critic Ignacio Echevarría; Catalina O'Hara is American visual artist Carla Rippey. And, of course, the visceral realists of the novel are the infrarealists of the 1970s.

The third and last part of the novel—"The Sonora Desert"—is less than a hundred pages long and comprises the final entries in Madero's diary, which narrate the protagonists' trip to the desert and their search for the forgotten poet Cesárea Tinajero, founder of an obscure group of poets in the 1920s and missing since then. This group was also known as visceral realists and was an offshoot of the historical estridentistas. The two groups of visceral realists represent different historical moments of a continuous pursuit of modernization in the social, political, and cultural spheres. The link between the Mexican avant-garde and modernization is explicitly stated by one of the narrators: "Stridentism and visceral realism are just two masks to get us to where we really want to go . . . to modernity . . . , to goddamned modernity" (433). *The Savage Detectives* is dedicated to Bolaño's wife and son and has an epigraph from Malcolm Lowry, author of *Under the Volcano* and another writer lost in Mexico, like Cesárea Tinajero, the novel's protagonists, and perhaps like Bolaño himself.[2] The novel's title refers both to Belano's and Lima's search for the forgotten poet Cesárea Tinajero and to the readers' "detection" of Belano and Lima in the novel's middle section.

In the passage between the diary and the testimonial forms of the novel there is a shift in the degree of authority granted to the respective narrators. Madero narrates from a first-person point of view but never abuses the authority usually granted to such a narrative perspective. His narrative modesty, sometimes verging on naivete, allows him to set up an easy complicity with the reader.

Some of the narrators of the middle section, on the other hand, speak with a greater degree of authority when they pass judgment on other characters or on controversial cultural and political topics. Their discourse, however, is implicated in a system of checks and balances supported by the novel's polyphonic narrative strategy. Perspectives and opinions are not cut and dry but open to question. Furthermore the events narrated in Madero's journal are condensed in one place and in a short period of time, whereas the events recounted in the central part of the novel are dispersed among various continents and countries and occupy a much larger temporal frame.

The overall plot of the novel covers twenty years, the first four months of which are detailed in Madero's diary. The first section of the diary (covering the last two months of 1975) focuses on the diarist's experiences after he joins the visceral realist group. This is the part of the novel that most resembles a bildungsroman because the experiences recounted are mostly experiences of initiation—leaving home, joining a new group of friends, the first steps on the way to a literary career, the first sexual and romantic liaisons, early intimations of danger and physical violence, the thrill of the nightlife, urban exploration, and so on. The Font household—composed of an extravagant and half-crazy paterfamilias, his wife, and their two daughters—plays a large role in these early experiences and also fulfills a structural function by supplying common ground to a variety of characters and plot events. The whole first part of the novel takes place in Mexico City.

The last entries of the diary cover the first two months of 1976 and focus on the search for Cesárea Tinajero in the northern desert. The search party is made up of Madero, Belano, Lima, and the prostitute Lupe, whom the three friends gallantly save from her pimp before leaving the capital, an act of generosity that forces the trio to flee for their safety. The pimp and a corrupt cop pursue the poets and tangle with them just when they make contact with the elusive founder of visceral realism, who is accidentally shot and killed in the melée. Both pursuers also die at the hands of their intended victims. Before this dénouement the "savage detectives" learn that in the 1930s Cesárea had been a schoolteacher in Santa Teresa (Bolaño's version of García Márquez's Macondo or Faulkner's Yoknapatawpha), that she read a lot and kept a series of notebooks where she wrote prose but not poetry, that she left the school and worked in a canning factory, that when the factory closed she ran a stall where she sold medicinal herbs—by which time she had become grossly fat—and that she lived in Villaviciosa. That's where the searchers find her and watch her die as they try to fend off their pursuers. Cesárea's death brings the novel's main plot to an end but opens up a new and much broader narrative cycle that lasts twenty years and focuses on the trajectories of Belano and Lima, who separate after the desert killings and eventually take off for Europe, Africa, and the Middle East.

Madero ends his journal with some reflections on Cesárea's notebooks, which he finds in her modest dwelling, and on the fate of Belano and Lima, who have hurriedly returned to Mexico City in the murdered pimp's car. His last three entries contain three rectangular drawings and one question repeated three times: "What's outside the window?" The question is answered the first two times but left unanswered the third time around. Unlike the first two rectangles—drawn with solid lines—the third rectangle or window is drawn with broken lines on all four sides, perhaps suggesting some meaning that escapes proper framing and closure, despite the novel's firm architecture. The drawings recall Cesárea Tinajero's only surviving poem, a puzzling sequence of straight, wavy, and broken lines with a box floating or bobbing on top that Lima and Belano interpret for their host Salvatierra. The interpreters turn the box into a sailboat and claim to have solved the poem's puzzle. But the poem can still refer to a number of different things and suggest different meanings: Quetzalcoatl's ship, Captain Ahab's encephalogram, the whale's encephalogram, Einstein's impossible rectangle, a coffin, or the "desolation of poetry" (377).

In any event the answer to the riddle "what's outside the window?" may simply be: the open road. The invitation embodied in Bolaño's infrarealist manifesto—leave it all and head off along the roads—suggest this solution to the puzzle. The invitation is heeded by the novel's protagonists, who first set off in search of Cesárea Tinajero and then set out in other improvised directions. Belano and Lima try to explain to their interlocutor the reason for their desert trip, but their stated motivation is inconclusive: "we're doing it for Mexico, for Latin America, for the Third World, for our girlfriends, because we feel like doing it" (522). The search for Cesárea could also be a quest for origins or a suicide mission, since in that conversation the participants keep taking vigorous drafts of a mezcal called "Los Suicidas." It is surely not by chance that Belano's motivation for his trip to Africa later in the novel is to get himself killed, a reasoning that recalls the consul's death wish in Lowry's *Under the Volcano* but that might also be the root cause of the travelers' nomadism, not only Belano's but also Lima's: "He had lost something and he wanted to die, that was all" (514). In the novel the experience of loss translates into the experience of disorientation, which is already inscribed in the title of the first part of the novel: "Mexicans Lost in Mexico." The desert, furthermore, is an effective spatial metaphor for the experience of disorientation, a space with no markings and seemingly no history.

The narrative gives plenty of indications that the search of the "savage detectives" is counterproductive. Cesárea's status as a poet, for one thing, fails to hold up to scrutiny. No one knows her as a poet in the places where she lived,[3] and her devotees are less than ecstatic when they find her: "Seen from behind, leaning over the trough, there was nothing poetic about her. She looked like a rock or an elephant" (570). Furthermore Cesárea's one surviving poem is a nonverbal artifact, an infantile drawing that may be a parody of the typographic games typical of avant-garde poetry, including the poetry of the estridentistas.[4] Furthermore Cesárea is often referred to as the mother of visceral realism, so that her violent death is a kind of matricide. But her symbolic role as mother is compromised by her name, which suggests a difficult birth.[5] There are other mother figures in the novel. Auxilio Lacouture, for example, declares herself to be the mother and protector of the young poets of Mexico and is acclaimed as such by her brood (182). And Rosario wants to mother the young Juan García Madero when he moves in with her. She says to him at one point that she did not like to see him "standing at the bar writing, like an orphan" (80–81). In fact both the absence of the mother and the proliferation of mother figures point to the same end, namely the orphaned predicament of the visceral realists,[6] who also lack a father figure: "all poets, even the most avant-garde, need a father. But these poets [the visceral realists] were meant to be orphans" (161).[7] Motherless and fatherless Belano and Lima break with visceral realism and strike out in different directions for the next twenty years.

Ulises's Odyssey

Ulises Lima's trajectory begins in Paris and is recounted in chapter 7 by a number of different "witnesses" of his temporary stay in the city. The fact that Paris is the first stop in Lima's wanderings beyond Mexico is not random, given the cultural and symbolic importance of the French capital for Latin American writers since late nineteenth-century *modernismo*—the Latin American version of French symbolism and Parnassianism, not to be confused with Anglo-American or Brazilian modernism, which are later movements related to the avant-garde. A significant number of *modernista* and avant-garde writers from Latin America made their temporary home in Paris at the turn of the twentieth century and well into the 1930s and 1940s. In *The Savage Detectives* the surviving estridentista Amadeo Salvatierra notes the hullabaloo caused in the Mexican press by Manuel Maples Arce's first trip to Paris (as the leading exponent of the avant-garde in Mexico, Maples Arce could not miss out on such an opportunity) and remarks that he himself used to visit Paris in dreams (334). Paris remained a magnet for Latin American writers well into the years of the Boom. In one of his later novels—*The Bad Girl*—Mario Vargas Llosa captures his fascination with Paris in meticulous detail. Cortázar's *Hopscotch* is structured as a metaphysical and esoteric dialogue between Paris and Buenos Aires, a structure similar to a later novel by Carlos Fuentes—*Distant Relations*—that brings Paris and Mexico City together in a Gothic embrace. And some of the best work by Peruvian novelist Alfredo Bryce Echenique—author of *Guía triste de París* ("A Melancholy Guide to Paris")—portrays the sentimental education of Latin Americans who intrude into French space.

The trip to Paris was really a pilgrimage or rite of passage for writers of many stripes during and after modernismo. It was also a social ritual for wealthy families. Avant-garde writers like Vicente Huidobro, Juan Emar, César Vallejo, Miguel Ángel Asturias, and Alejo Carpentier (the originator of magic realism or *lo real maravilloso*) traveled to and lived in Paris for significant periods of time, though in different economic circumstances. The city was not hospitable to all its guests to the same degree. The myth of Paris as a cultural or personal *promesse de bonheur* had a darker side to it which was not ignored by the very same travelers who sojourned in the French capital and celebrated its glories. Around the turn of the twentieth century, modernista poet Rubén Darío, for example, warned his Latin American compatriots not to exchange their native land for the streets of Paris unless they brought plenty of gold with them. Otherwise they would experience only misery, hunger, and rejection, a lesson that was bitterly learned by Uruguayan author Horacio Quiroga in his one and only trip to Paris (in 1900), whose incidents he recorded in a travel journal. Quiroga was so penniless that he could not afford ten *centimes* to buy a new notebook in which to continue his journal entries and had to depend for food on the charity of friends and creditors, whose only wish—if one is to read between the lines—was to see the embarrassing visitor back in his own country. In the 1950s a still unknown García Márquez complained of being mistaken for a Turk in Paris and treated poorly. Parisian high society might have welcomed wealthy and cultured visitors from across the ocean but reserved pejorative epithets (like *métèque*) for the common foreign guest. One may suppose that in the current era of undocumented immigration such epithets have become more common.[8] (In some of his poems Bolaño writes about the problems he had in his early years in Spain with his Chilean passport and work permits; in *The Savage Detectives,* Belano is turned away from a university archive in Hermosillo because his papers are not in order.)

The Paris that Ulises Lima experiences is not the glittering "City of Light" but the city of immigrants, exiles, and starving poets who live in crowded and foul-smelling *chambres de bonnes* and who help one another survive or exploit one another in the process. For the native inhabitants of that city Latin American transients are unwanted *metecos*. As one of these transient poets says: "it was then that I was suddenly overcome by the full horror of Paris, the full horror of the French language, the poetry scene, our state as unwanted guests [*metecos,* in Spanish], the sad, hopeless state of South Americans lost in Europe" (215). Even exchanges among poets from Mexico and France are strained because of the asymmetrical relationship between Latin American and French culture. The Peruvian poet who approaches his French counterparts with a modest request for the address of an older and admired local poet or with an article for potential publication in a Parisian magazine is rebuked. His offer to translate a poem by one of the young French authors and publish it in a Peruvian journal is useless. And Ulises Lima meets with indifference when he shares the details of his search for Cesárea Tinajero with Michel Bulteau, one of the authors of an early 1970s neovanguardist manifesto and a fellow traveler of the Beat generation. Lima actually owns Bulteau's *Manifeste électrique,* but Bulteau's response to his story is less than generous: "a story of lost poets and lost magazines and works no one had ever heard of . . . or at least no longer of the slightest importance here, in Paris, in the 1970s. A story from the edge of civilization" (221). The dialogue between Lima and Bulteau is difficult because the former is not fluent in either French or English, a circumstance that makes him into a "barbarian." Clearly the "civilized" French poets admired by the Mexican visitor are no "savage detectives" like their Mexican and Chilean counterparts. The dialogue is also difficult because there is a social and political difference between Latin American and French poets, as one of the Latin Americans lost in Paris remarks: "I remember Ulises liked the young French poets. . . . We . . . thought they were disgusting. Spoiled brats or drug addicts. You have to understand, Ulises, I would say to him, we're revolutionaries, we've seen the insides of the jails of Latin America. So how can we care about poetry like that?" (214).

In the novel's polyphonic structure, this question remains open to interpretation. There is certainly a difference between conceptual art and a visceral poetic reaction to the experience of imprisonment and political repression. But the difference can get lost in practice. For one thing conceptual art (and poetry) played a role in the resistance against Pinochet in the late 1970s in Chile. And for another not all is well with the revolution in Bolaño's view. There is no more powerful symbol of revolutionary malaise in his writing than the execution of Salvadoran poet Roque Dalton at the hands of his own guerrilla confederates in 1975. Bolaño traveled through El Salvador on his way to Chile in 1973 and is supposed to have met Dalton and his future murderers during his brief stay in that country. The story has been repeated endlessly by many reviewers and commentators in the United States and elsewhere, but it is inaccurate. Bolaño himself never affirmed that he had met the Salvadoran poet in person, though he did indicate that he had met his future murderers during his stay in El Salvador. Furthermore he could not have met Dalton before arriving in Chile in September 1973 because Dalton did not return to El Salvador until December of that year, when Bolaño had already spent four months in Chile after surviving a few days of imprisonment following the Pinochet coup.[9] At any rate Dalton and Bolaño's trip to El Salvador are referenced twice in *The Savage Detectives,* once on page 91 (when the narrator-diarist admits to stealing a book by the

Salvadoran author from a Mexico City bookstore) and a second time on page 134 when a different narrator remembers meeting Belano for the first time and listening to him talk about his trip through Guatemala and El Salvador.

Bolaño also passed through Nicaragua on the trip he undertook through Central America on his way to Chile. At that time the country was still ruled by Anastasio Somoza, whose dictatorship would come to an end in 1979 with the victory of the Frente Sandinista de Liberación Nacional. Two years into the Sandinista regime Ulises Lima lands in Managua as part of a delegation of Mexican poets who have come to show their support for the people of Nicaragua.[10] But instead of taking part in the conference scheduled for poets of both countries and discuss issues presumably related to the revolution, Lima disappears during the trip and only reappears two years later in Mexico. Has the leader of a rebellious poetic gang like the visceral realists abdicated his political responsibilities? This implicit breach between poetry and revolution is widened in the discussion between the leaders of the Mexican delegation and the Sandinista police inspector who shows up to investigate the disappearance of the "comrade writer" (315). The discussion, which begins as a progressively louder disagreement on the relative strength of Mexican and Cuban cigarettes, escalates into a conflict between poets and revolutionaries: "It was as if he [the police inspector] were saying: we revolutionaries smoke strong tobacco, real men smoke strong tobacco, those of us with a stake in objective reality smoke real tobacco" (316), an argument that condemns poets to the subjective dimension of reality and expels them from the political realm. The gap between the sheltered life of the man of letters and the hardy life of the soldier is at the core of the debate between arms and letters that Bolaño mentions in his Caracas address with respect to *Don Quixote*. In Latin American literature the contradictory situation of intellectual revolutionaries came to the fore in the epistolary exchange, at the end of the 1960s, between Julio Cortázar—who belatedly became a supporter of the Cuban revolution—and Roberto Fernández Retamar, the czar of the Cuban cultural bureaucracy.[11] But in the context of *The Savage Detectives,* the breach between hard-line revolutionaries and poets has a less polite component because it recalls, at least tangentially, the murder of poet Roque Dalton at the hands of his own guerrilla correligionaries.

In chapter 38 of *Don Quixote* (first part) Cervantes insinuates that men of letters (members of the lettered elite, that is, as distinct from penniless novelists like himself) have it easier than soldiers because they receive appointments from the state in accordance with their elevated status, whereas soldiers—members of the unlettered class—have to fend for themselves. Cervantes's grievance must have sounded like music to Bolaño's ears. Bolaño, who for twenty years was a literary outsider, constantly rails against writers who get too close to the state, the bureaucracy, and even the university for a source of income. Such writers, he argues, become subservient to specific political or ideological interests that thwart their poetic freedom. The visceral realists (like the infrarealists of literary history) never found a place in the cultural field, which means that they were never co-opted by any official discourse or institution: "the visceral realists weren't part of any camp, not the neo-PRI-ists or the champions of otherness [an indirect reference to Paz's poetry], the neo-Stalinists or the aesthetes, those who drew a government salary or those who lived off the university . . . , the Latin Americanists or the cosmopolites" (330). But the Mexican poets who visit Nicaragua do not enjoy such freedom from official ties. They constitute an official group—the "peasant poets"—bound by a personal bond to their leader Julio César Álamo, who is introduced at the beginning of the novel as the poetry workshop teacher who gets on the wrong side of the visceral realists: "Álamo had personally invited his best buddies, namely the peasant-poet gang" (308).

In the fictional code of the novel Álamo stands for Juan Bañuelos, the actual leader of a poetry workshop at the Mexican National University in the 1970s. Bañuelos is also one of five poets represented in an anthology called *La espiga amotinada* ("The Rebellious Stalk"), a poetry collection published in 1960 that gave rise to a minor literary movement of the same name. (A second anthology— *Ocupación de la palabra* ["Occupation of the Word"]—appeared five years later with the same lineup of poets.) The peasant poets of *The Savage Detectives,* therefore, are the *espiga* poets of the 1960s Mexican cultural scene. (These poets did not survive the decade as a group.) The word "espiga" would seem to justify the scornful epithet "peasant poets" directed at Bañuelos's group by the novel's implied author. Bañuelos's poetry is markedly regionalist and more traditional in form and concept than any avant-garde program would contemplate. Childhood, the Chiapas landscape, and Mayan mythology supply many of the themes present in Bañuelos's poetry. The nature of his poetry and the fact that the author has had a distinguished literary career explain the enmity between the "peasant poets" and the hopelessly marginal infrarealists, who failed to make a dent in the Mexican literary field. In the Nicaragua episode of *The Savage Detectives,* then, the politics of revolution takes second place to the cultural politics that structure the Mexican cultural field.[12]

Between his visits to Paris and Managua, Ulises Lima makes two other stops in the novel. One is at the French fishing port of Port Vendres, where Belano is waiting for him and helps him find temporary work on a fishing boat. (Incidentally this will be the last meeting between the two friends.) Lima, a landlubber who has never been on a boat before, sets out to sea with the local fishermen, a dejected bunch that had not caught anything in many previous sallies. But for the two weeks that the Mexican fishes with them, the fishermen's nets are miraculously full: "none of us had ever seen that before . . . , few of use could believe what had happened" (247). As one critic points out, this scene recalls the biblical miracle of the multiplication of the fish and ties in with the novel's epigraph, which mentions Mexican salvation through the action of Christ the King (see Solotorevsky 160–62). The epigraph, from Lowry's *Under the Volcano*, refers to the *cristero* war of the late 1920s, but the theme of national salvation, modulated by the perceived failure of industrialization in modern Mexico, resonates in other passages of the novel. Cesárea is unemployed when the canning factory where she works shuts down, and a minor character avows that "this country is a fucking mess. . . . The police don't do what they are supposed to do and neither do the hospitals or the morgues or the funeral homes" (341).[13]

The narrator of this section of the novel wonders why Ulises cannot stay longer in the village after bringing the fishermen such good luck, to which Lima responds that he has enough money for what he needs, which is "to buy a plane ticket to Israel" (247). He proceeds to Tel-Aviv, hoping to reconnect with a girlfriend from Mexico City: "Ulises told her that he loved her. Claudia's answer was that she already knew. I came here because of you, Ulises said, I came because I love you. Claudia's answer was that he could have written her a letter. Ulises found that highly encouraging, and he wrote a poem that he read to Claudia at lunch" (265). The poem is about a Mediterranean city that could be Tel-Aviv, and a bum or a mendicant poet but does not have much effect on Claudia because she is living with someone else. The poet's presence increases tension in that household. The visitor is forced to find work or leave. He chooses the latter, wanders around Israel doing odd jobs, and briefly returns with an unexpected guest, an Austrian drifter that Lima picks up during his wandering: "A month later, Ulises Lima showed up. With him was a huge guy, almost six and a half feet tall, dressed in all kinds of rags, an Austrian Ulises had met in Beersheba. . . . The guy's name was Heimito. We never knew his last name . . . , although Claudia said there was a writer called Heimito von Doderer, Austrian too" (272). Heimito prefigures the Benno von Archimboldi of *2666*, a German writer born Hans Reiter (Benno von Archimboldi is a pen name) who is also described as an unusually tall and corpulent individual.[14]

Ulises's last appearance in the novel is his encounter with Octavio Paz in a Mexico City park that the latter was known to frequent. (Rafael Vargas includes photographic testimony of Paz in Parque Hundido in his *Octavio Paz: Entre la imagen y el nombre*.) This section, dated October 1995, is narrated by Paz's secretary and confidante Clara Cabezas, from whom her boss requests a ride to the park. Clara is taken aback by the request, because in her view that destination is not a safe place, and speculates that the park "must bring back some memory for him" (475). At the park "Don Octavio" walks "in wider and wider circles," sometimes stepping off the path into the grass. A man unknown to the narrator comes from the opposite direction also walking in circles until his path crosses that of the eminent poet. The man turns out to be Ulises Lima, who is there apparently to face the bête noire of the visceral realists. The meeting is bound to be tense because the visceral realists, of whom Paz has never heard, were in the habit of interrupting readings by Mexico's premier man of letters and even threatened to kidnap him. But the two men sit down quietly on a bench and end their brief meeting by shaking hands. Their dialogue is not reported by the narrator, but the handshake amounts to a realization by the former visceral realist that his struggle against Mexico's canonical poet was futile. In fact this section of the novel is steeped in Paz's life and poetry. Not only is Parque Hundido a place linked to the poet's biography; Clara's name recalls the themes of clarity and transparency that characterize Paz's poetry, whereas her surname connotes the intellectual bent of Paz's poetic discourse; and the walking around is a playful reference to the circular form of one of Paz's major poems, "Piedra de sol" ("Sunstone"), which begins and ends with the same lines: "A crystal willow, a water poplar, / a high spout bent by the wind, / a firmly rooted but dancing tree, / a course like that of a winding river / that advances, retreats, takes the long way around / but is always on time." The theme of return is also prevalent in Paz's poetry.

The last news concerning Ulises Lima's whereabouts come from the "only expert on the visceral realists in Mexico" (519), a character that in the last chapter of the novel's middle section recapitulates the fate of the individual members of the group. This self-styled scholar notes that Ulises Lima still lives in Mexico City and that during a visit to the capital he went to see him and was scared by Lima's unfocused response (520). A report by another witness is equally negative: "Two years after he disappeared in Managua, Ulises Lima came back to Mexico. Not many people saw him after that, and when anyone did it was almost always by accident. For most he was dead as a person and a poet" (344). Mexico City is no Ithaca for Bolaño's Ulises. There is no Penelope to be rescued from unwanted suitors or throne to be reclaimed, as Ulises fails in his attempt to regroup the surviving visceral realists. The figure that Lima cuts at the end of his life is not so much that of the poète maudit but that of an orphan adrift in the world. It is ironic that both Octavio Paz and Mario Santiago—the real-life inspiration for Ulises Lima—died in 1998, the same year in which *The Savage Detectives* was published. But Paz was given a state funeral while Santiago's body lay in a morgue for days before someone recognized and claimed it.

Belano's Travails

If Bolaño inscribes the theme of wandering in Ulises Lima's name, he makes a similar symbolic gesture regarding Arturo Belano's first name, which refers to Arthur Rimbaud, the visionary French poet who gave up poetry at the age of nineteen and became a colonial tradesman and arms dealer in Africa. Rimbaud is a subject of conversation among the visceral realists, and one of his poems—"Le Coeur volé"—is quoted in full in *The Savage Detectives* and given a convoluted interpretation by Ulises Lima (140–45). Rimbaud was restless and rebellious enough to leave home on several occasions, and walk or ride long distances through the French countryside as a way to escape from conventional family life. He wandered penniless through the streets of Paris. His rebellion against established morality and provincial values and his conflation of poetry and revolution found fertile ground in the neo-avant-garde movements of the 1960s and 1970s. Having quit writing poetry at nineteen, furthermore, Rimbaud's image for posterity is that of a perennially young poet, a poet who never aged—an image that accords well with the effervescence of avant-garde movements. And his sympathies for the Communards of 1871 align him with the student revolts of the 1960s, including the one in Mexico that resulted in the events described in chapter 4 of *The Savage Detectives.* No wonder, then, that Arturo Belano emulates Rimbaud and ends up disappearing in Africa. Moreover he does so after giving up on visceral realism and poetry in general, and long after burying the revolutionary dream that underlay his poetic vision.

Belano and Lima are parallel figures who break with their poetic and revolutionary ideals, though they do so at different times and places and in different circumstances. As discussed in the previous section, Lima's indifference to the revolutionary ideal is manifested in his trip to Nicaragua, during which he goes missing instead of joining the celebration of the Sandinista triumph. And Lima's polite meeting with Octavio Paz confirms the end of his commitment to the poetics of visceral realism and the end of the movement itself.

Belano's break with the visceral realists, on the other hand, is attested in a letter dated 1977 and quoted by Felipe Müller, Belano's close collaborator in Mexico and later in Barcelona: "Nineteen seventy-seven was the year Arturo Belano found work as a night watchman at a campground. . . . I think that was the summer when the two of us broke with visceral realism. We were publishing a magazine in Barcelona . . . and we wrote a letter announcing our resignation from visceral realism. We didn't repudiate anything, we didn't bad-mouth our friends in Mexico, we just said we weren't members of the group anymore. Mostly we were busy working and trying to get by" (224–25). Belano develops a work ethic that his pal Ulises does not have, an ethic that is reflected later on in the articles he writes for a Spanish newspaper. As the narrator of the African chapter notes, Belano became a "stringer for a Madrid newspaper that paid him next to nothing for his pieces" (497). The fact that Belano gives up poetry and starts writing novels before becoming a journalist reaffirms his break with visceral realism, though the relevant narrator notes that Belano's switch from poetry to prose is not forced by material circumstances: "He was writing a novel and I was writing my journal and poetry and a movie script. . . . We weren't writing for publication but to understand ourselves better or just to see how far we could go" (386–87).

This disclaimer embodies a different kind of ethic than the work ethic that Ulises lacks. It takes for granted and reasserts literature's independence from the marketplace and from any institutional restraints that might affect creative freedom. The assertion of literary autonomy is important in a novel so deeply concerned with the commodification of literature in the contemporary publishing industry, as chapter 23 demonstrates. The chapter is set in the Feria del Libro, Madrid, July 1994, and opens with a serious critical reflection on the fate of literary works in an ideal world devoid of marketing and institutions (like the book fair itself) and composed only of the Work, Readers, and Critics (all capitalized). But the next seven sections of the chapter bring the Work back to reality and insert it in the circus-like milieu of a book fair where authors are sellers, readers are buyers, and poems and novels are categorized according to accepted consumer standards. Thus even the crazy poet Barrendoaín— doped, depressed, and in constant need of his nurse—has his share of readers, "those who feed on my madness to nourish their madness" (466). And the editor Morales complains that there is too much poetry around and that poetry does not sell (188)—presumably sane poetry. As Cobas Carral and Garibotto point out, this chapter contrasts with the assessment of literature put forth in García Madero's diary. In the latter artistic conceptions are defined by how they articulate ethics and aesthetics in the revolutionary context of the 1970s; but in chapter 23 artistic production is redefined in terms of its marketing potential (Cobas Carral and Garibotto 179). Or as another critic puts it, the chapter marks the transition between a romantic conception of literature and literature as a profession (Pastén 428). The commodification of literature depoliticizes literary production (in the same way that the advertising industry "recuperated"the revolutionary ideas of the historical avant-garde), but the opposite is no less true. Visceral realism has no marketing potential and can therefore be revolutionary; but its very marginality prevents it from having an effect on the public sphere.

In *The Savage Detectives* depoliticization goes hand in hand with the loss of faith in revolutionary utopia. This theme is synthesized in the "airport story" that Belano tells Felipe Müller at the end of chapter 23 right before leaving for Africa to join the ranks of the many characters who disappear in the novel. The story is about two Latin American writers who committed themselves to the revolution and ended up being its victims. One of these writers seems to be the Cuban Reinaldo Arenas: "The Cuban was a different story. He was gay and the revolutionary authorities weren't prepared to tolerate homosexuals. . . .

It wasn't long before he was dragged through the shit and madness that passes for a revolution" (470). The authorities make sure the writer loses his job and is unable to publish and finally throw him in jail. "One day he escaped. He made it to the United States. His books began to be published . . . but he and Miami weren't made for each other. He headed to New York. He had lovers. He got AIDS" (471). The other writer is a Peruvian poet who comes "unglued" when the Maoist terrorist organization Shining Path begins its campaign of destruction in Peru in the early 1980s: "The former admirer of the Gang of Four and the Cultural Revolution was transformed into a believer in the theories of Madame Blavatsky. He returned to the Catholic Church" (470). The narrator's conclusion, upon hearing these stories, is that the "dream of Revolution" is a "hot nightmare."

It is ironic then that Belano dives headlong into a continent convulsed by civil war. The Africa of *The Savage Detectives* is a mirror image of Latin America at its worst. Angola, Rwanda, Zaire, and Liberia are just as much the heart of darkness as Central America, Colombia, the Southern Cone, and Peru were in recent decades, not just a "hot nightmare" but the veritable "end of the world, human insanity, the evil nestled in every heart" (502). The narrator of the African chapter is a member of Belano's generation and admits to having read too much Marx and Rimbaud, like his congeners. If Marx provided a rationale for waging revolution, Rimbaud gave the revolutionary struggle a poetic and visionary touch. The novel does not really portray African politics, but if there is any kind of politics underlying the chaos and violence that the Western reporters experience, it is a fallen politics, a politics devoid of any redemptive purpose. This is not the utopian revolution that the romantic characters of the novel had in mind but a kind of barbarism that is all too familiar to Latin American reformers and writers. Borges, who is mentioned in the chapter as a literary favorite shared by the narrator and Belano, was one of the many authors who wrote on the topic of civilization and barbarism.

In his 1943 "Poema conjetural" ("Conjectural Poem") Borges imagines the violent death of one of his cultured ancestors at the hands of barbarous gauchos and points out that at the moment of death the poem's hero, one of the leaders of Argentine independence, has an epiphany that reveals to him the meaning of his life: "I've met my destiny, / my final South American destiny," are the words that spell the poem's epitaph." And in his most famous story, "The South" (1953), Borges tells the story of Juan Dahlmann, a second-generation Argentine who suffers a life-threatening accident and is rushed to a hospital. As Dahlmann dies in the hospital he dreams of a heroic death in the pampa, in a knife duel with the degraded descendants of the gauchos who once fought against the Indians in the countryside south of Buenos Aires.[15] Belano's travails in Africa, then, do not just recapitulate Rimbaud's itinerary but follow the Borgesian script as well. Much is made in the chapter of Belano's need for medicines—which recalls Dahlmann's medical treatment—and his vocation for death is mentioned more than once. One must remember Bolaño's statement in his Caracas address about literature being a dangerous game. In *The Savage Detectives* writing is not a white-collar profession whose aim is social respectability but a desperate métier that brings the writer face to face with danger and death. Belano is initiated into this dance with death in the Sonora desert when he has to fight off Lupe's pimp (and ends up killing him) and goes looking for death in Africa, one might say, in order to meet his writerly destiny.

Eviscerated Realism

Belano and Lima are not the only characters in the novel who renounce their identities as visceral realists. There is a third visceral realist who breaks with the group: Cesárea Tinajero, although this part of her story dates back to the 1920s. She is the founder of the original group, the editor of the single issue of *Caborca*—the magazine that compiled the group's work—and the author of the only surviving visceral realist poem from that period. Cesárea's life is divided into two. The first half takes place in Mexico City in the 1920s and the second in Sonora in succeeding decades. The 1920s was the decade when Mexico began to recover its political stability after the revolution of 1910 and also the decade of the estridentistas, whose founding manifesto is from 1921. The revolutionary government had the same objective as the artistic avant-garde, namely to bring the country into the modern era. In fact the estridentistas were supported by the governor of the state of Veracruz, General Heriberto Jara, who in the novel appears as General Diego Carvajal. Cesárea is a speechwriter for the general, and they both mix easily and frequently with the artistic crowd led by Maples Arce. The alliance between art and politics goes smoothly until Cesárea breaks with her correligionaries, at which point, says Salvatierra (the narrator of Cesárea's visceral realist years), "everything was sliding inexorably toward the edge of a cliff" (432).

Belano and Lima's trip to the desert in search of Cesárea Tinajero—whom no one regards as a poet in the places where she lives—is a journey back in time, a trip through preindustrial Mexico that reveals modernity as a mirage. Cesárea works as a schoolteacher but disagrees with the implementation of the government's educational reform. Then she works in a canning factory until the factory shuts down and she is unemployed, a sign that industrialization did not solve the country's problems. And she ends up selling medicinal herbs in a village market, a traditional occupation well outside the parameters of development theory. In fact she thinks that the Mexican revolution will take place sometime in the twenty-second century (434). The desert is a metaphor in the novel for the failure of modernity. One of the projects of the estridentistas, and one in which Cesárea was involved, was the design and construction of a futuristic city called Estridentópolis, a project that never left the realm of dreams: "And then I started to think again about Stridentopolis, about its museums and bars, its open-air theaters and newspapers, its schools and its dormitories for traveling poets, dormitories where Borges, Tristan Tzara, Huidobro and André Breton would sleep" (336). But in the present of that future, as critics have pointed out, Cesárea lives in a house that does not even have electricity, let alone dormitories for traveling poets (Cobas Carral and Garibotto 172). (Electric contrivances, furthermore, were ubiquitous objects in avant-garde poetry.)

Literature is the grand theme of *The Savage Detectives,* not just authors and books but literature as a way of experiencing and looking at the world. All the passions of the characters (including love, sex, and revolution) are filtered through a literary vision. There is hardly a character in the novel that is not in some way related to the practice or critique of literature. Belano and Lima may have given up on their commitment to visceral realism by the end of the novel, but they never make a clear distinction between the pursuit of literature and the pursuit of life. They do not write or publish and are not always regarded by others as poets, but they could point at their ethic—fusing art and life—as their true poetic work. The novel, as Bolaño says, can be viewed as a farewell letter to a literary generation, a generation that came of age in a disenchanted world and that failed to revive the spirit of the historical avant-garde, which by then had died a heroic death. Yet there is one feature of avant-garde discourse that Bolaño retains in *The Savage Detectives,* and that is its prophetic quality, which Bolaño turns into his own personal myth. The narrator of Cesárea's life during the avant-garde decade points out, referring to her, that some women have the ability to predict the future (223). The same narrator notes that even a rough and illiterate man like General Carvajal was "convinced that Picasso and Marinetti were the prophets of something" (333). And Cesárea herself speaks mysteriously of the times to come, and when asked what times would those be, she answers "sometime around the year 2600" (565), thus pointing the way to Bolaño's posthumous memorial of twentieth-century evil, 2666.

Chapter 6

Two Dramatic Monologues

Amulet and *By Night in Chile*

After finishing *The Savage Detectives,* Bolaño set out to write two shorter novels that resemble each other in form while differing markedly from their predecessor. *Amulet* was published the year after *The Savage Detectives*—in 1999—but it is internally dated September 1998, a symbolic date in the context of the novel. The narrative core of the novel takes place in September 1968, the date when the Mexican army took over the campus of Mexico's largest university (the UNAM, or Universidad Nacional Autónoma de México) and arrested hundreds of students on strike against the government. Two weeks later the same army under the same general perpetrated the student massacre of Tlatelolco, where an undetermined number of student protesters were shot point blank by soldiers and paramilitary agitators. By noting when the manuscript of the novel was finished, Bolaño is able to commemorate and memorialize the victims of two of the most tragic weeks in modern Mexican history. (It is not irrelevant to this outbreak of political violence that the Olympic Games were to be inagurated in Mexico City on October 12 of that same year. The army detachment involved in the student massacre was the Batallón Olimpia, a batallion specially trained to maintain order during the games.) *By Night in Chile,* on the other hand, was published the year after *Amulet*—in 2000—and focuses on the complicity between the literary institution in Chile and the Pinochet dictatorship. Both novels are about 150 pages long. Bolaño himself pointed out the formal similarities between them when he said that they both have the same musical and dramatic structure, each one partaking of the qualities of chamber music and of dramaturgy, and each one narrated by a single voice that is "unstable, capricious, and resigned to its fate" (Braithwaite 115).

Both novels, furthermore, were to be part of a trilogy, but the third panel of the tryptich—a short novel to be called "Corrida" ("Bullfight")—never materialized. It is important, however, to point out some differences between *Amulet* and *By Night in Chile.* The former, for example, is much closer to *The Savage Detectives* than the latter and is in fact an expansion of chapter 4 of the middle part. Those ten pages of *The Savage Detectives* are a mere sketch of the hundred and fifty pages of *Amulet,* which are more oracular in tone and more visionary in content. These qualities contrast with *By Night in Chile,* which is less visionary than its companion novel and more introspective than oracular. Not only that but Arturo Belano—the author's alter ego in *The Savage Detectives* and *Amulet*—disappears from the pages of the Chilean novel, to be replaced—as the author's stand-in—by the phantasmic figure of the "wizened youth" who repeatedly stirs the ethical conscience of the novel's narrator. Finally the narrative discourse of *Amulet* continually addresses a listener placed outside the novel (which correlates with the oral tone of the narrative), whereas *By Night in Chile* strikes the reader as an undirected interior monologue (Solotorevsky 49).

Despite this distinction both novels are dramatic monologues, a lyric form that H. M. Abrams defined as a lengthy speech by a single person and that, in its fullest form, is characterized by three features: the speaker is not the poet but a fictional character; the speech is addressed to an auditor or auditors about whom nothing is known except for the clues included in the poetic discourse; and the main principle controlling the poet's choice of words and themes is to reveal the speaker's temperament and character. But Abrams goes on to clarify that the second feature—the presence of a silent auditor—can be omitted (85–86). Thus the addressee is present in Robert Browning's *The Last Duchess* (1842) but absent in T. S. Eliot's *Love Song of J. Alfred Prufrock* (1915), two of the most famous dramatic monologues in Anglo-American literature. The use of the dramatic monologue in novels like *Amulet* and *By Night in Chile* once again speaks to Bolaño's penchant for blurring genre boundaries in his works.

Amulet: Cassandra among the Poets

As is common knowledge, an amulet is a magic charm, a device that protects against evil and misfortune. Bolaño's title refers to the collective song of the "ghost-children" who march to their death at the end of the novel: "and that song is our amulet," says the narrator (184). The ghost-children are the young sacrificial victims of the many repressive regimes (and equally repressive revolutionary movements) that have dotted the Latin American political landscape in recent decades, though in the novel these youths sacrificed on the altar of social change and civil liberties are specifically identified as the striking Mexican students who were dislodged from the university and later massacred by the army at Tlatelolco, a place where ritual human sacrifice was practiced in Aztec times. (The novel's narrator seals her identification with this lost generation when she states that she "lost her teeth on the altar of human sacrifice," 35.) The sacrificial victims were warriors captured by the Aztecs in their *guerras floridas* against enemy city-states. Captured enemy warriors were offered to the gods, but the practice of waging nonlethal campaigns and then sacrificing the enemy also had a dissuasive effect on the enemies of the Aztecs. It has been argued that the extreme reaction of the Mexican government leading to the Tlatelolco massacre of October 1968 had a similar intent. That event was a turning point in modern Mexican history, delegitimating the revolutionary rhetoric that had dominated Mexican politics since the 1920s and compromising the future of the ruling PRI party. Bolaño, however, is not so much concerned with the political fallout of the Tlatelolco massacre as he is with extolling the abnegation and generosity of the Latin American youth who give their lives for a just cause. Poetry is their form of expression, and a novel like *Amulet* a memorial to their virtues. The novel is both a eulogy and an elegy, a vision of a tragedy foretold projected by a narrator who is a symbolic mother to the orphan poets and whose tone evokes the world of Greek drama.

One of the important books that came out of Tlatelolco was Elena Poniatowska's *Massacre in Mexico,* a compilation of testimonies bearing on the Mexican student movement of the 1960s and on the government repression it endured.[1] One of the voices heard in that collage is that of a literature student who tells the story of a certain Alcira, a fellow student who "locked herself in one of the lavatories at University City and stayed there during the entire two weeks that the Army occupied CU [Ciudad Universitaria]," sleeping on the floor between the toilets and the washbowls and with nothing to sustain her except water from the faucet (65–66). This Alcira, however, was not a Mexican student but a Uruguayan teacher (called Alcira Soust Scaffo) who arrived in Mexico in 1952 and met Bolaño's family in 1970. According to a friend's testimony, Alcira was about forty at the time and went around dressed as a hippie. She seemed highly intelligent and worked translating French at the university (Maristain, *Bolaño: A Biography* 49–50). Bolaño lost touch with her in 1976, but her voice and image stayed with him for two more decades, to the point where Alcira became the narrator of *Amulet.* The urban legend woven around her is the core of the novel's plot, but Bolaño enriches the story with much added detail and turns the character into a mix of the oracular Cassandra and Julio Cortázar's female lead La Maga in *Hopscotch.*[2]

Alcira's name in the novel is Auxilio, a name prefigured in the novel's epigraph but lost to the English-speaking reader. The epigraph is from Petronius's *Satyricon* and reads: "In our misery we wanted to scream for help, / but there was no one there to come to our aid." (In Spanish, "aid" is translated as "auxilio": "Queríamos, pobres de nosotros, pedir auxilio; pero no había nadie para venir en nuestra ayuda.") Auxilio introduces herself as a Uruguayan emigré (her full name in the novel is Auxilio Lacouture) and then tells the story of the university's takeover by the army: "I was at the university on the eighteenth of September when the army occupied the campus and went around arresting and killing indiscriminately. No. Not many people were killed at the university. That was in Tlatelolco" (22). She then explains that the army invasion caught her by surprise in the bathroom reading some poems by Pedro Garfias (1901–67)—a Spanish poet exiled in Mexico after the Spanish Civil War—and that she had to hide there until the soldiers abandoned the premises, which was not until September 30, two weeks later: "I knew that I had to resist. So I sat down on the tiles of the women's bathroom and, before the last rays of sunlight faded, read three more of Pedro Garfias's poems, then shut the book and shut my eyes and said: Auxilio Lacouture, citizen of Uruguay, Latin American, poet and traveler, resist" (32). Many of Garfias's poems are about the Civil War and salute the republican militias that resisted Franco's coup. But in Bolaño poetry in general is an act of resistance both to historical violence and to what Frankfurt critical theorist Theodor W. Adorno denounced as the "totally administered society" and the capitalist commodification of life.[3] Bolaño is not a stranger to Borges's contention that reading is a more civilized activity than writing. Auxilio reads poems in the lavatory and thus symbolically opposes the barbarism of the army's actions. But she also writes poems on toilet paper and exclaims: "Because I wrote, I endured" (175), a line that recalls Chilean poet's Enrique Lihn's well-known poem about poetry and resistance "Porque escribí," whose last line is "Because I wrote I am alive."

The narrative returns time and time again to this primal scene of imprisonment and refuge, Auxilio's "season in hell." The narrator is *fixated* in the bathroom space in both a physical and psychological sense. In that abject space of human waste she bears witness to history and safeguards the autonomy of the university. When a soldier walks into the bathroom, Auxilio climbs on the toilet and lifts her feet "like a Renoir ballerina," as if she were about to give birth: "and in a sense, in effect, I was preparing to deliver something and to be delivered myself," says the narrator (29). (The theme of deliverance is inscribed in the cover of the original Spanish edition, which features a painting by Belgian symbolist artist Fernand Khnopff—based on a Christina Rosetti poem—called "Who Shall Deliver Me?") Throughout the novel Auxilio toys with the idea of being the mother of Mexican poetry and of Mexican poets, but what she is about to deliver as she squats on the toilet is nothing less than History, which elsewhere is described as a "horror story." When the soldier walks out of the bathroom without seeing her, the birth is over (31). The equation between history and excrement is not so surprising if one remembers that the original title for *By Night in Chile*—another novel concerned with historical crimes—was to be "Shit Storm." At any rate that bathroom space on the fourth floor of the

Faculty of Philosophy and Literature is the last redoubt in which "to defend the autonomy of the National Autonomous University of Mexico" (30).

Amulet, however, is not a stationary novel. Critics have already pointed out that spatial fixity is in tension with the urban itineraries traced out by Auxilio, sometimes by herself and sometimes in the company of her young protegés, members of the nocturnal race of bohemian poets (see, for example, Solotorevsky 36). Critics who focus on the itinerant aspect of the novel point out that a differentiated map of Mexico City emerges through the narrator's continuous errancy (contrasting the diurnal space of the university with the nocturnal environment of dangerous neighborhoods, for example), and that themes such as exile and migration are articulated as variations on urban nomadism (Manzoni, "Recorridos urbanos"). The itinerant aspect of the novel is not limited to its content but informs its narrative discourse as well, whose basic shape is that of the spiral: "Avance en espiral o en línea recta vacilante," writes one critic— "forward movement in a spiral or in a steady straight line" (Manzoni, "Reescritura como desplazamiento" 178). In fact it could be said that the reading method employed by Auxilio as she undergoes moments of panic in her bathroom stall applies to the whole novel: "then my reading started to speed up and soon it sped out of control, the verses flying past so quickly I could hardly take anything in, the words were sticking to one another" (27) This panicked reading forced by circumstance turns into a method for writing visions and premonitions.

The "free-fall reading" that the novel forces on its readers implies that time is not linear but either fractured or condensed in an eternal present: "I started thinking about my past as if I was thinking about my present, future, and past, all mixed together and dormant in the one tepid egg" (32). This peculiar treatment of time is particularly marked in the narrator's oneiric visit to surrealist painter Remedios Varo. Chapter 9 begins with the narrator's recollection of her being back in the women's bathroom in September 1968, where she was thinking about the adventures of the half-forgotten Remedios Varo, who had died in Mexico City in 1963, when the narrator was still living in Montevideo, according to her own statement. But then she questions this statement and speculates that she—the narrator—may have been living in Mexico City after all, volunteering as an occasional housemaid for Spanish poet Pedro Garfias. Satisfied with this speculation, the narrator reboots the narrative and asks the poet for the painter's address. Auxilio has never met Remedios (the similar meaning of the names may or not be a coincidence), but she finds her way to the painter's house and is invited in. The next line implies that the visitor has come from the future: "She is fifty-four years old. Which means that she has a year left to live" (107). The topsy-turvy nature of time in the novel is more than a question of narrative strategy, since the narrator has visions of both the past and the future. If Auxilio is able to remember the future, it is because history keeps repeating itself.

The novel, however, does have a recognizable plot or, at least, a plot-like structure, since it begins with the narrator introducing herself and ends with a final vision of apocalypse. Everyday details coexist in the novel with visions, hallucinations, and nightmares. In the first chapter, for example, the passage between the everyday and the visionary does not take long. Auxilio is telling the plain facts of her life and describing the house where poets Garfias and León Felipe live,[4] when all of a sudden a trivial object—a vase—grabs her attention and shatters the illusion of normality: "I thought: I'm going to put my hand into the vase's dark mouth. . . . And I saw my hand move forward . . . , approaching its enameled lip, at which point a little voice inside me said: Hey, Auxilio, what are you doing, you crazy woman, and that was what saved me, I think, because straight away my arm froze and my hand hung limp . . . , a few inches from that Hell-mouth" (7–8). A similar vase, associated with visions of hell, nightmares, and—in two cases—with the works of Edgar Allan Poe, appears in three poems of *The Unknown University* (pages 80, 129, and 709). One of the other poems in this collection is called "In the Reading Room of Hell." The flower vase in *Amulet* is metonymically related to the books that line the shelves in the poet's living room, books that may hide another entrance to hell. The vase may ultimately be a Bolaño obsession, but it also recalls the search for the cracks and fissures of reality in the works of Julio Cortázar.

In this same introductory chapter, Auxilio—stressing her role as the mother of Mexican poets—reveals that she knew "Arturito Belano when he was a shy seventeen-year-old who wrote plays and poems and couldn't hold his liquor" (1–2). An autobiographical reading of this statement places the reference in the year 1970, but more important the narrator's affirmation reintroduces one of the protagonists of *The Savage Detectives* to a novel in which he plays a marginal but still important role. In comparison with ghostly characters like Remedios Varo and Lilian Serpas—personages taken from real life—Belano (who ironically is a fictitious entity) turns out to be a realistic character in the novel's system of verisimilitude. The narrator takes up young Belano's story in chapter 4, where she adds that he was proud that Salvador Allende had been elected president of Chile and that he was the author of a novel that he later burned. She introduces him to the poetry of American modernists Pound, Williams, and T. S. Eliot and takes him home one night when he is sick and drunk, at which point Auxilio meets Arturito's family.

Later in the novel the young man appears on four different occasions. Auxilio runs into him at the Casa del Lago (the location in Chapultepec Park, in downtown Mexico City, where the infrarealist gang used to crash poetry recitals by establishment figures) and introduces him to her friends as an "eighteen-year-old Chilean poet" (55); then she is saved by his unexpected intervention as she is walking along a deserted street in the middle of the night and is being followed by a stalker (67); later still she accompanies him to the bus station when the young poet decides to make a trip to Chile by land and sea in order to support Allende's revolution (69), a trip that Bolaño undertook in August 1973; and finally she follows him to help rescue a victim of the King of the Rent Boys, "a guy . . . who had a monopoly on male prostitution" (83) in Colonia Guerrero, a run down neighborhood in Mexico City.

The victim is a young homosexual poet called Ernesto San Epifanio, another character from *The Savage Detectives.* The King had bought Ernesto's body, and Ernesto asks his friend Arturo to help deliver him from the pimp's grasp. Arturo has just returned from Chile, where he came close to being tortured or disappeared in one of the detention camps set up in the wake of the military coup. His prestige as a Latin American macho revolutionary is at its height, and he has no choice but to accept the dangerous mission proposed by Ernesto, namely to pay the King a visit at the seedy hotel room where he holds court. The two poets are accompanied at a distance by Auxilio, who carries a knife and is there to witness the scene. The trio irrupts into the King's room, and Arturo demands not only Ernesto's freedom from sexual slavery but also the liberation of a sickly boy who cowers in a corner. The episode is tense but devoid of overt violence. Arturo wins the contest with the King by talking, by confidently telling stories about death: "it was the storyteller talking, not the booze" (98).

This particular episode, which occupies chapters 7 and 8, echoes the theme of deliverance from the nightmare of history that sounds throughout the novel. But it can also be read as a mythic descent into hell: "the Avenida Guerrero . . . was in every respect a damned river, a river of the damned, ferrying corpses and corpses-to-be, black automobiles that appeared, vanished, and then reappeared . . . , as if the river of Hell were circular" (90). One critic emphasizes the storytelling and poetic fabulation at the heart of the rescue and interprets this episode as a "comic, gay version of Orpheus and Eurydice" (Bogue 120). But he also warns that "the triumphant outcome of this mythic tale . . . hardly represents Bolaño's vision of the post-'68 poets' future or their standing in the world" (120). Indeed in the myth Orpheus's rescue of Eurydice fails. What is more important, the theme of historical deliverance in the novel is trumped by the discourse of apocalypse with which it ends and that is also dramatically evident in the visionary allusion to the title of what would be Bolaño's great posthumous novel, *2666:* "Then we walked down the Avenida Guerrero. . . . Guerrero, at that time of night, is "more like a cemetery than an avenue, not a cemetery in 1974 or in 1968, or 1975, but a cemetery in the year 2666" (86).

Greek myth and theater play an important role in *Amulet,* beginning with the narrator, Auxilio Lacouture, whom Bolaño described in an interview as a

"Uruguayan with a vocation for Greek dramatics" (Manzoni, *Roberto Bolaño* 33). In chapter 5 Auxilio dreamily reflects on her love life and evokes the story of her friend Elena and her Italian lover Paolo. Elena is an attractive and well-off recent university graduate who befriends Auxilio and drives her around the city in her car. Paolo is on a visit to Mexico waiting for the Cuban authorities to grant him a visa so that he can go travel to the island and interview Fidel Castro. This story is contextualized by numerous references to theater and poetry but at first sight seems digressive. Later in the novel, though, the names of Helen of Troy and Che Guevara come up, creating a web of internal references that integrates Elena's story into a larger pattern of meaning. The Cuban revolution becomes part of a historical series (involving the Mexican revolution, the Spanish Civil War, the Second World War, the Tlatelolco massacre, and the Pinochet coup in Chile) that seems to unfold from the mythic origins of the Trojan War. Myth and history converge in a spiral of destruction, one from which poets cannot remain aloof. The two "Trojan" poems included in the Barcelona section of Bolaño's *Unknown University* and discussed above in chapter 1 attest to the strong connection between history, myth, and poetry. The connection is a melancholy one because the Trojan poets of contemporary times have lost the spirit of epic poetry but remain caught in the upheavals of history.

The central Greek myth rehearsed in *Amulet* is that of Orestes and Erigone, which is told in chapter 11 when the narrator pays a nocturnal visit to Carlos Coffeen Serpas, the son of poet Lilian Serpas, who that night has decided to spend the night away from the apartment where she lives with her son. The narrator becomes the narratee. Coffeen (whose surname is almost a homophone of "coffin") tells the story of Erigone in the gloomy atmosphere of an apartment "which draws its sustenance from anti-life, from anti-matter, from the black holes of Mexico and Latin America, from all that once tried to find a way out into life but now leads only back to death" (137). This ominous atmosphere captures the themes of murder, rape, matricide, and revenge that characterize the story. Erigone is the niece of Helen of Troy and the most beautiful woman in Greece. She is the daughter of Clytemnestra—Agamemnon's wife—and Aegisthus, the lover Clytemnestra takes when her husband goes off to Troy. Agamemnon returns from Troy and the lovers kill him. Orestes and Electra—Agamemnon's children—avenge their father by murdering both their mother and her lover. Orestes proclaims himself king and falls madly in love with his half-sister, whom he rapes and impregnates one night. Electra advises him to get rid of Erigone because she carries the seed of Aegisthus's descendants. Orestes hires a guide to take Erigone away from the city and dispose of her in secret. But then he seems to backtrack and warns Erigone of the danger she is in. The story ends inconclusively. Erigone is seen leaving the city, but her fate is not revealed.

As a textual device, the Erigone story, which is partially an all-night conversation between Orestes and his intended victim, mirrors the frame story, an uneasy dialogue between the unstable Coffeen and Auxilio. As Coffeen recounts the Erigone myth to Auxilio, she grows increasingly unsettled by the tone and content of the narrative, as if she were about to become the sacrificial victim of a possibly deranged narrator: "I was at a loss for words, and for a moment . . . it seemed that Coffeen was Orestes and I was Erigone, which meant that the night would have no end, I would never see the light of day again, I would be incinerated by the black gaze of Lilian's son" (149). Like Erigone, Auxilio is at the crossroads of history, having become an involuntary witness to the crimes of history, particularly the violation of the university by the army and the student massacre that followed. *Amulet* is to a significant extent a testimony denouncing those crimes, a prophetic testimony given by a Cassandra-like figure that sees the repeated birth of history as the cyclical repetition of such crimes. The Erigone story in *Amulet* has been read as a political allegory in which the interests of the state (enacted through mad violence) clash with the ruler's individual desires (Bogue 123). That is, two forms of irrationality (lust and murder "most foul") cross swords in a bloody family feud in which a wife takes an illicit lover and murders a husband, leading to her children's equally murderous revenge on her, and leading further to a half-brother raping a half-sister and impregnating her with a potential enemy of the state. Auxilio is frightened during the telling of the myth because she is the witness of history confronting an avatar of the mad ruler who seeks to suppress any incriminating evidence. The novel begins with an admonition that "this is going to be a horror story. A story of murder, detection and horror. But it won't appear to be . . . although, in fact, it's the story of a terrible crime" (1).

In an earlier chapter the focus of the novel is on Carlos Coffeen Serpas's mother, the poet Lilian Serpas, who, at this point in time—explicitly identified as 1973—is walking the streets of Mexico City selling her son's drawings in cafés and bars. As the narrator says, Lilian Serpas had been "a reasonably well-known poet and a woman of extraordinary beauty" back in the 1950s (119). In actual fact, though, she was not Mexican as the narrator affirms but Salvadoran. The biographical Lilian Serpas lived in San Francisco in the 1930s and apparently arrived in Mexico with a government scholarship in 1940. She was married to an unsuccessful American painter called Carlos Coffeen and indeed had a son called Carlos Coffeen Serpas. Another son, Fernando, died tragically, and his death was blamed for his mother's deteriorating mental health. By 1978 Lilian was wandering the streets of Mexico City and begging for alms. Her hair was unkempt and dirty, and she dressed in rags. Her clothes often had cigarette burns because she was an inveterate and careless smoker. At the request of a charitable organization, she was finally admitted to a mental institution and died from a fall in October 1985.[5] Serpas obviously belongs to the lineage of the poète maudit and could have been part of the *Savage Detectives* gang were it not for her advanced age (she was born in 1905).

In the novel Lilian is a double of Auxilio: they move in similar circles, they are both itinerant artists, they both take occasional jobs to make ends meet, and they are both the "mothers" of Mexican poetry. But Lilian brings out the erotic life denied to Auxilio. One of her lovers, in fact, is said to have been Che Guevara himself, a statement that is somewhat plausible since Guevara was in Mexico in 1955, the year he met Fidel Castro. Auxilio and others are very interested to know what the famous comandante was like in bed, but all Lilian says is that he was "normal." The important point here is not the voyeuristic curiosity but Lilian's body, which brings together poetry and revolution. It is true that at one point the narrator states, referring to Lilian, that "poetry left her cold" (122). But this statement is not to be taken as a put-down of poetry but, rather, as the reiteration of a strange paradox in Bolaño's writing: poets do not have to write poetry to be considered poets, and they certainly do not have to publish. García Madero, the first narrator of *The Savage Detectives,* keeps talking about writing poems and even tells the reader how many poems he has written in one day, but none of these poems are attested in the novel. He is accepted into the visceral realist fraternity *before* any of his poems are read by the group members. In fact there are no visceral realist poems to be found in that novel, with the exception—if that is what it is—of Cesárea Tinajero's childish drawing of the straight, wavy, and broken lines. The poems actually printed on the page are by Rimbaud and Efrén Rebolledo, with the addition of two lines by modernista Mexican poet Amado Nervo. The poet's task is to live the life of a poet, as Lilian herself hints in *Amulet:* "These stints never lasted very long, because, as she told me, not without a certain sadness, when you're a poet and you have to live by night, there's no way you can hold a steady job" (121). And in chapter 10 she lives by night and turns up very late at the Café Quito to sit at a table with the young poets of Mexico.

The Guevara story is part of Lilian's legend, but Lilian's whole life acquires an aura of unreality in the novel. When the narrator tries to place their meeting at a specific time and place, the image of Lilian Serpas goes up in smoke: "it's eleven o'clock and through the smoke . . . I see Lilian arrive enveloped, as always, in smoke, and her smoke and that of the café eye each other like spiders" (124). And as time goes by and people start to leave the café, Auxilio is stranded in front of a half-empty cup of coffee. That is when "an evasive shadow . . . approaches my table and sits down next to me. How are you doing, Auxilio? says the ghost of Lilian Serpas" (126).

Lilian also appears as a ghost in a previous chapter when Auxilio goes to visit surrealist Catalan painter Remedios Varo and discerns a shadowy presence behind the drapes. Like Pedro Garfias and León Felipe, Varo was a Spanish exile in Mexico, where she arrived in 1940 fleeing from the Nazis (she was living in Paris at the outset of the Second World War) but also from the Franco forces in Spain, who by that time had already defeated the Republican side in the Civil War. Varo became an important painter in the 1940s and 1950s, and Bolaño alludes to the content of some of her paintings in the novel. When Auxilio goes looking for the artist's house, for example, she reaches a street "where all the houses seem to be ruined castles," a reference to the many works by Varo that feature medieval or fairy-tale castles (107). Varo also has many paintings of cats. Accordingly her living room and courtyard in the novel are populated by a variety of cats hiding behind curtains or taking a siesta.

Auxilio's visit is really a vision of Remedios Varo: "I was back in the women's bathroom on the fourth floor of the Faculty of Philosophy and Literature and it was September 1968 and I was thinking about the adventures of Remedios Varo" (106). The visit is precisely dated in 1962—a year before the artist died—but Auxilio already knows that Varo has only one year left to live. And at the end of the interview it is "implacably clear" to the visitor that Remedios Varo is dead (114). Varo herself had visions that materialized in her paintings: "I know that she has seen many bad things, the ascension of the devil, the unstoppable procession of termites climbing the Tree of Life, the conflict between the Enlightenment and the Shadow" (108). The gift (or curse) of vision sets up a complicity between the two women. While the narrator's visions disclose historical apocalypse, those of the painter announce her own death (109).

The main object of the conversation between Remedios and Auxilio is a picture covered with an old skirt, a huge skirt that seems to have belonged to a giant. This picture is neither Varo's last nor second to last, as the narrator suggests. It is probably not even by Varo. The skirt is lifted, but no sexual or reproductive organs are revealed—no "Origin of the World," to quote the title of Courbet's painting (1866). Instead what Auxilio sees is "an enormous valley, viewed from the highest mountain, a green and brown valley" (110). The sight makes her anxious because she senses that the scene is a prelude for something bigger and uncanny, like the "approach of an ice man, a man made of ice cubes, who will come and kiss me on the mouth" (110). These cryptic references are clarified at the end of the novel, when the narrator evokes a frozen landscape borrowed from Poe's *Narrative of Arthur Gordon Pym* and a valley that abruptly ends in an abyss.

This is the moment of Revelation in the novel. The ghosts of Remedios Varo and Lilian Serpas become the ghosts of a multitude of children on their way to the abyss: "I conjectured that they too had wandered through the snowy mountains, where they had met with one another and gradually gathered to form the army that was now moving across the field" (181). These children are drawn from two books that left a lasting impression on Bolaño: Marcel Schwob's *The Children's Crusade* and Jerzy Andrzejewski's *The Gates of Paradise*,[6] both of which narrate the Children's Crusade of the thirteenth century, one of the most durable legends to come out of the Middle Ages. According to the story, thousands of Christian children took it on themselves to liberate Jerusalem after the failure of the fourth Crusade, but when they managed to cross the Mediterranean they were sold into slavery on the shores of North Africa. At the end of *Amulet* Bolaño merges this fable with the sacrifice of a whole generation of Latin Americans who fought for their own kind of liberation in a different time and place. The "ghost-children" were united only by their generosity and courage, and they were singing as they marched down the valley and into the abyss: "And although the song that I heard was about war, about the heroic deeds of a whole generation of young Latin Americans led to sacrifice, I knew that above and beyond all, it was about courage and mirrors, desire and pleasure. And that song is our amulet" (184).[7]

These are the last words of the novel, and they convey the streak of romantic idealism that runs through all of Bolaño's work. The song the children sing is, of course, a reference to poetry. One of Auxilio's prophecies is that poetry will not disappear and that its "non-power shall manifest itself in a different form" (159). Bolaño states that when he speaks of the nonpower of poetry he is referring to "something that is self-evident: poetry is a sumptuary object, devoid of power. Poetic discourse . . . does not tend toward power. Toward revolution but never toward power."[8] W. H. Auden said something similar in his famous poem to the memory of William Butler Yeats: "For poetry makes nothing happen: it survives / In the valley of its saying where executives / Would never want to tamper."

By Night in Chile: A Phantasmagoria

Bolaño seems to have written *By Night in Chile* (or at least finished it) after his last trip to his native country in late 1999, when he was invited to the Santiago book fair. There is a reference in the novel to Chile's new socialist president, which can only be interpreted as an allusion to Ricardo Lagos, the Concertación candidate who won the second round of the presidential election in January 2000, the same year the novel was published. Lagos's election was the third such contest in Chile since the end of the military regime headed by general Pinochet, but it implied a more radical break with the dictatorial past than previous elections because Lagos was a member of the Socialist Party, whereas the two previously elected presidents belonged to the more centrist Christian Democratic Party. Lagos's election, however, did not imply a return to the Allende years (1970–73). During his term there was no revolutionary rhetoric and no nationalization of private industry. The government remained committed to a market economy but also made significant progress in the areas of human rights and political reform. The 1980 Constitution, drafted while the military were in power, was reformed in 2005 to make it more democratic, and a commission was set up to investigate the thousands of cases of torture and political imprisonment between 1973 and 1990.

The 1990s in Chile were the first decade of postdictatorship and of an emerging postdictatorial culture and literature often centered on the theme of traumatic memory and human rights. Ariel Dorfman's play *Death and the Maiden* (1992) was an iconic production of this period. Like *Distant Star, By Night in Chile* can also be read as a postdictatorship novel, though neither of the two is primarily concerned with overcoming the traumas of the past or making an explicit argument on behalf of human rights. Their treatment of dictatorship is uncanny, if the term is defined as "what one calls everything that was meant to remain secret and hidden and has come into the open."[9] What is disclosed in *Distant Star* is not only the criminal bent of the dictatorship but the complicity between art and violence, a collusion that implicates certain forms of the avant-garde. In *By Night in Chile* it is the tortured body of the militant that is accidentally exposed toward the end of the novel.

The title of *By Night in Chile* in Spanish is *Nocturno de Chile*. A nocturne is a romantic piece of music composed for piano that transmits emotions associated with evening and night. The opening sequence of the novel takes place in an estate in the far south of Chile where the night sky is brightly illuminated by the full moon. The narrator is struck by the scene and soon notices that the great national poet Pablo Neruda, who is also a guest in the estate, comes out of the house into the garden and recites verses to the moon: "There was Neruda and there a few metres behind him was I, and, between us, the night, the moon, the equestrian statue, Chilean plants, Chilean wood, the obscure dignity of our land" (12). The mood of the scene is nocturnal, in both the musical and poetic senses of the word. Aside from being a musical genre, the *nocturno* is a well-defined genre in Spanish and Latin American poetry. Poets like Rubén Darío, Xavier Villaurrutia, and Neruda himself cultivated the genre, but the most famous nocturno in Latin American poetry—and a poem actually quoted in the novel—is José Asunción Silva's "Nocturno III," a poem about the death of the beloved (or the poet's sister) that is as gloomy and musical as Poe's "The Raven."[10] The musical nocturne is gentle, more a crepuscular reverie than a harbinger of death. But Silva's poem, like the three nocturnos by Darío, is about death or the presentiment of death. Bolaño's prose in *Nocturno de Chile* has a foreboding character and a musical structure—provided by the periodical repetition of the phrase "Sordello, which Sordello?," which acts like a refrain, and of the reappearing vision of the "wizened youth"—that brings it close to poetry. The novel takes many liberties with the conventions of narrative prose and includes visionary images and passages that at times recall hermetic poetry more than a standard piece of prose fiction. But the title clearly refers to the long night of dictatorship that darkened the Chilean political landscape between 1973 and 1990.

By Night in Chile is an often delirious deathbed confession by a literary critic and Opus Dei priest who during the dictatorship collaborated with the Pinochet regime by agreeing to instruct the four members of the junta on the fundamentals of Marxism, but also by remaining silent in the years when serious human rights abuses were being committed all around him.[11] The narrator is called Sebastián Urrutia Lacroix, a name that mimics the surname of the most prominent Chilean critic of recent times, José Miguel Ibáñez Langlois. This critic, like his fictional counterpart, is an ordained priest, and he writes under the pseudonym Ignacio Valente. Like his real-life model, Bolaño's character also adopts a pseudonym, which he does in order to separate his poetic work from his critical writings: "So I adopted the name of H. Ibacache. . . . Urrutia Lacroix was preparing a body of poetic work for posterity . . . , while Ibacache read other people's works and explained them to the public" (25).[12] The narrator furthermore argues that Ibacache's "purity would be able to illuminate . . . the body of work taking shape verse by verse in the diamond-pure mind of his double: Urrutia Lacroix" (25). There is self-deception involved in the priest's self-characterization as "pure," but on a different level this passage suggests the phantasmic quality of characters and identities in the novel, as if all of them were like those shadows or silhouettes that the narrator sees dancing on the walls of the restaurant where he and his mentor, at one point in the novel, stop to eat dinner: "the people in the street rushed by . . . , casting their shadows one after another, more and more quickly, on the walls of the restaurant" (49). But the passersby are not the only shadows in the passage: "And that night . . . I returned from the house of our storyteller and diplomat, walking with Farewell's dissolute shadow" (38). "And once again I saw my father as the shadow of a weasel or a stoat scurrying from corner to corner in the house" (48).

The game of doubles proliferates in the novel. Valente's predecessor in the history of Chilean literary criticism was Hernán Díaz Arrieta, who wrote under the pseudonym of Alone. This is the critic who in the novel appears as Farewell, the homosexual, bitter, and sarcastic mentor of the young Urrutia Lacroix but who is also the living repository of the Chilean literary tradition. Farewell (which, in addition, happens to be the title of a well-known poem by the early Neruda) also has an alias, a family name by which he is known by the farmhands and peasants of his estate: González Lamarca. And the narrator too has a double in the novel, the spectral youth who keeps reappearing as a vision and who acts as the narrator's antagonist and critical conscience. The "wizened youth," whose voice periodically makes itself heard questioning or judging the narrator's actions and nonactions, is easily identified with Bolaño himself, as they were both born at about the same time, they both left their native country, and they are both writers. Bolaño thus inhabits his own novel as a ghost and at the same time establishes a critical distance between his own values and those of his narrator.

The folding and unfolding of alter egos stresses the phantasmagoric quality of the novel but also relates to Bolaño's fluid handling of the dramatic monologue form in this work. Whereas in *Amulet* the narrative discourse was directed at, and therefore framed by, an internal addressee, in *By Night in Chile* the narrator addresses no one in particular. The wizened youth is the narrator's potential addressee, but this spectral figure never materializes as a possible interlocutor. The novel, furthermore, has only two paragraphs. The first one runs from page 1 to page 130, and the second consists of only one line, the final line of the text: "And then the storm of shit begins." Bolaño had intended to title his novel "Tormenta de mierda" but was dissuaded from doing so by his editor Jorge Herralde and by Mexican author and friend Juan Villoro, one of whom suggested the actual title. It should be noted that the final line is not uttered by the novel's narrator but by an offstage voice that creates another level of discourse (or fiction) just when the novel ends.[13]

Despite its freewheeling narrative style *By Night in Chile* is far from anarchic. Bolaño himself points out the novel's structural design in the same interview quoted at the beginning of this chapter: "*By Night in Chile* is an attempt to construct the whole life story of a person in six or seven or eight scenes ["cuadros"]. Each scene is arbitrary, and at the same time—and paradoxically—exemplary; that is to say, a moral lesson can be drawn from it. Each scene may be read independently. All the scenes are joined by little branches or ducts ["tubos"] that at times are even faster and far more independent than the scenes themselves" (Braithwaite 115–16; author's translation). The reference to the "little branches or ducts" evokes the model of the rhizome, but the organization of the narrative space in terms of fixed and well-defined narrative sequences checks the horizontal growth of the intervening links and stabilizes a monologue of unusual fluidity.[14]

At least six "scenes" or sequences can be discerned in the novel, all of which put moral and ethical values in play. The novel's epigraph, taken from one of Chesterton's Father Brown stories ("The Purple Wig"), has a similar moral character: "Take off your wig," which may be read as an admonition to stop dissembling and be authentic. The novel as a whole questions the moral character of its narrator and the ethics of the literary institution at a time of political repression and state terror. Ibacache's idealized conception of himself and of literary criticism as a source of civilized values cannot survive the ethical contradictions injected by the military dictatorship. The narrator is certainly not a man of the people, but the fact that he undertakes an "examen de conciencia" (or self-examination) at the moment of death—inconclusive as it may be—partially redeems him.

The opening sequence of the novel (1–22) corresponds to the narrator's "literary baptism" at Farewell's southern estate (22). After introducing himself to the reader by name and nationality, the narrator goes on to remark that at the age of thirteen he heard God's call and decided to enter a seminary. He remembers meeting the famous critic Farewell at the time he was ordained, confessing his own desire to be a critic, and accepting the latter's invitation to join him and a few literary friends at his villa in the south of Chile, a property called *Lá-bas* ("Down There"). The name of the property is a reference to Joris-Karl Huysmans 1891 novel of the same title, which mostly designates a symbolic location, namely hell. Huysmans's novel has been aptly described as "one of the key texts of the Decadent movement of the 1890s and [one that] writhes with satanists, occultists, incubi (male demons), succubi (female demons) and intellectuals.[15]" Bolaño's novel does feature a number of intellectuals but no satanists or demons. However, Bolaño did state in an interview that *By Night in Chile* is "the metaphor of an infernal country" (Braithwaite 114), a statement that to some extent explains not only the choice of name for the hacienda but also the incidents leading up to the guest's arrival at the property. The young priest's arrival at Lá-bas is modeled after Jonathan Harker's arrival at Castle Dracula in Bram Stoker's novel. In both cases the narrative atmosphere is one of foreboding and dread, and in both accounts an envoy of the host is sent to meet the disoriented guest. In *Dracula* the coachman picks up Jonathan Harker at Borgo Pass; in *By Night in Chile*, the local version of a coachman meets Urrutia Lacroix at the main square of a town called Querquén: "I must have been a sorry sight standing there helplessly with my suitcase from the seminary. . . . I said a hasty prayer and headed for a wooden bench. . . . Our Lady, do not abandon your servant, I murmured, while the black birds . . . cried *quién, quién, quién*. . . . Then, at the end of the road, there appeared a sort of tilbury or cabriolet or carriage pulled by two horses . . . , its silhouette looming in the horizon . . . , as if that equipage were coming to take someone away to Hell" (6–7).

But the weekend gathering in which the incipient critic participates is not particularly hellish. The other participants milling around the grounds are young Nerudian poets (all with fictitious names) who depend on their master and mentor Farewell to break into the mainstream of Chilean literature, and the great Pablo Neruda himself, who easily dominates the scene. The narrator is awed by the poet's presence and mocks his imaginary antagonist—the wizened youth—because he, the young man, never had the chance to meet "any of our Republic major writers in a setting as elemental as the one I have just described" (12). Bolaño never met Neruda, who died in 1973 when Bolaño was living in Mexico. The quote above, therefore, seems to express Bolaño's genuine regret for not having had the chance to meet the larger-than-life Neruda, in whatever setting that meeting could have taken place. The reference to the "elemental setting" in the novel can be explained by the rural location of Farewell's estate but also applies to Neruda's *Elementary Odes,* the first volume of which appeared in 1954. (The historical time frame of the estate scene is the late fifties.) The three volumes of elementary odes contain some of Neruda's best poems, all of which are written in praise of the basic components of human and natural life: joy, air, love, the birds of Chile, fishes and vegetables, copper, earth, storms, autumn, books, time, fire, bread, poetry, and so on. There is even an ode dedicated to literary critics, but in this poem critics are chastised for abducting the poet's simple poems from their equally simple intended readers, the common folk.

Neruda's presence at Farewell's soirée is a key element of the narrator's "literary baptism." Other important elements are Farewell's unwelcome sexual advances and the narrator's short walks around the countryside, where he meets the local farmhands and peasants. Though he accepts breaking bread with a family of laborers in their "cabin" (9–11), Urrutia's impression of the local people is not a favorable one. He finds the men and women physically unpleasant, an impression that correlates with his later disapproval of Salvador Allende as president of Chile. (Allende was a middle-class professional, but his political posture was that of a man of the people.) Aesthetics and politics come together in a curious mix. In this context some readers may miss the irony of the "elemental meal" scene at the laborers' hut, to which Urrutia is invited in his role as a priest. This hosting family has a sick infant and hopes that a priest can alleviate the child's suffering. The priest, however, reacts brusquely to the family's request and suggests that if the child has not already died and they want to save him, they should call a doctor. Here the narrator unconsciously echoes the hope of the Chilean people, who in 1970 elected a "savior" (Salvador) who happened to be a physician.

Structurally the meal scene that unfolds between pages 9 and 11 takes the place of the formal dinner that Farewell has prepared for his guests and which is barely described in the following pages. The menu is described on page 13 but not the conversation around the table, which never reaches the status of a symposium. Even in its understated way, however, the banquet scene once again recalls the figure of Neruda, who was often depicted at the head of a table enjoying a long and succulent meal with friends and admirers.

Two other structural features should be noted in the opening sequence of the novel that foreshadow later sequences and events. One is the imagery associated with Farewell in the following passages: "Farewell's voice was like the voice of a large bird of prey soaring over rivers and mountains. . . . Unable to meet Farewell's penetrating gaze, I modestly lowered my eyes, like a wounded fledgling" (4–5); "then I looked up again and my seminarist's eyes met Farewell's falcon eyes" (5). This imagery will later "materialize" in the episode where specially trained falcons hunt down the pigeons that deface the churches and cathedrals that Urrutia has been charged with visiting in Europe. In addition falconry is a medieval sport, just as troubadour poetry is a medieval art form. One name that insistently appears in the novel's opening sequence (and throughout the novel) is that of the troubadour Sordello, an Italian poet-warrior of the early thirteenth century who figures in Dante's *Purgatory,* in one of Robert Browning's narrative poems, and in one of Pound's cantos. Sordello is probably mentioned at this point in the novel because Virgil and Dante run into him in the *Divine Comedy,* not in the *Inferno* but in *Purgatory.* Still, if Chile is a hellish country, as Bolaño states in the context of military dictatorship, then it may be said that the young apprentice Urrutia Lacroix runs into the same Sordello at Farewell's estate on his frustrated way to Paradise. Aside from its thematic content, the whole scene at Farewell's villa performs a crucial structural function that frames the novel in strictly formal terms. The weekend gathering of literary friends at Lá-bas directly points to the final sequence of the novel, namely the soirées held at the house of María Canales and her husband Jimmy Thompson, where literary conversation serves as a cover for the torture of political prisoners going on in the basement.

A new phase begins for the narrator upon his return to Santiago. He begins writing poems and publishing reviews of the major figures of Chilean literature between the middle of the nineteenth century and the poets and novelists of the 1950s and 1960s. One of the writers he reviews is Salvador Reyes, a diplomat and novelist who won the National Literature Prize in 1967 but who is remembered in the novel not as a particularly successful or widely read writer but for his meetings with Ernst Jünger during the Second World War, when Don Salvador was Chilean consul in Paris. As the narrator points out, Reyes is the only Chilean writer mentioned in Jünger's memoirs. In the novel's second sequence (25–38), the narrator and Farewell visit Don Salvador at his house and hear the story of those meetings in occupied France, which the narrator reports in his own voice. The transition between this sequence and the previous one is provided by the theme of purity. Ibacache surrounds the practice of literary criticism with an aura of purity and quotes Reyes as saying that Jünger "was one of the purest men he had met in Europe" (26). Jünger was the author of numerous literary works going back to the 1920s and a decorated war veteran (he was awarded the Iron Cross in 1916). He may have struck his Chilean counterpart as morally upright, but the impression he makes on the reader is open to question. The most substantial meeting between both writers takes place in the attic of an anorexic and probably undocumented Guatemalan painter who came to Paris to make a name for himself but is trapped in the city by the outbreak of the war. He spends his days "contemplating the street plan of Paris" (29) through his window, refusing what little food Reyes can bring to him, and working on a painting called "Landscape: Mexico City an Hour before Dawn," which shows his disorientation. Jünger is attracted to the attic by his own artistic curiosity but shows up in his Wehrmacht uniform. During the meeting Reyes displays his concern that the painter might have been arrested by the French police or, worse still, by the Gestapo. But even without this comment, the presence of a German officer in a novel like *By Night in Chile*—so eloquent on the subject of military dictatorship—would be ominous. Reyes's appreciation of his German counterpart might have been helped by the fact that Jünger actually bothers to read the translated copy of his work that he offers the German writer the last time they meet. The Guatemalan painter, on the other hand, never goes to the trouble of opening the novel that Reyes gives to him on a different occasion. This neglect is a blow to the author's vanity. Reyes does not return to the attic for two months after discovering the painter's indifference.

But literary vanity and the questionable nature of purity are not the only themes in this sequence. Heroism is explicitly highlighted with respect to "Captain Jünger, the First World War hero, author of *Storm of Steel, African Games, On the Marble Cliffs,* and *Heliopolis*" (26). Heroism can also be inferred with respect to the unyielding attitude of the Guatemalan painter, who stoically admits his personal defeat: "in its own way the painting was an altar for human sacrifice . . . , and in its own way the painting was an acknowledgement of defeat, not the defeat of Paris or the defeat of European culture bravely determined to burn itself down . . . , but his personal defeat" (35). Inescapably the artistic defeat of the "obscure Guatemalan" (35) casts a shadow on the heroic triumphalism of the "Teuton hero" (34), since the latter's laurels rest on the ashes of European culture. The Guatemalan's vision, imperfectly realized as it may be, also undercuts the Chilean writer's artistic inspiration: Reyes cannot see what the painter sees in the horizon and is afraid to ask and hear "what can't be heard" (31). It seems that the real hero in this sequence is the artist-as-martyr, especially since in Bolaño heroism is an attribute reserved for writers and poets, always at a disadvantage against the forces of history and the indifference of their contemporaries. After leaving Don Salvador's premises the narrator has a vision of "heroes setting out for immortality armed only with their writings" (39) and "a vision of torrential grace, burnished like the dreams of heroes" (38), epiphanies that lead into the novel's third sequence, the story of Heldenberg (39–48).

A motif running through the first two sequences of the novel and forming a bridge between the second and third (those "little branches and ducts") is the partaking or lack of food, a motif that serves a purely structural function. The narrator has a repast in the laborers' cabin, then he attends a more succulent meal at Farewell's manor, later he listens to a story where a Chilean writer and diplomat tries to keep an anorexic painter fed, and subsequently he and Farewell stop at a restaurant where the latter tells the former the story of Heldenberg. The story is about a wealthy shoemaker at the time of the Austro-Hungarian Empire who makes his way to the emperor himself and presents him wih a project to build a monument to the heroes of the empire on a hill whose property he has already secured by disbursing a large sum of money. The monument would function as a cemetery and museum. It would remember the heroes of the past by erecting statues in their honor, and it would serve as a burial ground for the heroes of the present and the future whose bodies would be carried there by civil servants and interred for all posterity. The emperor enthusiastically agrees to the project, and the shoemaker begins preparations for turning the hill into a mausoleum. He spends his entire fortune and dedicates every moment of his waking life to Heldenberg, but as time passes the initial exaltation of courtiers and common people alike dissipates, and the shoemaker finds himself increasingly forgotten. "The Emperor died. A war broke out and the Empire collapsed. . . . Nobody remembered the shoemaker anymore, except, at odd and fleeting moments, the lucky few who still had a pair of his splendid, long-wearing shoes" (47). Ultimately invading soldiers find the shoemaker's body in a crypt, "sitting on a grand stone seat . . . , his eye-sockets empty as if he never were to contemplate anything but the valley spread out below Heroes' Hill" (48).

Farewell's account of Heroes' Hill is, to some extent, historically accurate. Heldenberg is an actual memorial near Vienna built in the middle of the nineteenth century and conceived by entrepreneur Joseph Gottfried Pargfrieder, "an industrial pioneer who supplied the army with footwear" and the wealthy shoemaker of Bolaño's fable. The memorial contains busts and statues of rulers and military heroes and was meant to glorify the Imperial-Royal Army and the Habsburg dynasty. "Pargfrieder eventually had himself interred between the tombs of the two generals in a separate vault, where his embalmed corpse, dressed in knight's armour and seated in an upright position, keeps guard eternally as it were, watching over the glory of the House of Habsburg."[16] But the point of the story is, once again, the relation between art and time and between the artist and history. The shoemaker's arrival at the emperor's court is related in the same way as Salvador Reyes's arrival, in the previous sequence, at the embassy party where he meets the "Teuton hero" Ernst Jünger. Both the shoemaker and the Chilean writer have to make their way through layers of people and spaces—rooms, salons, vestibules—and cross many thresholds before arriving in the presence of the respective master figures of their stories.

The parallel descriptions on pages 26 and 40–41 make Reyes and the shoemaker into reflections of one another. In fact the shoemaker is described not just as a craftsman: he was "deeply absorbed in his work as only an artist can be" (45). Reyes is a forgotten writer in his country, surviving only in another writer's memoirs. The shoemaker is a forgotten artist in his own country, surviving only as a kind of statue in a pantheon in which he is the solitary hero. Forgotten artists, failed painters: the theme of both these stories is defeat, which gives the artistic enterprise a heroic aura. In Bolaño the image of the artist as warrior (embodied in historical figures like Archilocus and Sordello) is not infrequent.

The aftermath of this bit of storytelling is a disillusioned reflection by the storyteller himself—Farewell—who observes that books are only shadows, "nothing but shadows" (50). The restaurant where the Heldenberg story has been told now becomes Plato's cave: "Farewell and I stayed put and kept still . . . , while our eyes looked on . . . watching the shadow play, figures appearing and disappearing like black flashes on the partition wall" (49). But the dialogue that goes on between the two characters, far from being dialectical, becomes at times antagonistic, with Farewell debasing his protegé's subtler points. If Urrutia represents the mind in this conversation, then the older critic stands for the body, as his references to a gut ache, whores, screwing, and drunkenness make clear. The Socratic dialogue is undermined by a Rabelaisian discourse of the carnivalesque, one that emphasizes low bodily functions. The dialogue becomes truly bizarre when Father Urrutia—prodded by his fellow diner—shows off his knowledge of papal history and launches into a detailed history of Pius II. As it turns out, this seemingly outlandish digression is a functional link that leads into the novel's next sequence (60–79), in which Father Urrutia is charged by the mysterious Mr. Raef and Mr. Etah (palindromes of "Fear" and "Hate") to undertake a trip to Europe and report back on the preservation of churches. The pair is reminiscent of the conspiratorial Spaniards in *Monsieur Pain* and of the warders who come to arrest K. at the beginning of Kafka's *The Trial* (Logie 285).

Churches are architectural works of art and are meant to endure through time, thus suggesting immortality. But the immediate problem Urrutia encounters when he gets to Europe is "pigeon shit, the numbers of pigeons in Pistoia, as in many other European cities and villages, having increased exponentially" (69). The remedy that his fellow priests have found to fight the plague of pigeons is to rehearse the art of falconry and use the hawks as dive-bombers. Sometimes the birds have very funny names: the Pistoia falcon is called Turk, whereas the Turin exemplar is called Othello; the Avignon bird is Ta Gueule, and the terror of the Burgos sky is Rodrigo (probably named after Rodrigo Ruy Díaz de Vivar, El Cid).[17] But at least on one occasion the remedy is worse than the disease, as when a falcon called Fever by mistake mauls a white dove that was the mascot for an athletic competition, "and the athletes were visibly displeased or perturbed, likewise the local society ladies, who had sponsored the race and proposed the idea of opening the proceedings by releasing a dove" (77). And of course there is the theological issue of the Holy Spirit and the fact that pigeons, "in spite of their shitting, were God's creatures too" (73).

There is an obvious farcical element in the falcon episode, but the whole sequence has to be read on more than one register. One of the words used in the Spanish original to refer to the falcons in the novel is "azor," a word that easily evokes Chilean poet Vicente Huidobro's long avant-garde poem *Altazor* (1931). The poem is a contradictory search for poetic originality in which the speaker imagines himself as a hawk eagle fearlessly falling through the air into an abyss of shadows, where new poetic experiences may be found. The appearance of Huidobro's hawk symbol in Bolaño's novel is a reminder of the prominence of poetry in the author's vision of Chilean history. The symbol, however, also lends itself to a political reading. The pigeon hunt in *By Night in Chile* indirectly alludes to the persecution and killing of left-wing militants and sympathizers under the Pinochet regime (Draper 131). The flight of the falcons as they lock on their prey is reminiscent of the murdering aviator's aerial antics in *Distant Star.* And the jets that bombed the presidential palace in Santiago on September 11, 1973, were Hawker Hunters. The episode of Father Urrutia's visit to Europe's decaying churches, therefore, amounts to an ironic allegory of recent Chilean history. The priest's passive attitude regarding the extermination of pigeons suggests complicity with a regime of terror.

It is no surprise that the interval following Father Urrutia's return to Chile is filled in by a fast-moving history of political events between the election of Salvador Allende in 1970 and the military coup and its aftermath. This breakneck chronicle includes references to Neruda's Nobel Prize (1971) and to the poet's death a few days after the coup. It is significant that as Chilean socialist voters celebrate Allende's victory, Urrutia compulsively reads the Greek classics, though he also publishes a review of a novel called *White Dove* by local novelist Enrique Lafourcade. *Palomita blanca* (1971) is the story of a romantic liason between a working-class girl and a young man from the upper middle classes. The sentimental story is projected against the background of the political changes the country was going through halfway through Allende's term. (Allende's term should have lasted six years but was cut in half by the coup.) It was immensely popular at the time, but its inclusion in *By Night in Chile* probably has more to do with the dove symbol—a clever device to induce thematic coherence—than with the success of Lafourcade's novel.

The fifth sequence of *By Night in Chile* comprises the lessons in Marxism that Urrutia is asked to impart to the members of the military junta (85–102). The bearers of this strange request are the same Mr. Raef and Mr. Etah who had previously asked for the priest's assistance in the matter of the decaying churches. Urrutia prevaricates and reveals he has no sympathy for Marxism and is no expert on the subject. But the mysterious envoys insist and convince him that by assenting to their request he would be fulfilling his patriotic duty. The lessons are meant to give the military leaders an idea of the enemy they are fighting and go on for ten weeks. They present Urrutia with a moral dilemma: "Who would have thought you'd come to this, Sebastián?" asks the priest from himself (90). And at the end of the course he wonders, "Did I do the right thing or not. . . . Did I do my duty, or did I go beyond it?" (101).

The question receives no answer, but the theme of the collusion between right-wing intellectuals and the military regime is expanded in the novel's final sequence, the most uncanny of them all if "uncanny"—to reiterate—is defined as the public exposure of that which should remain secret. The novel's culminating section focuses on the literary soirées held at the house of a Chilean woman writer and her U.S. husband (106–27). The character called María Canales in the novel is, in point of fact, Mariana Callejas, the wife of U.S. citizen Michael Townley, who was a special agent for Pinochet's secret police and was involved in several high-profile assassinations outside the country in the 1970s, including the car bombing of former Allende ambassador Orlando Letelier in Washington, D.C., in 1976. Callejas was in fact a writer and, as stated in the novel, was awarded a short story prize in 1975. Townley appears as Jimmy Thompson in the novel. The couple owned a house on the outskirts of Santiago that was regularly attended by writers and visual artists but also served as a clandestine detention center where political prisoners were tortured, sometimes as the literary parties were in progress.

Bolaño's treatment of this shocking topic in recent Chilean history is sustained and masterful. The hostess is described as extremely welcoming, young, pretty, and talented, and as someone very much in touch with the artistic and literary goings-on in the country. She has two very young sons (one called Sebastián, like the narrator) and is devoted to her husband, "who worked as a salesman or an executive for a firm that had recently set up a branch in Chile" (108). The narrator explains that critics and writers needed to gather and talk, and that in a city emptied by a military curfew, there were few places to go and satisfy this gregarious impulse. María Canales's house, he suggests, lent itself perfectly to these occasions. He clarifies that he met the hostess by chance and is careful to explain that everybody and not just him was acquainted with her (107). After the guests would arrive, María's children would come down to say hello and when they went back up to their bedroom, the party would begin in earnest, "with the hostess serving whiskies all round, Debussy on the record player, or Webern performed by the Berlin Philharmoniker" (108), a not so subtle reference to the Nazis' taste for classical music and high culture in general. In the first few pages of the story the narrator knows he is touching on a controversial subject but withholds some of the crucial information relating to the more sinister aspects of those civilized meetings. Furthermore the narrative act is an attempt at exculpation. The narrator states that it was only months after he stopped attending the literary evenings that a friend told him what was really going on in the basement while writers and artists discussed themes relating to the avant-garde in the living room upstairs. The secret is partially exposed when a guest gets lost looking for the bathroom and walks into a dingy room where a tortured body is tied to a metal bed. "And then democracy returned," the narrator explains, "and it was revealed that Jimmy Thompson had been one of the key agents of the DINA [Pinochet's secret police or Dirección de Inteligencia Nacional], and that he had used his house as a centre for the interrogation of prisoners" (121). There is no mystery as to whether Thompson's wife was in the know: "María Canales had known about it for a long time, of course. But she wanted to be a writer, and writers require the physical proximity of other writers" (122).

As in *Distant Star,* Bolaño refuses to absolve writers and artists who take cover in the networks of power and fail to examine the ethical ground of art. (In *Amulet,* on the other hand, poets and artists form a solid unified block against the state.) The narrator asks the same question that is asked in any country dominated by state terror, whether it is Nazi Germany, the Argentina of the Dirty War, or Pinochet's Chile: what did people know about the human rights abuses going on? And why did those who knew not speak out? He suggests that many of the regular guests at the couple's receptions knew what was transpiring beneath their feet: "Why didn't anyone say anything at the time? The answer was simple: Because they were afraid. I was not afraid. I would have been able to speak out, but I didn't see anything, I didn't know until it was too late" (122). If every document of civilization is at the same time a document of barbarism, the narrator—speaking on behalf of his multiple identities as ordained priest, critic, and poet—tries to place himself on the side of civilization. But it's not clear if the narrator's argument is good enough to convince the "wizened youth," his moral antagonist.

The Canales episode concludes with the narrator's last visit to the house of horrors, long after its secrets have been revealed. He comes mostly as a priest, perhaps to offer consolation or seeking to alleviate his own conscience. The lady of the house still lives there, but the house has lost its luster and might soon be demolished. The visitor asks the owner if she has finished her novel, to which she responds in the negative but adds that she plans to continue with her literary career. The visitor's next question is whether she knew what was going on in the basement. María admits it, and when the priest asks her if she has repented, she answers, "Like everyone else" (125). Then she volunteers details about two of Jimmy's victims who died in the house while being subjected to the electric prod, and defiantly asks the priest if he wants to visit the basement. That question marks the end of the interview. The narrator squeezes the woman's hand and advises her to pray but fears not to have put enough conviction in his advice (126). María, however, has her own conviction, which she expresses in her farewell to the priest: "That's how literature is made in Chile" (126).

Upon leaving, the narrator takes María's assessment to heart but decides that Western literature in general, regardless of its national origins, is made in the same way, "at least what we call literature, to keep ourselves from falling into the rubbish dump" (127). This is a more nuanced view of the literary endeavor, one that allows for some glimmer of hope in the redemptive power of literature. The narrator has one last imaginary dialogue with the wizened youth, in which he tries to convince his alter ego or younger self that a single individual is no match for history, thus diluting his own point about the salvational possibilities of the artistic calling. He himself is on the side of history. But the wizened youth is a rebel and refuses to listen, implicitly denying that literature is produced out of torture and murder, or needs to seek the protection of a coercive state. The question about the ethics of writing and the politics of the literary institution brings to an end the series of moral "lessons" that, according to Bolaño, may be drawn from each of the individual sequences making up the novel and from the novel as a whole. St. John Perse said that it is enough for the poet to be the bad conscience of his times—a definition that fits Urrutia Lacroix like a glove.[18] By contrast the female narrator of *Amulet* embodies the good conscience of her times.

The closing sentence of *By Night in Chile* brings up a different set of formal and thematic questions. To repeat a point made earlier, the statement "And then the storm of shit begins" constitutes the entirety of the second paragraph of the novel and is uttered by a narrative voice that is not that of Sebastián Urrutia Lacroix. Urrutia is a homodiegetic narrator, whereas the impersonal narrator that utters the final sentence is heterodiegetic.[19] The gap between the two narrative voices—the last of which is difficult to distinguish from the voice of the implied author—is duplicated by a shift in verbal tenses. The end of the paragraph immediately preceding the final line is in the past, whereas the novel's closing statement is in the present: "And then faces flash before my eyes at a vertiginous speed, the faces I admired, those I loved, hated, envied and despised. The faces I protected, those I attacked, the faces I hardened myself against and those I sought in vain.—And then the storm of shit begins" (129–30). And, in addition, there is also a thematic shift—or antithesis—between these two passages since the idea of beginning contrasts with the sense of an ending brought by death (and by the literal end of the novel). There is also a contrast between the profane tone of the novel's ending and the lyrical connotations of its title.

Finally the expression "storm of shit" brings back to mind the episode of the pigeons and the churches, but by the end of the novel its reach surpasses any one of its episodes. The storm of shit is really the dust raised by Bolaño's visit to Chile in 1999—his second visit since he left the country in a hurry in the first months of the dictatorship—during which he attacked and was attacked by many local writers who, according to Bolaño, were "licking ass nonstop to hang onto their scraps of fame." The details of the controversy aroused by Bolaño's visit are recounted in "I Can't Read" (*The Secret of Evil*).

The Stories and a Short Lumpen Novel

During his lifetime Bolaño published two short story collections and was able to finish a third one that appeared the year of his death. *Llamadas telefónicas* ("Phone Calls"), the first of the three, was published in 1997 and was followed a few years later by *Putas asesinas* ("Murdering Whores," 2001). The translated versions of these twenty-seven stories were collected under two different titles: *Last Evenings on Earth* (2006) and *The Return* (2010), but their original source and order of publication were disregarded. This reshuffling, however, should not affect reading of the stories because neither *Llamadas telefónicas* nor *Putas asesinas* were conceived as organic wholes. Bolaño's third collected volume was *El gaucho insufrible* (2003), which was integrally translated into English as *The Insufferable Gaucho* (2010). The stories contained in Bolaño's fourth and last short story collection were gleaned from the author's computer files by Spanish critic Ignacio Echevarría and published posthumously as *El secreto del mal* (2007; *The Secret of Evil*, 2012).

Two Uncollected Early Stories

Bolaño's earliest published story, however, antedates all these collections and is not included in any of them. Nor has it been translated. The story in question is called "El contorno del ojo" ("The Contour of the Eye") and finished third in a Spanish regional competition in which Bolaño entered in the early years of his career, when he depended on income from literary prizes to make ends meet. The story, which is now available on the Internet, was originally published in Valencia in a hard-to-find collective volume entitled *Encuentro en Praga* (1983), which includes the five winning entries in that competition. Of interest is that "Sensini," the opening story of *Llamadas telefónicas*, tells the story of "El contorno del ojo" without referring to it by name. "Sensini" itself won first prize and a "very modest sum of money" (Vila-Matas, "Blanes" 154) in a later contest sponsored by a Basque foundation (1996).

"El contorno del ojo" is the first story Bolaño ever published, but it is not the earliest extant story written by Bolaño. Pride of place belongs to "Diario de bar" ("Bar Diary"), a story dating back to 1979 that was published only in 2006 as an appendix to the author's first published novel, *Consejos de un discípulo de Morrison a un fanático de Joyce,* written in collaboration with Antoni García Porta. In the preface to this publication García Porta gives Bolaño full credit for being the sole author of the story and recalls that "Diario de bar" was meant to be part of a larger collaborative effort between him and Bolaño that at some point ran out of steam.

These early stories have vastly different settings, but they are both written in the form of a diary. Furthermore both their protagonists are writers, and both end in suicide. "Diario de bar" is set in Barcelona in 1979 and features a character—Mario—who closely resembles the Bolaño of those days. Mario is young and Chilean and has no residence permit to be in Spain. He stays up nights writing stories and early every morning goes for coffee at the local bar, where he listens to the owner talk about what's going on in the neighborhood. He finds out that a Chilean student has jumped to his death from a seventh floor and that the neighbors thought that he, being one of the few Chileans around, might be the suicide. The story thus sets up a double mise-en-abyme: Mario is a projection of Bolaño to the same extent that the unnamed Chilean fatality is a projection of Mario. As if to stress this projective symbolic strategy, Mario himself jumps to his death at the end of the story. Among the scribblings that keep Mario awake at night is a diary. Conventionally a diary is a first-person account of its keeper's thoughts, feelings, and daily experiences. But "Diario de bar" is narrated in the third person by a narrator who keeps his distance from the characters' inner lives, including that of Mario himself. Mario, therefore, is not the narrator but the focalizer (or "reflector") of the story. Plot events, characters, and setting are all viewed through him; yet he always remains distant enough from the reader that the reasons for his suicide remain inscrutable.

If the laws of verisimilitude are to be respected, a diarist cannot record his own suicide, but he can announce it, as is the case in "El contorno del ojo." This story takes place in a Chinese village in 1980 and is narrated by a middle-aged military officer and war veteran who is also a prestigious author of literary works. Chen Huo Deng has retired to the countryside after thirty years of military service to recover from a physical and mental breakdown. In the village he observes the routine activities of the locals; receives the visits of the town commissar, the local doctor, young army officers interested in his literary works, and the village schoolteacher; collects newspaper clippings about unusual events going on in China; takes long bicycle rides in the countryside; and writes his journal. As distinct from Mario's journal in "Diario de bar," Chen's diary is written in the first person and records the author's private musings, feelings, and impressions. It also goes into some detail concerning the diarist's sexual encounters with the schoolteacher. In the last entries of the diary, the author matter-of-factly stamps the announcement of his impending suicide. Despite the private nature of his writing, Chen ultimately makes his diary available to the local authorities. He leaves it on a table with the rest of his papers and poems and heads to the forest looking for a secluded spot to hang himself.

As in "Diario de bar," the motivation for the protagonist's suicide is barely sketched. Bolaño is not concerned in either story with psychological realism but with the connection between writing and self-destruction. A revealing moment in "El contorno del ojo" occurs when Deng's physician sees in the protagonist's daily writing routine "an excellent sympton" of his recovery. The doctor is only partially right. Writing is a symptom but not one that necessarily leads to the patient's recovery. The protagonists of these two Bolaño stories are early and only partially achieved reflections of the self-destructive type of artistic personality that recurs in later phases of Bolaño's writing.

The Collected Stories: Some Generalizations

Bolaño's stories display a great variety of techniques, themes, characters, narrative voices, situations, formats, and locations. *The Secret of Evil* is the most heterogeneous of the author's short story collections, which is not surprising given that the book was cobbled together from an assortment of undated files found on Bolaño's computer. But the point about variety applies to all four of the author's short story collections. Among these, only *Llamadas telefónicas* observes some kind of structural order. The book is divided into three groups of stories, each of which is preceded by the title of one of the members of that group ("Phone Calls," "Detectives," and "Anne Moore's Life"). The other three volumes display their contents in no apparent order. But even in *Llamadas telefónicas,* and despite the relative thematic coherence that one may find in the separate sections, the order is more apparent than real. Why, for example, is the title story not included in the final section of the book, since "Phone Calls" is an unhappy love story like the four entries in that cluster? And why is "Clara" located in the last third of the book instead of finding a place in the book's opening section, since phone calls play such an important role in the development of the story? Ultimately, though, neither critics nor translators have paid much attention to the order of the stories or to their original source in either *Llamadas telefónicas* or *Putas asesinas,* though the first five stories of *Llamadas telefónicas* were incorporated together and in the same original order of appearance in *Last Evenings on Earth.*

Bolaño wrote most of his stories in the first person. Only one major story— "The Insufferable Gaucho"—is written in the third person and in past tense.

("The Troublemaker" and "The Days of Chaos," both from *The Secret of Evil,* are minor stories written in the same classic format.)[1] The first-person narratives, in turn, may be subdivided into autofictional and "heterofictional" stories. Stories such as "Sensini," "The Grub," "Enrique Martín," and "Mauricio ('The Eye') Silva" fall into the autofictional category to the extent that they make use of autobiographical details relating to Bolaño's life in Gerona, Mexico, and Barcelona. But it should be noted that Bolaño never flaunts the first person as would an author interested in crafting an autobiographical project through his fiction. Even in "Colonia Lindavista," a story that feels like a memoir of the author's early days in Mexico City, Bolaño's narrator projects himself in a modest and unobtrusive way. Bolaño never attempted to turn his life into a literary myth and was, in fact, averse to autobiographical writing. The only biographies or autobiographies he respected were (or would be) the ones written by great detectives or great criminals (Braithwaite 100–101). The autobiographical element in Bolaño's stories is low-key. If autofiction "involves not just an awareness, but a *celebration* of the fictionalization of the self in writing," (Boyle 18), then it might be best to steer clear of the autofictional label to categorize Bolaño's stories. Bolaño's "autobiographical" narrators are not autodiegetic as much as homodiegetic; in other words they are not the heroes of their own stories but characters who tell the stories of other characters from a limited perspective. The distance between the narrating self and the other protagonists varies. Sometimes the narrator is intimately involved with a lover (in stories like "Phone Calls," "Cell Mates," and "Clara"); at other times he simply frames a story told by an acquaintance ("Mauricio ['The Eye'] Silva," "Snow"); and at still others the distance between the narrator and the narrated characters is extreme (as in "Labyrinth," a story about various French writers and intellectuals found in a photograph). But even in the stories about love the narrator's focus is outside himself and his knowledge of the situation is limited.

If in Bolaño's autofictional stories the first person narrator keeps a low profile, the autofictional narrator entirely disappears in the stories narrated by fictitious characters. Texts such as "Prefiguration of Lalo Cura," "Police Rat," and "Dentist" are "heterofictional" because they are narrated from a first-person perspective that has no apparent connection with the author's lived experience. Finally some of Bolaño's heterofictional stories are narrated by female characters—for example, "Joanna Silvestri," "Daniela," "Suntan," and "Muscles."

The cognitive deficit that typifies Bolaño's autofictional narrators is remarkable in stories like "Cell Mates" and "Clara." In these stories the narrating character cannot fully account for the behavior of the female protagonists, a limitation that creates or preserves the enigma driving the narrative act. The narrator of "Cell Mates" begins by establishing a bizarre analogy between his experience and that of Sofía, a woman he meets later in life and with whom he has a love affair. Both protagonists happen to be in jail the same month of the same year but in cells thousands of miles apart. He spends time in a Chilean detention camp after the coup while she is in one of Franco's jails in Spain for protesting against government policy. There are hints from the beginning that Sofía always had "psychological problems," and after she becomes addicted to tranquilizers her behavior becomes particularly erratic. As the narrator tries to explain his lover's behavior, he returns to the prison analogy that helped create a bond between them but confesses that the meaning of that coincidence escapes him: "I've never been any good at analogies" (*The Return* 63). And later in a fit of anger Sofía herself points out to him that he has no idea what is happening between them and that he is in no position to judge her: "What would you know about me?" (65). The reader is in the dark about the facts too and has to accept at face value what appears to be Sofía's return to normality at the end of the story.

Like "Cell Mates," "Clara" is also a story about a woman with "psychological problems" whose relationship with the narrator deteriorates over time. It is a more expansive story than "Cell Mates" but also a less successful one. In order to cover the twenty plus years of Clara's life, it must resort to the summary form, a narrative style that detaches both the narrator and the reader from the plot and the characters. Perhaps in an unconscious ironic twist the narrator at one point criticizes Clara as narrator of her own life: "Her voice was as cold as ever . . . , the voice in which she recounted her life with the detachment of a bad storyteller, putting exclamation marks in all the wrong places, and passing over what she should have gone into" (77). Bolaño is most emphatically not a bad storyteller, but "Clara" does lack the fully developed individual scenes—the showing as opposed to the mere telling—that make "Cell Mates" a compelling story. In any event the protagonist is diagnosed with cancer and disappears at the end of the story, leaving her family—and the narrator—wondering why she would do such a thing and where she might have gone. It is true that the narrator of "Clara" is less involved with Clara than the narrator of "Cell Mates" is with Sofía and therefore knows less about her. But in both cases the limitations of the first-person point of view are equally responsible for the cognitive gaps. One final note on this topic is that the cognitive deficit of homodiegetic narrators is more marked in Bolaño's autofictional stories than in his heterofictional ones.

These cognitive gaps can be related to what one critic calls the "poetics of inconclusiveness," a practice that presumably characterizes Bolaño's work as a whole and not only the stories or novels that the author clearly left in an unfinished state (Ignacio Echevarría wrote this in the "Preliminary Note" to *The Secret of Evil*). In "Advice on the Art of Writing Short Stories" Bolaño advocates writing stories three or five or fifteen at a time so as to avoid getting stuck on the same story (*Between Parentheses* 350). Some critics would argue that this bulk approach to writing stories explains the incomplete condition of many of them. But a poetics of inconclusiveness is easily confused with a poetics of implication, a term that more faithfully reflects what Bolaño does in stories like "Cell Mates" and "Clara" (and in others like "Sensini," "Last Evenings on Earth," and "Dentist"). The ending in this type of story, as well as its meaning, are implied in all that comes before the denouement but not made explicit. Bolaño, in other words, liked to write *around* an enigma without fully resolving it, so as to avoid the comforts and shortcuts of commercial literature. This approach is in line with Chris Andrews's statement regarding Bolaño's short fiction: "[Bolaño] cultivates suspense more than curiosity, and surprises the reader by confounding expectations rather than by revealing withheld information" (71). The notion of inconclusiveness should be limited to Bolaño's work in progress or to fragments of text that remained forever unfinished, either as a result of the author's early death or of his loss of interest in some of his projects.

To reiterate one of the points made above, over half of Bolaño's fifty-three collected stories are narrated in the first person, but sometimes it happens that the author's alter ego (B, Belano, or Arturo Belano) appears in stories narrated in the third person and in the present tense. (The only exception to this rule is a minor story called "The Days of Chaos.") Some examples are "A Literary Adventure," "Phone Calls," "Last Evenings on Earth," "Days of 1978," "Vagabond in France and Belgium," and "Death of Ulises." One may imagine that at least some of these stories are narratologically reversible and that they might have been narrated in the first person by the same B, Belano, or Arturo Belano.

Other elements contribute to the variety of approaches found in Bolaño's stories. Their protagonists, for example, can be male or female, young or old, real or fictitious, rural or urban, and they can be dead or alive. ("The Return" is a ghost story told by a narrator who has recently died of a heart attack.) They can also belong to a different species, as in "Police Rat," a Kafkan fable narrated by a rat. When they belong to the human species, Bolaño's characters have different nationalities and occupations. They can be Chilean, Mexican, Spanish, French, Russian, North American, and so on, and their occupations run the gamut from writers and middle-class professionals to gangsters, prostitutes, policemen, lower-middle-class wageworkers, porno stars, and soccer players. Some of these characters are political exiles and immigrants and, thus, reintroduce a theme that has been present in Bolaño's writing since the Barcelona poems of the late 1970s. The theme of political violence that had been fully developed in *Distant Star* reappears in the stories with exiles (like "Mauricio ['The Eye'] Silva") and in others like "Scholars of Sodom."

This last one is a metafictional reflection by a first-person narrator on the story he is writing or at one point planned to write on Trinidadian author V. S. Naipaul's visits to Argentina in the years immediately preceding the military coup that launched the Dirty War in March 1976. The point of the story is (or was to be) that Naipaul sensed the horrors to come under military rule as he walked the streets of Buenos Aires at a time when the political atmosphere was already poisoned—extrajudicial killings, forced disappearances, systematic torture, the theft of babies, and so on. The title relates to the controversial article that Naipaul actually wrote as a result of his Argentine sojourns ("The Return of Eva Perón") and to the author's interpretation of local political violence in terms of Argentine sexual customs, and particularly in terms of the sodomy that—according to him—characterized heterosexual relations.

Love, eroticism, and pornography constitute another prominent thematic cluster in Bolaño's stories. Characteristically in these stories, the characters' sexual relations and emotional bonds are perturbed by mental or physical disease often followed by death or willed disappearance. "Joanna Silvestri," for example, is about the love-and-sex relationship between real-life porno stars John Holmes and Moana Pozzi (the "Joanna Silvestri" of the title), both of whom died at an early age, he of AIDS and she probably of liver cancer.[2] "Cell Mates" and "Clara" both deal with disturbed female protagonists. Other female figures in Bolaño's stories either suffer from criminal violence ("Phone Calls") or enact it ("Murdering Whores").

The first four stories of *Llamadas telefónicas*, however, are about literature and literary ethics. They are stories peopled by writers, readers, and critics, and motivated by the personal and institutional politics (and miseries) of the literary life. These are "Sensini," "Henri Simon Leprince," "Enrique Martín," and "A Literary Adventure." Three of these feature either a recognizably autobiographical narrator or B, one of the author's alter egos. On this account these three stories have been related to the "book fair" chapter in *The Savage Detectives* (chapter 23) as further examples of the writer's predicament vis-à-vis the publishing industry and the marketing of literature (Cobas Carral and Garibotto 183). All this material, therefore, foregrounds issues such as the price paid for literary success or failure, the desirability of mainstream notoriety or marginality, and the ultimate meaning of the literary vocation.

The three stories in particular operate like miniature fables regarding the contemporary writer's options given the commodification of literature: to accept the rules of the market and write what sells; to withdraw from the market and labor in secret to produce a personal literature that may never see the light; and to irrupt into the market breaking some of its rules (Cobas Carral and Garibotto 185). But "Henri Simon Leprince" is not such a different case, even if it is narrated in the third person without any mention of the author's biography or alter egos, set in occupied France during the war, and unaware of any such thing as the commodification of literature. The story, however, does deal with the writer in the public eye and with the difference between successful and failed authors. It argues that minor writers are an invaluable "supplement" to major writers at a time of historical crisis and highlights authorial ethics by having the protagonist choose his friends and enemies at a time when choosing one side or the other in a war zone is a matter of life and death. The title character opts to work for the resistance and is rewarded with a mediocre existence but mostly with the right to write: "In his heart, Leprince has finally accepted his lot as a bad writer, but he has also come to understand and accept that good writers need bad writers if only to serve as readers and stewards. He also knows that by saving (or helping) several good writers he has earned the right to sully clean sheets of paper and make mistakes" (25).

The title character of "Enrique Martín" is another bad writer but one who cannot turn his loyalty to poetry and his good intentions into symbolic gain, like Leprince. Martín can never shake free from certain poetic influences and sullies countless clean sheets of paper imitating earlier poets and writing badly in both Castilian and Catalan. He ends up secretly entrusting his manuscript to the care of a friend—a narrator that resembles Bolaño in many respects—and commits suicide. B, in "A Literary Adventure," is an unsuccessful author who cannot abide by the sanctimonious pontificating of a successful colleague and decides to mock him in one of his books. The mockery is supposed to go undetected by most, but B is never sure whether A—his famous rival—is able to discern it. A, at any rate, suddenly begins to publish favorable reviews of B's work and elevates B's public stature to a level unforeseen by the parodist. B keeps trying to meet A until he finally succeeds. Bolaño refrains from describing the meeting that brings the story to a climax (or anticlimax), but the implication is that B accepts his rival's superiority and prepares to receive his blessings. Another implication is that A and B recognize themselves in each other to the extent that they both sacrifice their previous beliefs for their fifteen minutes of fame: "Yet A and B are not entirely dissimilar. They both come from lower-middle-class or upwardly mobile working-class families. Politically both are left-wing" (42). More than once Bolaño railed against writers who took up literature for the sake of social advancement. In "A Literary Adventure" he may be trying to exorcize that particular ghost.

A Brief Anthology

Bolaño was not a casual practitioner of the short story genre, as the distracted reader might surmise when opening a collection like *The Insufferable Gaucho* or *The Secret of Evil* and finding there a mix of true-to-form stories, conference papers, and fragments of unfinished stories or works in progress. He was well acquainted with the tradition of the short story and with some of its great-est practitioners in Latin America and elsewhere, beginning with Poe, going through the likes of Horacio Quiroga, Borges, and Cortázar, and ending in more recent times with Raymond Carver—not to mention Kafka. There is no critical consensus regarding which of Bolaño's stories are his best, so any choice of a Bolaño canon has a subjective element in it. Yet there are some stories that appear more often than others in Bolaño criticism and that would form the core of whatever canon is eventually erected. These include "Sensini," "Mauricio ('The Eye') Silva," "Last Evenings on Earth," and "The Insufferable Gaucho." Others, like "Two Catholic Tales" and "Dentist," deserve individual attention on account of their technical prowess or because they display unexpected ap-proaches to narrative logic.

"Sensini"

"Sensini" is Bolaño's Ur-story, the one that most critics would consider the cornerstone of his short story production. It is not only a fully accomplished story but also represents the heroic phase of an author who struggled in obscu-rity for two decades and had to find less than heroic ways to make ends meet while he persevered in his writing. Even externally this story has a foundational character, since it is the opening salvo in the the author's first short story collec-tion to be published in Spanish. In addition it is a story that effortlessly brings together personal, literary, and political themes that resonate broadly through Bolaño's work.

Sensini is the made-up name of Argentine writer Antonio Di Benedetto (1922–86), author of the much admired novel *Zama* (1956) and a victim of the Argentine Dirty War of the 1970s. He was imprisoned and tortured by the military regime because he wrote for a provincial newspaper that was inves-tigating police repression in the years leading up to the coup. He was eventu-ally released after spending months in prison and went into exile in Spain. In Madrid, Di Benedetto scratched a living by doing some editorial work and oc-casionally collecting prize money from the provincial competititons that he en-tered with his stories. Bolaño, of course, was also sending stories to provincial competitions in those years but with less success than the more experienced Di Benedetto, the difference being that at the time Bolaño was an unknown writer and Di Benedetto had established himself as an important writer in Argentina before he became an exile. Di Benedetto returned to his native country in May 1984 when he accepted an underpaid job in the cultural bureaucracy. He died in Buenos Aires two years later. His daughter Luz and wife, Graciela, were at his side.

In "Sensini" it is difficult to know where reality ends and fiction begins. Is the epistolary exchange between the Bolaño-like narrator and the exiled Argentine writer based on actual fact? Probably not. Sensini has a wife and daughter in the story, but their names—Carmela and Miranda, respectively—do not correspond to those of Di Benedetto's real-life wife and daughter. He also has a son called Gregorio who is said to be the issue of the writer's previous marriage and to have disappeared during the dictatorship. When his body is discovered in a mass grave, Sensini decides to return to Argentina. The narrator surmises that Gregorio's name comes from Kafka's *Metamorphosis,* a speculation that punningly refers to the way Di Benedetto's signature novel was received by at least one Spanish critic, who called the novel's protagonist (Diego de Zama) a "colonial Kafka." (Zama is called "Ugarte" in Bolaño's story, which takes place in colonial Paraguay. Its protagonist is a colonial bureaucrat who waits in endless anguish for a transfer that never comes.) In turn it may be surmised that in the sense made explicit by the story Gregorio is a fictitious character. Gregorio, however, implicitly stands for a real victim of the dictatorship. At one point in the story, the narrator asks Sensini about poet Juan Gelman, whose son Marcelo was abducted by the military in August 1976 along with his pregnant wife, Claudia. Marcelo, like Gregorio, was never seen again. Gelman's granddaughter surfaced in March 2000 with the name given her by her foster parents, María Macarena. Bolaño's story also mentions other Argentine writers who were disappeared or killed during the Dirty War, namely Rodolfo Walsh, Haroldo Conti, and Francisco Urondo.

The story's point of departure is factual enough. The narrator states that at the time the story is set (which—judging from internal evidence—appears to be 1981) he was poorer than a church mouse and was forced to send stories to literary competitions in the hope of claiming some prize money. He wins fourth prize in one of these contests, and when he receives the anthology containing the winner and the six finalists, he runs across the name of Luis Antonio Sensini, an Argentine writer whom he had read and admired and who was older than him by three decades. (As remarked at the beginning of this chapter, the actual anthology was called *Encuentro en Praga* and includes only five winning entries. Bolaño's entry won third and not fourth prize. Di Benedetto's story is called "Intensa mirada filial"—"Intense Filial Gaze"—and is about the death of a son.) The narrator gets Sensini's address in Madrid and begins a sustained epistolary exchange with him. The letters include news about the writer's barebones existence in Madrid and soon include photos of his whole family. In one of those letters Sensini announces that the body of his disappeared son has presumably been found and that he must return to Argentina to find out the truth about his death. He adds that he's taking his wife with him but leaving his daughter Miranda behind. The narrator does not hear from Sensini again and eventually finds out that he died in a hospital. Years later he hears a knock on his door at midnight, and when he opens it he sees Miranda waiting to be let in. She had kept her father's address book and is taking the opportunity to visit some of the people he knew as she travels through Europe with her fiancé. The narrator and Miranda talk through the night about Sensini's literary reputation and death. Nothing in particular is revealed, but the conversation takes on the character of an understated epiphany: "Miranda was leaning on the balustrade, looking at the lights of Girona. . . . Suddenly I realized that we were at peace, that for some mysterious reason the two of us had reached a state of peace, and that from now on, imperceptibly, things would begin to change" (*Last Evenings on Earth* 17–18). It is not so much the meeting with Miranda but the passing of a great and neglected writer that creates the conditions for this glimpse of an anagnorisis.

There is something of Borges's "The Aleph" in this ending. At the beginning of that story the narrator has a painful epiphany triggered by the death of his impossible beloved Beatriz Viterbo: "I realised that the wide and ceaseless universe was already slipping away from her and that this slight change was the first of an endless series," he notes (15). "The Aleph" is one of Borges's fantastic and metaphysical stories, but it is also one that deals with literature, the literary life, and the literary institution. Carlos Argentino Naderi is the writer at the center of "The Aleph" (though the story is continually shifting gears and displacing its narrative focus) and is a parody of a writer like Antonio Di Benedetto. The latter, furthermore, is not involved in any literary or metaphysical speculation but standing squarely in the midst of state terror. The historical predicament of writers is a theme that greatly interested Bolaño; he was an independent and anarchic writer who despised any sort of institution that brought writers officially together but who at the same time professed sympathy and affect for fellow writers who were victimized by circumstance in the pursuit of their vocation. Bolaño probably realized at some point that the success of his story was bound to expand the circle of Di Benedetto's readers and open the latter's work to renewed scrutiny.[3]

"Mauricio ('The Eye') Silva"

Like "Sensini," "Mauricio ("The Eye") Silva" is the autofictional story of a political exile, not Argentine this time but Chilean; and it is set not in Spain but in Mexico, where the protagonist meets the narrator of the story, who is clearly identified as the young Bolaño. But unlike Sensini, Silva does not return to his native country when the dictatorship comes to an end. He leaves Mexico for Paris and later travels around the world as a freelance photographer, a profession that gives him his nickname. He rents modest apartments in several European cities and spends more than a year in India on an assignment that changes his life and that is the core of the story. "The Eye Silva" is also the lead story of *Putas asesinas,* Bolaño's second collection of short stories. The stories of that collection, as one critic notes, "pose questions about what it means to imagine a community that is no longer national, and thus no longer the extended national community of exile or diaspora, but rather a global community of strangers and wanderers" (López-Vicuña 81–82). Silva starts out as an exile from the Pinochet regime when he is in Mexico, but as time passes he sheds his identity as an exile and becomes simply a displaced person, perhaps a transnational stranger or a cosmopolite. The same critic writes that in *Putas asesinas* Bolaño "explores the forms of affect that displaced individuals share" (81), a statement that is particularly relevant in the context of the story.

The relationship between Silva and the narrator is based on sympathy and mutual understanding. They are both Chilean expatriates, which helps bring them together, but the narrator's impression of Silva is all the more positive to the degree that the latter is not a typical Chilean exile. For one thing Silva is ostracized from the exile community because he is a homosexual, a condition that he discloses to the narrator in confidence but that Silva's fellow exiles were in the habit of whispering about: "In spite of their left-wing convictions, when it came to sexuality, they [the exiles] reacted just like their enemies on the right, who had become the new masters of Chile" (*Last Evenings on Earth* 107). Silva also shows patent sympathy for the Indian children that he saves from degradation and profusely cries for the many that he could not save.

The narrator's role in the story is rather passive. "Bolaño" is really a frame narrator, a device that allows for someone else to tell the story or a significant part of it. For the most part, the narrator plays the role of narratee. It is Silva who tells the narrator the central part of the story when they reencounter each other in Berlin many years after they initially met in Mexico. By this time the young "Bolaño" has become a famous author who has been invited to Berlin to give a talk. As in all autofictional stories, and certainly in Bolaño's treatment of the genre, the line between reality and fiction is quite thin. The "genetic" myth of "The Eye Silva" is that the fictional Silva tells a fictional Bolaño a story about a cruel and apocryphal Indian ritual that a short time later the real Bolaño sits down to write. But the story's Orientalism is hardly innocent. The unreal world of India proves not to be so unreal after all, despite its exotic trappings. Silva is a man intent on avoiding violence, even at the risk of seeming a coward. Unfortunately "violence, real violence, is unavoidable, at least for those of us"—says the narrator—"who were born in Latin America during the fifties and were about twenty years old at the time of Salvador Allende's death" (106). Violence catches up with Silva in India, a country that in the story is presented as an exotic foil to Latin America, both the same and other.

The core of Silva's story is its narrator's accidental discovery of a "barbarous underground cult" (López-Vicuña 84) dedicated to a castrated god that demands pure male bodies, bodies of children devoid of sexual organs. Silva comes upon this cult because he has accepted an assignment to document the red light district of the unnamed Indian city where the action takes place. He steps into the temple where the ritual castrations are performed at the very moment when one is about to be enacted. When he realizes the monstrosity of the situation, he cannot refrain from taking a photo of one of the young victims, at which point he knew he was damning himself for all eternity" (115). This realization is an inversion of the primitive belief that taking a photo of someone is tantamount to capturing that someone's soul, a belief very much in evidence in Julio Cortázar's famous story "Blow-Up" ("Las babas del diablo," in Spanish).[4] But Silva, in Bolaño's story, acts to redeem himself and to palliate the violence of this world by rescuing two of the children and protecting them for as long as they lived. (They die soon enough after their escape when the plague hits the village where all three were hiding.) Silva passes himself off as their father, but the experience has transformed him into something else: "Mother, he said, and sighed. At last. Mother" (117). At the end Silva reintegrates himself into Western culture, having purged himself of pity and fear by telling the story twice and "sobbing" or "crying" both times.

"Last Evenings on Earth"

This story could be called autofictional if it were narrated from a first-person point of view, but as it is, authorial representation is delegated to a third-person narrator that refers to the protagonist simply as B. The dispassionate system of reference together with the impersonal narrative strategy creates a distance between author and character and between character and narrator. It would also create a distance between character and reader if it were not for the fact that the story is consistently focalized through B, which in practical terms means that readers can easily identify with the protagonist and experience the same vague sense of dread that haunts him. The story is about a mostly failed attempt between father and son to bond through a vacation trip to the famed beach resort of Acapulco. In light of this content, it might be tempting to attribute the use of the impersonal designation B to the fact that the story is told after the fact, when the connection between father and son has already been broken and when B is already someone else. Whether it was broken before the trip or during does not really matter in this case. But this attempt to integrate form and content is only partially convincing since the story is told in the present tense and not as a series of completed events in the past. The trip to Acapulco is taking place in the here and now of the narrative present, as if the narrator (or the protagonist) were trying to elucidate its meaning just now and not in the time frame of the actual trip.

The story is very precise about its internal and external chronology and invites the reader to make connections with the author's life. Thus father and son plan to start their drive from Mexico City precisely at six in the morning. B has to sleep in his father's house the night before because—by implication—they do not live together. (The biographical side note here is that Bolaño's parents separated when the family lived in Mexico City.) The year in which B and his father leave the city for a short holiday is specifically given as 1975, and it is specifically noted that this was a year after B's trip to Chile, in which he came close to death more than once, as the narrator relates later on: "That was in 1974 and B had not yet turned twenty-one. Now he is twenty-two and his father must be about forty-nine" (*Last Evenings on Earth* 148). (Bolaño returned to Mexico in January 1974. His plane landed in Acapulco before heading east to Mexico City.) Father and son spend a week in Acapulco sharing a hotel room, going out to eat, and swimming in the ocean. The father insists on going out looking for female company, but B is not too keen on it. In one of their sallies, B's father—a former boxer, like Bolaño's father—falls in with an ex-diver who admires the former's physique and athletic past. The ex-diver is a local resident who shows the visitors around and takes them to the suburbs to experience the real Acapulco and eat local food. Toward the end of the story the group ends up at a dive that is a sordid combination of bar, gambling den, and whorehouse. B is accosted by whores while his father plays cards and wins hand after hand. When he gets up and wants to leave, two of the losers block his way demanding he stay and play a few more hands. The ex-diver has apparently decided to take the strangers' side during the confrontation. B's father prepares to face the strangers blocking his way and calls his son to his side to protect him. The story freezes at the culminating moment: "Then his father walks toward the door stooping slightly and B stands aside to give him room to move. Tomorrow we'll leave, tomorrow we'll go back to Mexico City, thinks B joyfully. And then the fight begins" (157).

The ending of the story is reminiscent of the ending of *By Night in Chile*, which is this: "And then the storm of shit begins." The verbal formula is the same, but its contextual function is different. Whereas in the novella the final statement comes after the story has run its course, in "Last Evenings" the brawl is part and parcel of the story being told, and its outcome should decide the fate of the main characters. Chris Andrews points out that Bolaño's story ends the same way that Borges's "The South" does, namely by suspending the outcome of a climactic duel (80). The logic of Borges's story demands that its protagonist Juan Dahlmann die fighting like a gaucho in the pampas. Likewise the logic of Bolaño's story requires that father and son leave the premises unharmed.

Part of this logic is that "Last Evenings on Earth" is, from its very title, an account of a disaster that repeatedly looms over the horizon without ever materializing itself. The ominous signs are everywhere: B gets a weird presentiment during a nighttime conversation with a strange woman in the hotel terrace: "Something approaching over the sea. Something advancing in the wake of the dark clouds invisibly crossing the Bay of Acapulco" (140). B's father goes swimming in rough seas and disappears from view for a protracted period. From B's point of view this episode bodes ill because he is intently reading a book on French surrealism that details the death by drowning of a minor poet (Gui Rosey) who could no longer wait for a visa to escape from Nazi-occupied France to the United States or Mexico. For B too Mexico—or Mexico City—becomes a safe haven at the moment of the crucial fight, as the quote above makes clear. At the end of the swimming episode, and as if steeling himself for a disaster to come, B disconsolately thinks that "there are things you can tell people and things you just can't" (148). On a different night, B's father goes out by himself, and his son waits anxiously for his return. But the father does return from his nocturnal excursion. The most extended threat is the climactic barroom brawl, but here too the disaster announced by the story's title fails to materialize.

Could this disaster be the final act of alienation between father and son and the breaking of the filial bond? The story states the separation theme more than once. At the beginning of the trip father and son stop to eat at a roadside café. B's father goes around the back to the kitchen to see how the owners prepare roasted iguana, and B, observing his father from behind a curtain, has "the intermittent impression that this curtain separates not only the kitchen from the restaurant area but also one time from another" (132). The narrator invokes the time of childhood when B's father presented his son with a horse whose name B had forgotten but recalls after asking his father. (The horse is a biographical detail that Bolaño has mentioned in more than one of his interviews.) This is the time that has become severed from the present and the future. Later in the story father and son go boating, and B's father loses his wallet in the water when the boat capsizes. He dives to retrieve it and takes a long time to resurface. B dives in turn and passes his father on the way down to the bottom of the ocean. They each follow their own trajectory (in opposite directions) without meeting in the process: "They look at each other as they pass, but can't alter their trajectories" (149). A short time later B thinks that a new phase has begun, a phase ruled by "deities of ice" in the tropical heat of Acapulco, a sense of being at odds with his progenitor: "*disaster* he would say, a private disaster whose main effect is to drive a wedge between B and his father: part of the price they must pay for existing" (150). Father and son are carried by different currents and seem already to have spent their last evenings together. It is well known that Bolaño did not have a close relationship with his father after he moved to Spain.

And yet the end of the story once again foils the impending catastrophe announced in the title. That is the separation between father and son is not as final or disastrous as one might expect. B's realization of filial estrangement is qualified by an equally important realization that comes to him when he discerns his father's protective stance at a moment of danger: "he sees himself as a Gui Rosey, a Gui Rosey buried in some vacant lot in Acapulco . . . , but then he hears his father . . . and he realizes that unlike Gui Rosey he is not alone" (157). The story may be "paradoxical," as Andrews claims in his book on Bolaño (80), but it may also be that literature and life do not always coincide.

"The Insufferable Gaucho"

The narrator of "Sensini," a barely disguised Bolaño, tells how as a young man he kept up with Argentine writers by reading as many of their works as he could find in magazines and secondhand bookshops in Mexico City, including "pirated anthologies of Buenos Aires writing, probably the best writing in Spanish of the twentieth century" (*Last Evenings on Earth* 3). We may assume that the narrator's assessment of Buenos Aires writing can be applied to all Argentine literature, to writers from the interior (like Antonio Di Benedetto himself) as well as to those from the capital city. Bolaño's infatuation with Argentine literature is also evident in "The Vagaries of the Literature of Doom," a mock-serious assessment of that country's national literature (included in *Between Parentheses*). In that text Bolaño takes stock of Argentine literary history after Borges and, without dismissing some of its leading figures, recommends that one and all reread the master, whose work he locates or relocates at the center of the canon.

"The Insufferable Gaucho" is another of Bolaño's incursions into Argentine literature. The story is a critical pastiche of two of Borges's best-known stories ("The South" and "The Gospel According to Mark") but also of a number of other texts by authors as diverse as José Hernández (author of *Martín Fierro*),[5] Leopoldo Lugones (the influential early twentieth-century writer who elevated the protagonist of Hernández's narrative poem to the level of national myth), Juan Rodolfo Wilcock, Antonio di Benedetto, José Bianco (frequent collaborator of *Sur*, the premier journal of the Buenos Aires intelligentsia for many decades beginning in the early 1930s), and Julio Cortázar (see Faverón Patriau for a detailed study of the story's intertextuality). "The Insufferable Gaucho" is not only a creative reimagining of the Argentine literary canon but also an updating of its historical frame of reference. Bolaño's story is set during the economic crisis that affected Argentina in 2001 and caused riots in the streets as well as the removal of an elected president (Fernando de la Rúa). Understanding this story implies projecting it against the background of its many intertextual references but especially against the background of the two aforementioned stories by Borges.

Juan Dahlmann, the protagonist of "The South," is a descendant of German immigrants who considers himself profoundly Argentinian. He is a quiet and unassuming librarian at a municipal branch of the National Library but has a strong identification with one of his nineteenth-century heroic ancestors, a creole officer who died on the frontier of Buenos Aires in the wars against the Indians. Dahlmann owns a somewhat dilapidated *estancia* (a ranch or estate) in the countryside that is a memento of that heroic past and of that place and time. The story is set in 1939, a date that has world-historical connotations (the beginning of World War II) but also personal significance, since that was the year when Borges suffered a head wound and nearly died from blood poisoning. Dahlmann too gets blood poisoning after receiving a cut in his forehead from the edge of a recently painted door. He is taken to a hospital where doctors shave his head, strap him to a stretcher, shine bright lights in his eyes, stick him with needles, and examine him to the point of nausea. One day they tell him he can leave the hospital and go convalesce at his country estate. At this point the story bifurcates into dream and reality. Dahlmann ostensibly leaves the hospital and takes a train to his *estancia*, but there are plenty of clues embedded in the story that suggest another reading of the plot, namely that Dahlmann never recovers from his illness and dreams his trip to the South as he lies dying in the hospital.

"The Insufferable Gaucho" is a linear and not a bifurcated story like "The South." Bolaño "joins" Borges's story in progress, as it were. The junction between both stories is Dahlmann's trip to the South. In fact it is when Bolaño's protagonist arrives at his destination in the middle of the countryside that he remembers Borges's story for the first time.

Dahlmann gets off the train and heads to a nearby general store in search of transportation to his ranch. He decides to eat at the store and is importuned by a group of local louts. He tries to ignore them, but one of the peons gets up and begins to insult Dahlmann in a loud voice. A very old gaucho—a symbol of the old South—is intently watching the scene and throws a dagger at Dahlmann's feet: "it was as if the South had decided that Dahlmann should accept the duel." Dahlmann picks up the dagger and walks out to the plain prepared to die: "He felt, as he crossed the threshold, that to die in a knife fight, and charging under a big sky, would have been a liberation for him, a joy and a celebration, in the first night of the sanatorium, when they stuck him with a needle. He felt that if he could have then chosen or dreamed his death, this is the death that he would have chosen or dreamed." In one of his poems ("The Conjectural Poem"), Borges enacts a similar scene in which an intellectual like Dahlmann fulfills his "South American destiny" by dying violently at the hands of a barbarian horde. The poem's hero is Francisco de Laprida, a historical figure who tried to bring enlightened government to the United Provinces of the River Plate in the decade following independence and who lost his life in 1829. Laprida was an ancestor of Borges. Dahlmann, on the other hand, is a fictitious alter ego of the author who attempts to endow his life with meaning by imagining an authentically creole death in a knife fight in the open plain. The South in Borges's story represents the solid foundations of Argentine nationality not only because of its historical role in the consolidation of the Argentina nation but also because the epic confrontations of gauchos, Indians, and the state are the stuff of literature and myth. Bolaño's protagonist has read about the South (partially in Borges's stories), but he will have a sometimes comically hard time fitting his romantic image of the South to his actual experience in the pampa.

Bolaño's protagonist is Manuel Pereda, a widower, exemplary father, and retired judge "with a record of honesty, in a time and place that were hardly conducive to such rectitude" (9). Pereda's son is a successful writer who teaches at a U.S. university but comes back to Buenos Aires to keep an eye on his father, who has become accustomed to a life of solitude and is showing signs of premature ageing. Among other diversions Bebe (the son) takes his father to literary gatherings "where authors basking in the glory of some municipal prize held forth at length about the nation's destiny" (12). Pereda is proud of his son's literary success and firmly believes that he and Borges are the best Argentine writers. One day the Argentine economy collapses, bank accounts are frozen, demonstrators riot in the streets, millions are left without a job, and the president is forced to resign. (This happened at the end of 2001 when two new words entered the national vocabulary: *corralito*—which referred to the restrictions imposed on bank account holders—and *cartoneros*—the shantytown dwellers who would invade the streets of downtown Buenos Aires at night looking for recyclable materials.) At first Pereda joins the protestors but ultimately decides to go back to the country and settle for a while in his ranch Álamo Negro. Like Dahlmann's recollections of his estate, Pereda's mental images of his ranch "had blurred and faded, leaving only a house with a hole in the middle" (14). But the former judge reckons that nothing could be worse than staying in the city.

Dahlmann's trip to the South is also a journey to the past, not only to the protagonist's childhood but also to a time when the Argentine nation was in the process of consolidating itself through the extermination of the "barbarians" that threatened the isolated outposts of "civilization" on the southern border of Buenos Aires. The "conquest of the desert" was completed in 1884, which was also the period when gauchos became practically extinct and survived mostly as a literary and nationalist myth. (This archetypal gaucho is the one that Dahlmann encounters in "The South" and that provides him with a knife.) The first person Pereda runs into when he arrives in the country is a childhood friend who celebrates his playmate's return and points him in the direction of the ranch. But Pereda sees something strange during his train ride to the pampas: rabbits, rabbits in pursuit of other rabbits, running in tandem "like cyclists in the Tour de France" (16). What he does not see surprises him even more: cattle. Rabbits are the most obvious intertextual link between Bolaño's story and stories by Cortázar, Wilcock, and Di Benedetto, but in the context of the "The Insufferable Gaucho" itself rabbits go hand in hand with a parodic demystification of the pampa that will become more acute as the story progresses. In Bolaño's pampa rabbits proliferate throughout the territory and have displaced the horses and cattle that in gauchesque literature are inseparable from the figure of the gaucho. This altered situation makes it difficult for Pereda to behave like a gaucho among gauchos, especially when he notes that the few remaining and mostly decrepit gauchos in the locality would rather play Monopoly at the corner store than do the things that gauchos are supposed to do—like drive cattle, engage in knife fights, and display horsemanship. Pereda's conviction that the whole country is "debased" is aggravated by his disenchantment with the pampa.

Thus Pereda is initially a misfit in the modern-day (or realistic) pampa, though at times he catches a whiff of the way things used to be. For example he walks by a corner store and hears someone strumming a guitar inside, "just as he had read in Borges. For a moment he thought that his destiny, his screwed-up American destiny, would be to meet his death like Dahlmann in 'The South'" (22). But unlike Borges's protagonist, Pereda does not meet a heroic ending or any other kind of death in the South. At the end of the story he goes back to Buenos Aires to sell his house and must decide whether to stay in the city or move back to the countryside. (He chooses the latter and hopes to do something for the poor gauchos who have learned to accept him.) It is ironic that the only time Pereda gets to wield and use a knife in the story is upon his temporary return to Buenos Aires, when he wounds an obnoxious writer at the café where he used to go with his son. On a previous occasion, he wants to settle a dispute with a group of gauchos in the way he has read in books, but when he tries to provoke them by pulling out a knife, "the old guys recoiled in fear and asked what he was doing" (35). He is understandably depressed: "Pereda felt that the shame of the nation or the continent had turned them into tame cats. That's why the cattle have been replaced by rabbits" (35).

There is another aspect of Pereda and some other incidents in "The Insufferable Gaucho" that evoke Borges's "The Gospel According to Mark," which—like "The South"—is a story about a *porteño* (or inhabitant of Buenos Aires) going off to the plains and dying there. The protagonist Baltasar Espinosa (whose name is ostentatiously symbolic in the context of the story) is a young medical student with a great capacity for public speaking who at the request of a cousin agrees to spend a season in their family's country estate. The ranch is kept up by a foreman who is part of a family of three: father, son, and not the Holy Ghost but a daughter of uncertain paternity. The Gutres are mestizo and illiterate, in fact barely articulate. They live in the present and have no sense of history. The cousin leaves for Buenos Aires right before a flood hits the area. The ranch is isolated for many days, and the isolation creates some intimacy between Espinosa and the Gutres. One day Espinosa cures the girl's pet lamb with some pills he had brought from Buenos Aires, winning the family's undying affection. Another day he discovers an English Bible in the house and starts to read the parables to the Gutres after their evening meal. By now Espinosa has grown a beard, unknowingly setting himself up for the sacrificial scene with which the story ends. One night he dreams of the Flood, and hammer blows—which he associates with the building of the Ark—wake him up. He is told that the roof of the toolshed has caved in but that the beams are being fixed. Meanwhile the girl is given to him for one night (Bolaño reiterates a similar episode in "The Insufferable Gaucho") after which the elder Gutre asks Espinosa if Christ allowed himself to be sacrificed so that all men could be saved. He answers in the affirmative and adds that even the Roman soldiers who hammered the nails in were saved. Espinosa keeps reading to the Gutres the chapters of the crucifixion until he is finally led into the toolshed, which is without a roof because the beams had been pulled down to make a cross. Espinosa had unwittingly become the Messiah of the pampa.

Bolaño's Pereda inherits Espinosa's messianic traits but in a farcical way, as the character's fantasies involving his triumphant return to Buenos Aires make clear: "What should I do, Pereda wondered, take the train or ride? That night he could hardly sleep. He imagined people thronging the sidewalks as he made his entry mounted on José Bianco [the name of his horse]. His entry into Buenos Aires, as he imagined it, had the ambience of Christ's entry into Jerusalem or Brussels as depicted by Ensor." (In 1888 Belgian painter James Ensor executed a painting of Christ entering Brussels during a carnival parade.) In the end Pereda arrives in the city dressed as an odd combination of gaucho and rabbit trapper and commits an act of what might be considered gratuitous violence. Thus he resembles the El Chivo character in González Iñárritu's movie *Amores perros,* which was released in 2000, more or less at the same time when Bolaño was writing his story. El Chivo is a former guerrilla fighter and ex-con who has turned into a hitman but who acts as an avenger in the third segment of the movie. Pereda is a former judge who understands soon enough that in his country the bench is not a throne from where justice can be dispensed. He gradually develops a Quixote complex and begins to understand that he went to the pampas to fight windmills. At the end of the story he wonders if he should stay in Buenos Aires and become a "champion of justice" or go back to the country—where he knows he does not belong—and do what he can for the poor gauchos of modern-day Argentina.

But Cervantes's immortal knight is not the only model for Pereda's self-appointed mission. On his way to the pampa Pereda sits next to a man who looks half-Indian and who is reading a Batman comic book, a passing reference that parodies Pereda's later superhero image. Postmodern theory established long ago that the blending of high and popular culture is a defining trait of contemporary art and literature. In *The Language of Postmodern Architecture* (1977) architectural theorist Charles Jencks referred to this feaure of postmodern culture as "double coding." Thus the coexistence of Borges and Batman in the same cultural space generates a peculiarly postmodern form of irony that Bolaño applies in his text to demystify the literature of the gaucho. Other contemporary Argentine novels, like César Aira's *The Hare* and Sergio Bizzio's *En esa época* ("At That Time"), share Bolaño's demystifying spirit.

"Dentist"

Stories like "Last Evenings on Earth" and "The Insufferable Gaucho" have a clear focus and feel like a finished and well-rounded product. "Dentist," however, is a different kind of narrative, one whose center of gravity is difficult to find and that seems to be built on the model of Brownian motion. "Dentist" is really three stories in one, each one crashing into and colliding with the other two in a way that challenges the reader—if not the narrator—to find their overall unity.

The story is narrated by an anonymous first-person heterofictional narrator who takes a few days off from work to visit a college friend out of town. The narrator lives in Mexico City and appears to be a literature or philosophy professor. He needs a break to get over a breakup with his longstanding girlfriend. Thus he visits his old college friend in Irapuato, a provincial city located in the state of Guanajuato, northwest of Mexico City. In their university days both friends were blind admirers of Mexican novelist Salvador Elizondo, an important experimental writer of the 1960s whom neither one reads any longer but whose name brings back nostalgic memories. The narrator's friend is a bachelor and a successful dentist who has his own private practice but who also donates his time to treat the destitute in a public clinic.

The dentist is not going through one of the best moments in his life. He feels guilty over the death of a patient—an old Indian woman whose treatment was mangled by a student volunteer at the cooperative—and had a humiliating encounter with a painter whom he admires and buys engravings from. At a party the painter calls him a homosexual for not wanting to participate in a ménage à trois, and has his gangster friends dangle him over a balcony. But the most significant aspect of the dentist's life in the present of the story is his relationship with a young Indian boy (Ramírez) endowed with a precocious literary talent. The dentist meets the boy while fixing his teeth at the dental cooperative and becomes infatuated with the stories he writes. The narrator suspects that his friend might be homosexual after all but accepts the latter's invitation to visit the boy's shack and read some of his work. He reads a four-page story and is impressed by the author's ability to condense masses of material in such a brief space: "when I got to the end, I felt as if I had read a novel" (*Last Evenings on Earth* 207). Bolaño's story is about twenty pages long but also feels as if it could have been a novel. The plot is split up into three disparate strands (the old Indian woman who dies of cancer of the gums, the painter who humiliates the dentist, and the precocious Indian boy) whose unity is not easily apparent. The dentist's review of another of the boy's stories is really a mise-en-abyme of Bolaño's story as a whole: the first part of that story is about a child who has to look after his younger brothers and sisters, but then the plot swings around and "smashe[s] itself to pieces." The story then becomes a narrative about "the ghost of a schoolmaster trapped in a bottle" and gets more complicated when new characters appear: "a pair of shady faith healers, a twenty-year-old girl on drugs, a guy reading a book by de Sade and living in a wrecked car beside the highway." The dentist's laudatory final comment on the story applies to Bolaño's story as well: "All this in one story" (204).

Bolaño was aware that he did not always know where the limits of a short story were. He tells an interviewer that if he did not have what he calls a *contraire* when sitting down to write a story, the story could easily turn into a six-hundred-page novel. He specifically alludes to "Anne Moore's Life" when referring to a story that has the potential to explode into a long novel; and he illustrates what he means by a *contraire* when he reveals that the story "Detectives"—totally written in dialogue—is a prose fiction version of Nicanor Parras's "Saranguato," a dialogic and extravagant poem that proceeds by way of negation and contradiction (Dés 150). It's impossible to know whether "Dentist" has a "shadow" or "reverse"—and, if it does, whether it has one or three of them—but the point of the story seems to be to find a common center for its three narrative strands.[6] Not only that but the knot that would tie all the stories together would have to exemplify or incorporate the somewhat cryptic theory of art espoused by the dentist in one of his conversations with the narrator. The dentist insists that art comes from life stories and that it may be defined as "the story of a life in all its particularity" (191). Then he clarifies that he is referring to the secret story of a life, at which point his interlocutor looks up in surprise and demands further enlightenment. The secret story—to paraphrase the dentist—is the one we'll never know, although we're living it from day to day, thinking we have things under control and that what we overlook doesn't matter. But, he emphatically concludes, "every single damn thing matters!" (192), referring by implication to how a seemingly incidental detail like the botched operation on the Indian woman has affected him.

Chris Andrews points out that Bolaño's stories do not fall into familiar patterns but yet manage to hold the reader's interest by generating and sustaining narrative tension while remaining puzzling and inconclusive (75). In turn, and along with Andrews, this echos the previous point that "Dentist" generates narrative tension by juxtaposing three seemingly disparate stories and making their interrelationship problematic. Andrews's approach to "Dentist" is by way of Ricardo Piglia's well-known theory of the short story, according to which all stories tell two stories, a visible one and a secret one. The classic story (Poe, Cortázar, Borges) has a closed structure and strives to produce a surprise ending by letting the invisible and half-suggested plot emerge from the interstices of the manifest story and reveal itself at the end. The modern story, on the other hand, gives up on the surprise ending and focuses on the tension between its narrative components.[7] Clearly "Dentist" belongs to the second category, not only because it brings together more than one plot but also because its implicit artistic theory involves the notion of a "secret story." Is the secret of the story revealed at the end? The answer would have to be yes but only through a glass darkly. The narrator has a dream after the "supremely literary night" he has spent with his friend at young Ramírez's house and for "barely a second" understands "the mystery of art and its secret nature" (209). But this illumination leaves no trace in the waking world, an outcome already suggested at the beginning of the story when the narrator states that the Indian boy "wasn't Rimbaud." As Andrews concurs the "relations among the components remain enigmatic" (79). The narrator's ineffable revelation supersedes a more comfortable reading that would make repressed homosexuality the key to the story.

"Two Catholic Tales"

Critics have paid little or no attention to one of the minor stories in *The Insufferable Gaucho* but one that nevertheless shows Bolaño's technical prowess in a distinctive light. In terms of content, the story is hard to fit in Bolaño's universe, which is partially the reason why its technical aspect stands out. In fact it is the technical aspect of the story that renders it familiar to Bolaño readers because the displacement of perspective and focalization that characterizes its construction recalls many novels by Bolaño—ranging from *The Skating Rink* to *The Savage Detectives* and *2666*—that use a similar technique.

As its name indicates, "Two Catholic Tales" is a dyptich. Its "panels" are called "The Vocation" and "Chance," respectively, and they are both narrated in the first person but by different narrators. Each narrator appears as a third person in the other's narrative, which provides a double vision of both narrators by the end of the story. One vision is provided by internal focalization— the kind provided by the standard first-person narrative—and the other by an external focus on the narrator who now becomes a character and is perceived from a distance. In Bolaño's story this perspectival displacement affects the kind and even the amount of information available to the reader regarding the identity and motivation of the two protagonists. Thus it is only at the end of the second part that the narrator of the opening section is given a physical description as "a fat, ugly adolescent" (119). Until then most of what is known about this character is that he likes movies and that he is possessed of a religious vocation. By the same token, the mysterious "monk" that the adolescent narrator follows in the first part as he returns from the movies is given his full identity and motivation only in the second. The shocking nature of this revelation is enhanced by Bolaño's indirect presentation of events. This is one of the very few Bolaño stories that feature a surprise ending in the manner of Poe, Borges, or Cortázar. It actually runs against the grain of Bolaño's handling of narrative tension. To repeat the statement by Andrews quoted above: "[Bolaño] cultivates suspense more than curiosity, and surprises the reader by confounding expectations rather than by revealing withheld information." "Two Catholic Tales" excels at withholding information and thus creating a narrative puzzle.

The story is puzzling both structurally and thematically. Its narration tends to approach the paratactic mode, a tendency that is partially checked by having the narrative clauses follow one another in a numbered sequence. The mathematical ordering, then, seems to correct the non sequitur appearance of both sections. Both parts of the story make progress and advance in a roughly linear form, but the logic of the numbers is elusive, to put it mildly. Narrative clauses can be one word long or consist of several sentences. Both sections, furthermore, are narrated in the form of a dialogue, but in both the dialogue is controlled (reported) by the first-person narrator, which at times creates a deliberate (though temporary) confusion as to who is speaking. In sum the story is characterized by three structural features: its division in two parts (with an attending perspectival shift), the fragmentary nature of its narrative sequences, and a dialogue controlled by what is essentially a narrative monologue.

Thematically, as implied above, the story is puzzling because it seems to fall outside the usual Bolaño parameters in terms of characters, themes, motivation, and location, though the reader remains aware that the story is basically a crime story, a staple of Bolaño's narrative. Strictly speaking there is very little narration in the first part of the story. The narrator first introduces himself as an anxious seventeen-year-old who has frequent conversations with his friend Juanito—mostly about the movies—and who is haunted by images relating to the martyrdom of St. Vincent, "deacon to Bishop Valero, tortured by the governor Dacian in the year 304" (103). These images do not seem to come out of the movies as much as out of the genealogical fantasies of the narrator's aunt, who traces her family lineage back to the fourth century. The narrator sets down information on Juanito's mother and father and on his own religious vocation, as he seems headed for the priesthood. Whatever narration there is in this section involves a trip to the movies with Juanito on a snowy afternoon. After seeing a Clark Gable film, both friends separate and return home. It is dark and freezing cold in the streets. On his way back, a strange figure catches the narrator's attention on account of his attire and because there is no one else around at that time of day and in that weather: "Then I saw him. Just a shadow at first. But it wasn't a shadow, it was a monk" (110). In the second half of the story it is revealed that the monk is no such thing but a psychotic criminal. For now, though, the reader is taken in by the narrator's devotion. He imagines that the monk is a Franciscan who perhaps has just given the last rites to a dying person or is on his way back from visiting a sick child. The monk is barefoot: "His immaculate footprints shone in the snow like a message from God. I started crying" (111). The narrator follows the monk into the local train station and observes that he comes out of the bathroom with a pair of shoes on. He watches the monk jump on the train with surprising agility, and when he himself leaves to return home he looks for the monk's footprints but fails to find any trace of them.

This part of the story is retold from the monk's perspective in the second Catholic tale. The fake monk takes over the first-person narrative pronoun and reports on a dialogue with an "old guy" who calls him Vicente, like the saint with whom the first narrator is obsessed. This part of the text is a carbon copy of the beginning of the opening section, in which the original narrator gives his age and notes that his life is a "continual shuddering" (103). At the beginning of "Chance," the new narrator lets us know that he is old though not yet sixty and asks his interlocutor why he is shaking—he could have said "shuddering"— all the time. The conversation is partially a rambling discourse on life in the asylum, from which at least Vicente, if not the old man too, seems to have es- caped: "I remembered the years in the asylum: the injections, the hosing-down, the ropes they used for tying us up at night" (112). Before being committed to an asylum, Vicente had been a beggar hanging around church buildings and a devout Catholic to boot. And just as the original narrator was fascinated by St. Vincent, the narrator of the "Chance" section identifies with Santa Barbara, another saint who suffered persecution (she was locked in a cell and eventually decapitated). Now a certain Commissioner Valle (probably Juanito's father, who is a "police commissioner") is after the escapee, which prompts his inter- locutor to give him some commonsense advice: "Get out of here, Vicente. . . . Get some clothes to make you blend in" (116).

In his escape the fugitive enters a house in search of food and warmth and sees a friar reading a missal sitting next to a naked child stretched out on a bed. The former inmate does not understand the scene that he's confronted with and in a fit of rage stabs both the friar and the child. He then rummages through the room and finds a clean habit hanging in a closet. The references to the fugitive's blood-covered footprints on the snow implicitly connect "Chance" to "The Vocation," a connection that is expanded further in the last few paragraphs of the story: "I realized that someone was following me. . . . My pursuer was a fat, ugly adolescent. Who was I? That didn't matter at all. . . . I could have killed the boy. . . . But why bother?" (119–20). At the end it is revealed that the "monk" goes into the train station bathroom to wash his bloodstained old shoes—a piece of information that the original narrator was unable to know from his external perspective—and that he takes the first train passing through, regardless of its destination.

"Two Catholic Tales" is obviously a twist on Matthew Lewis's *The Monk* (1796) and a notable addition to Bolaño's Gothic catalog, a collection that also includes the mock-Gothic story "The Return," "The Room Next Door," certain descriptions in "Cell Mates," and the "Dracula" episode of the last part of *2666*. It might also be regarded by some as a twist on Luis Buñuel's surrealist ironies directed at the Catholic Church in films like *The Andalusian Dog* (1929) and *Viridiana* (1961), especially given the suspicious physical proximity in Bolaño's story of a supposedly chaste friar and a newborn infant. (The child's mother is temporarily out of the house.) The story's ironic title would endorse such readings. Ultimately, though, the story should be accepted at face value and read as a partial refutation of the poetics of inconclusiveness that some critics have made too much of when trying to understand Bolaño.

From Story to Novel: "Muscles" and *A Little Lumpen Novelita*

"Muscles" is one of the unfinished stories retrieved by Bolaño's editors from the author's computer files after his death and included in *The Secret of Evil*. It is remarkable because it is an early and incomplete draft of the last novel Bolaño was able to publish before he died, *Una novelita lumpen* (2002), a short novel recently translated into English as *A Little Lumpen Novelita* (2014). It therefore lends itself to a comparison with its fully achieved version through which can be understood part of Bolaño's creative process, and particularly his ability to transform and adapt fragments of his work to a new set of needs. A similar process of transformation and adaptation can be seen in the relation between the last chapter of *Nazi Literature in the Americas* and *Distant Star,* or in the expansion of one of the sections of *The Savage Detectives* into *Amulet*. But a closer look at these examples—and others, such as the conversion of "People Walking Away" into *Antwerp* or the relation between *The Woes of the True Policeman* and *2666*—reveals that Bolaño does not rework previously existing texts in the same way or following a single preestablished method. Each case has to be examined on its own. The transformation of "People Walking Away" into *Antwerp,* for example, implies a (not necessarily successful) transition between poetic prose and prose narrative; *Amulet* is a 150-page expansion of a ten-page fragment with the aim of striking a more prophetic or visionary narrative tone; *Distant Star* involves a metafictional and autofictional transformation of "The Infamous Ramírez Hoffman," and so on. The case of "Muscles" is different. The examples of *Antwerp, Distant Star,* and *Amulet* all involve rewritings of previously finished works or chapters of works. But "Muscles" is an unfinished story whose full meaning is brought out only by and through a process of revision and expansion.

The protagonists of the story are Marta and Enric, a pair of adolescent siblings who are brought closer together when their parents die in a road accident. The story takes place in Barcelona and is narrated by Marta, who is several years younger than her brother but acts as his caretaker. Marta is a well-rounded character in her own right, but the focus of the story is mostly on Enric. The older brother was closer to his parents than his sister and in consequence is more afflicted by their tragic death. He is obsessed, for example, by the fact that he and Marta are now orphans and breaks up for no apparent reason with his first and only girlfriend, a friend and coworker of Marta's at a hairdressing salon. Enric reads the pre-Socratic philosophers during breakfast, works at an auto repair shop during the day, and spends his free time every day working out at the neighborhood gym. He is heavily into bodybuilding. When he was younger, the narrator informs us, he dreamed of playing Maciste when he grew up—Maciste being the Hercules-like hero of many Italian sword-and-sandal movies of the 1960s. Brother and sister live alone in their home until one night Enric invites guests over for dinner. The guests are two South Americans—or sudacas—who have no fixed residence, have no stable job, and—we are led to believe—do not have their papers in order. At Enric's invitation they stay on for an indefinite period of time, although their status as permanent guests often clashes with Marta's wishes. She worries about their influence on her brother and hears suspicious noises at night coming from her brother's bedroom. She respects the law of hospitality (by not evicting the guests) but does not behave like a gracious hostess. At times it seems that she is one more guest in her own home. The guests, however, are not exactly the "guests from hell" of the cliché. Every so often they impress Marta as likable and harmless characters down on their luck, an impression that makes it difficult for her to treat them with outright hostility. They are considerate enough, for example, to show up one night with a heap of provisions for a meal that they themselves prepare. But, as Marta quickly suspects, the provisions are stolen. She joins the dinner party, nevertheless, out of love for her brother, who is delighted with his friends' manners and with his sister's acquiescence. The story is left hanging at the point where the guests show up with the stolen provisions and sit down to dinner with Marta and Enric.

"Muscles" is slightly altered, expanded, and completed in *A Little Lumpen Novelita*. The main characters remain the siblings, but their age difference has been dismissed, and they now live in Rome and not in Barcelona. Their parents die in a car and not in a bus accident, as they do in the story. The narrator is still the sister but she is now called Bianca (her brother remains nameless). The unexpected guests are no longer sudacas—one is from Bologna and the other is either Libyan or Moroccan. They both take turns to become Bianca's lover at different times during their stay. By comparison in the story the sexual option is merely latent. The guests not only put an end to Bianca's virginity but also introduce the theme of lawlessness in the novel, just as they do in the original story. In "Muscles" they steal food from a grocery store; in *A Little Lumpen Novelita* they talk Bianca into becoming a paid sexual companion to an older man who lives by himself and who is thought to have a safe box full of money and jewels hidden somewhere in his house. The man happens to be none other than the mythical Maciste that Enric wanted to emulate in "Muscles"—not the actual movie character, of course, but an actor who played the role of Maciste back in the 1960s. This Maciste, a former Mr. Universe who went by the name of Franco Bruno in the movies, enters the novel precisely at its midway point and is the protagonist of the last eight chapters. Like the siblings' parents, he also had an accident and is now blind, a fact that is hidden from Bianca until it is too late for her to turn back and upset the plotters' scheme. She visits him periodically and develops a real interest in his life (even imagining toward the end that she is his bride) but never stops looking for the safe box, which she never finds. The criminal scheme, however, becomes more and more secondary as the novel progresses and Bianca's patience regarding her unwanted guests and their ploy is in increasingly shorter supply. In the end Bianca decides she is not in love with Maciste and rejects his last payment for the sexual favors she has rendered him. She says farewell and tells him that she is going to start a new life. She returns home and with his brother's acquiescence expels the intruders, never to see them again.

The outcome of the plot is announced in the opening sentence of the novel: "Now I'm a mother and a married woman, but not long ago I led a life of crime. My brother and I had been orphaned. Somehow that justified everything." *A Little Lumpen Novelita* is, in fact, a miniature bildungsroman that narrates the female protagonist's integration into conventional middle-class society after surmounting a traumatized youth characterized by aimless sex and a poorly conceived criminal scheme. We do not know what happens with the brother except that his sister keeps him away from bad company and saves him from a life of crime. It should be noted that the shape of things to come is a theme present in the story since its earliest conception. At the beginning of "Muscles" both Enric and Marta fear being devoured by the "black hole of time," just as their parents had been, along with the lost works of antiquity to which Enric alludes in his morning conversations with his sister. The black hole image recurs at the end of *A Little Lumpen Novelita* when Bianca looks at the night sky and discerns a hole where she can fit, "a shadow that was my shadow." By that point in the novel brother and sister have gotten their bearings and face the future—uncertain as it may be—with renewed confidence.[8]

It should also be noted that Bianca's path to the future is the result of a moral decision, precisely the kind of moral decision that Ana—the antiheroine of *Consejos de un discípulo de Morrison a un fanático de Joyce*—fails to make. Ana dies as the outlaw that she was in her short life, without remorse and without redemption. As a type of cold-blooded killer, Ana is like the murdering whore of Bolaño's story by that name. But Bianca has a moral dimension that is reminiscent of *By Night in Chile*, a novel that shows a marked concern with the ethics of character. Bolaño's insistence on the "moral lesson" that can be drawn from each of the episodes that make up the novel should be remembered. In that text Father Urrutia is a guilt-ridden actor in a political drama that surpasses him, but his deathbed confession is an ethical act. Bianca is guiltless since, as she herself says, her orphanhood justified everything. Still it is striking that two novels as different as *A Little Lumpen Novelita* and *By Night in Chile* should converge on the theme of morality.

This does not make Bolaño a moralizing author, of course. In fact the moral "turn" in *A Little Lumpen Novelita* has an ironic twist that implicates the author in an ethical sleight of hand. The novel's epigraph, taken from Artaud's *Le Pèse-Nerfs* (*The Nerve Meter* 1925), is an invective against writers and particularly modern writers: "All writing is garbage. People who come out of nowhere to try and put into words any part of what goes on in their minds are pigs. All writers are pigs. Especially writers today." Through this epigraph Bolaño is playfully throwing mud on himself and including himself in the writers' pigpen, the reason being that *A Little Lumpen Novelita* was a work commissioned by publisher Mondadori in 2000 as part of a series called Año Ø. The series involved several young Latin American writers who were invited to contribute a novel or some other type of work to be set in a world city at the time of the millennium. Trips were paid for and the money probably shown in advance. Bolaño took the opportunity to travel to Rome and contact Colombian author Santiago Gamboa, one of the contributors to the series and a friend who happened to live in Rome at the time. Gamboa has stated that Bolaño visited him at the end of October 2000 with his pregnant wife, Carolina, and notes that he did not seem interested in the city itself, not even in Civitavecchia, where he asked his host to take him because Stendhal had spent time there. According to Gamboa, Bolaño's way of doing tourism was to talk, smoke, and look at the ground the whole time.[9] It is not a surprise that the Rome of *A Little*

Lumpen Novelita feels like a movie set and is interchangeable with any other city on the map. Only a few superficial references "characterize" the city as such. And as was pointed out before, the early draft of the story is set—much more convincingly—in Barcelona.

Still Rome was the only city in which a story featuring Maciste could have taken place, since the Maciste character originated in a 1914 Italian film called *Cabiria* and returned to the screen many times during the 1960s in the *peplum* films shot in Italy. Therefore Bolaño's brief sojourn in Rome may be considered a "research" trip, which is probably how Bolaño himself regarded his visit to the Eternal City. It is likely, however, that Bolaño was somewhat bothered by the possible contradiction between his writerly ethic and the crass marketing and commercialism involved in the Mondadori proposal. So he externalizes his mea culpa by prefacing the novel with Artaud's epigraph. But, as it is plain to see, this mea culpa involves a fair amount of self-irony and falls short of a full apology.[10]

Finally the lumpen character of the novel deserves some attention, though there is nothing surprising in it in view of Bolaño's literary and personal history. To begin with, Bolaño defined himself as a nomadic Chilean from the lower middle classes (Braithwaite 90). Then infrarealist poetry has more than once been described as lumpen on account of its affinity with barrio culture and street jargon, an affiliation that Bolaño reaffirms when he describes himself— or his poetic persona—as a "nomadic proletarian" in one of the poems of *The Unknown University* (181). This poem is dedicated to his mother and was written during Bolaño's early years in Spain, when his social circle included sundry representatives of what is usually classified as the lumpen proletariat. But more to the point, the title of Bolaño's novel is a critical allusion to José Donoso's *Tres novelitas burguesas* (Barcelona: Seix Barral, 1973), a collection of three short novels set in Barcelona of which Bolaño disapproved because—according to him—they lack narrative tension and mark a moment of decline in Donoso's narrative production (Madrigal 194).

The three novelitas are a minor work by Donoso standards, but they are quite interesting in their own way. They represent Donoso's engagement with the *gauche divine* ("the divine left") of the 1960s and early 1970s, a movement of progressive artists and intellectuals from the upper ranks of the Catalan bourgeoisie that heralded the social and political changes that Spain would undergo after Franco's death (1975). Donoso's approach to this social class was sympathetic but also ironic. Literarily these novellas derive from Balzac and, more directly, from nineteenth-century English domestic fiction and the novel of manners. (One of them starts with a disguised allusion to Jane Austen's *Pride and Prejudice*.) The three novelitas were translated into English as *Sacred Families,* a somewhat misleading title since—with one exception—Donoso's characters in that book are not portrayed as parents but mostly as dysfunctional partners in married couples.

In his own *A Little Lumpen Novelita,* on the other hand, Bolaño explicitly ties Bianca's moral conversion to the character's pledge to save her brother from bad company and thus reconstruct the familial bond severed by her parents' tragic death. The family is more "sacred" in Bolaño than in Donoso, despite the unfavorable social milieu in which Bolaño's characters are forced to operate. Biographical-minded readers would be tempted to relate this thematic feature to the fact that Bolaño's wife was expecting at the time the novel was composed. Perhaps this is stretching the role of biographical meaning in understanding Bolaño's fiction too much. But it is true that the outcome of *A Little Lumpen Novelita* implies a more settled vision on the part of its author than the denouement of an early novel like *Consejos de un discípulo de Morrison a un fanático de Joyce.*

Chapter 8

2666

Bolaño's Global Novel

In an essay published in 1989 on the state of the novel, Chinese American author Maxine Hong Kingston calls for a renovation of the genre by admonishing writers to devise the lineaments of a new narrative form that she calls the global novel. This new form would emerge out of the tradition of the national novel and represent a kind of organic growth of a genre traditionally enclosed by national borders: "The dream of the great American novel is past. We need to write the Global novel. Its setting will be the United States, destination of journeys from everywhere. . . . Refugees from Southeast Asia and South America are coming to the last place that you would think North Americans would make unlivable, the United States. We shut the borders, migrants drop from the sky, as in *The Satanic Verses,* a pioneer Global novel for which the author has risked life and art" (39–40). More broadly the global novel would respond to an ethical and specifically humanist impulse that the author illustrates by means of a reference to Mario Vargas Llosa's *The War of the End of the World* (1981), a novel set in the backlands of Brazil at the end of the nineteenth century that recounts the efforts of the Brazilian government to destroy a religious community bent on challenging the republican principles of a nation that had just become a republic a short time earlier. Kingston describes the rebellious community as "a community with no property, no money, no taxes, no hunger, and no marriage" (41) and implicitly blames the Brazilian government and army for warmongering. She uses Vargas Llosa's novel as a moral example: "the Global novelist of the future has to imagine the commune winning so that there will be no war and no end of the world" (41). The choice of example accords well with an apocalyptic strain in Kingston's own writing that makes the creation of the global novel an urgent matter: "the hands of the clock are minutes away from nuclear midnight" (37).

Being an accomplished novelist herself, Kingston cannot but be concerned about the formal aspects of the global novel. Since she charges this genre with propagating ideas about world peace, she is naturally concerned with how "to write a novel that uses nonviolent means to get to nonviolent ends" (37). Novels are supposed to be about things happening to people and are expected to be full of action and crisis, precisely the kind of excitement that *The War of the End of the World* delivers through hundreds of pages. Kingston repeats William Burroughs's assertion that there is no such thing as a great Buddhist novel. She also invokes the creative writing adage that "the loaded gun in an early chapter has to go off later on," and wonders how to break that rule (37–38). Ultimately the danger with the global novel is that it "has to imitate chaos: loaded guns, bombs, leaking boats, broken-down civilizations, a hole in the sky, broken English, people who refuse connections with others. How to stretch the novel to comprehend our times—no guarantees of inherent or eventual order—without it falling apart?" (40).

Kingston's essay and the notion of a global novel constitute an appropriate point of departure to discuss Bolaño's gigantic *2666*, a nine-hundred-page novel in the English translation that moves easily through time and space (and cuts across national literatures), and that takes historical and social violence as its main theme. Its apocalyptic tone is already figured in the title, which combines a dystopian vision of the future with the numerological sign of the devil. In Bolaño's work the date 2666 first appears in *Amulet,* in the passage where Arturo Belano and his homosexual friend Ernesto San Epifanio (followed by the narrator Auxilio Lacouture) venture into the domain of the King of the Rent Boys with the purpose of freeing Ernesto from the clutches of the pimp (see chapter 6 above): "Then we walked down the Avenida Guerrero. . . . Guerrero, at that time of night, is more like a cemetery than an avenue, not a cemetery in 1974, or in 1968, or 1975, but a cemetery in the year 2666, a forgotten cemetery under the eyelid of a corpse or an unborn child, bathed in the dispassionate fluids of an eye that tried so hard to forget one particular thing that it ended up forgetting everything else" (86). The context of the date 2666 is cryptic but a reference to historical amnesia and to the mass graves of the Second World War, to the murders of Ciudad Juárez, and to the often anonymous dead of the military dictatorships of the Southern Cone may be discerned in it. (The future and morbid date may also refer to Bolaño's awareness that his novel would be a posthumous one.) The image of the apocalyptic cemetery, furthermore, may have been suggested by the Oscar Hahn poem mentioned in the first chapter of this book. The poem may be found in Hahn's book *Imágenes nucleares* (Santiago: Ediciones América del Sur, 1983) and is called "Reincarnation of the Butchers." Its first stanza goes like this: "And I saw that the butchers on the third day, / on the third day of the third night, / began to blossom in the cemeteries / like murky lilies or lichen."

In *2666* Bolaño responds in his own way to some of the fears articulated by Maxine Kingston in her essay on the global novel. Both authors project a global vision of history as a catalog of horrors, Vietnam being the Kingston equivalent of Bolaño's Second World War. But at the same time Kingston's notion of the global novel has to be qualified in order to serve as a significant point of departure for the study of Bolaño's *2666*. For one thing it is doubtful that readers will find in Bolaño's magnum opus any secret impulse to promote world peace and understanding. In compensation, though, readers will find a fascination and an obsession with finding the roots of the criminal violence that can manifest itself in the Europe of the Second World War just as much and as virulently as in the Mexico of neoliberalism and globalization.

Perhaps more to the point is the double fact that Bolaño's global novel did not emerge out of the tradition of the great national novel, nor is it located in the United States. The Savage Detectives can only in jest be considered the great Mexican novel of the 1990s or a novel with the same national prestige of Carlos Fuentes's *The Death of Artemio Cruz* (1962) or Juan Villoro's *El testigo* ("The Witness," 2004), both of which read at times like Mexican national allegories. It stands to reason that the author of a great national novel should be a citizen of the nation in question. In fact Bolaño's position as an outsider and an expatriate both in Mexico and Spain put him in a favorable position to write just the kind of global novel that Maxine Kingston and others have been speculating about since the 1980s, even if each novelist has a different conception of this flourishing genre. As to the second fact pointed out above, it should not be surprising that world novels—despite their wordly identity—can still be attributed to a single geopolitical location as Kingston suggests, and that the genre of the global novel can form part of "American studies," for example, or some similar nation- or region-bound discipline such as the (yet to be baptized) "Latin American world novel." *2666* is set both in Europe and Latin America, and it is significant that its actions and characters converge in a border town. Bolaño's Santa Teresa is a fictionalized version of Ciudad Juárez, Chihuahua, the border city where the *maquiladora* industry started in 1965 and where the *femicides* of the 1990s took place.[1]

Finally it will be evident that Kingston's fears about the formal chaos that might be incurred by novels that spread themselves over a heterogeneous and multitudinous range of global issues are unfounded in the case of Bolaño's *2666*, for here is a novel that branches out in any number of directions but that is held together by a subterranean network of connections, some more subtle than others. The textual network or web is not a rhizome. There is a central character, a central location, and a central sequence of events. At bottom the novel is the story of Benno von Archimboldi and of how this German writer with the unlikely name ends up in Santa Teresa at the time of the women's murders. There is also a central vision. In Bolaño's own words, *2666* is a "grand vision of horror."[2]

Prelude to *2666*: *Woes of the True Policeman*

This posthumous work was published in Spanish in 2011 and in English the following year. As Larry Rohter put it in his *New York Times* review of the novel, if *Woes of the True Policeman* were a music CD rather than a novel, "it would undoubtedly be described as a collection of outtakes, alternate versions and demos"[3]—mostly of *2666*, one should add. The protagonist is the same Amalfitano of Bolaño's masterpiece, though in *Woes of the True Policeman* he is married to a different woman and his marriage ends differently: not because he is abandoned by his wife (as in *2666*) but because the wife dies of cancer. (The wife's name in *Woes of the True Policeman* is Edith Lieberman, a name that recalls the Edna Lieberman of Bolaño's poetry—see chapter 1; in *2666* Amalfitano's wife is called Lola, a name that also appears in the poetry collected in *The Unknown University*.) A secondary protagonist of the novel—although he never appears on scene—is a disappeared French writer by the name of J. M. G. Arcimboldi, whom Amalfitano translates into Spanish and whose works are glossed in the fourth chapter of the novel.

Despite certain obvious differences, it is impossible not to connect this Arcimboldi with the Benno von Archimboldi of *2666*, just as it is not to think of French novelist J. M. G. Clézio, one of whose novels—*La Quarantaine* (Paris: Gallimard, 1995)—has as its protagonist a family by the name of Archambau. One more important point in this regard is that the femicides of Santa Teresa play a role in the plot, though this part of the novel is considerably shorter than its counterpart in *2666*. ("The Part about the Crimes" is the most extensive section of *2666*.) Since the murder of women in Ciudad Juárez began in 1993, at least part of *Woes of the True Policeman* can be dated to the mid-1990s.[4] (Another important date in this respect is 1989, the year when the Berlin Wall came down. The first part of *Woes of the True Policeman* is entitled "The Fall of the Berlin Wall," and it is not impossible that this historic date marks the beginning of the novel's composition.) On a smaller scale, both *Woes of the True Policeman* and *2666* feature a visit to a nightclub or circus magician who has some mysterious relationship with either the Arcimboldi of the first of these two novels or the Benno von Archimboldi of *2666*. In this latter novel, the magician is called Doktor Koenig and disappoints the visiting critics who were hoping he would be the Archimboldi they were looking for. Finally *Woes of the True Policeman* is divided into the same number of parts (five) as *2666*, each having its own heading.

The "outtakes" of *Woes of the True Policeman* also relate to other works by Bolaño. The explosive opening chapter, for example, is included in *The Savage Detectives,* where in the form of a reported monologue it is attributed to a different character than in *Woes of the True Policeman.* (The content—Bolaño's delirious "theory" on the gender of literature—reads like a set piece. One is led to believe that if novels are heterosexual and poetry homosexual, it's because the latter functions as a minor genre in the literary marketplace when compared with the former.) Furthermore Padilla's letter about Raoul Delorme and the sect of barbaric writers (in the second chapter of *Woes of the True Policeman*) is expanded in chapter 10 of *Distant Star,* a novel in which Padilla (Amalfitano's student lover) does not appear as a character. Many other instances of self-cannibalizing may be identified: thus the story about the rape of Rimbaud reappears in *The Savage Detectives;* the anecdote about the recruit from Seville who ends up on the wrong side of the war in 1941 becomes one of the stories included in *The Return* ("Another Russian Tale"); the therapeutic "pilgrimage" that Elisa undertakes to the psychiatric hospital of Mondragón at the end of the novel is the same trip that Amalfitano's unhappy wife Lola takes in the second section of *2666;* and the Pancho Monge of *Woes of the True Policeman* seems to be a version of the Lalo Cura of *2666* (and of the story "Prefiguration of Lalo Cura," also included in *The Return*).

The editorial history of *Woes of the True Policeman,* as explained by Bolaño's widow in the note appended to the text, is convoluted. According to the editor, Bolaño started to work on this project in the 1980s and kept working on it until the time of his death. She states that the individual chapters show different degrees of completion but that they were all transcribed from an original handwritten manuscript, revised, and sometimes polished in a third (computerized) version. But then she adds that there was not one but two "original" manuscripts, and that one was more complete than the other. The more elaborate manuscript was organized in separate folders, to which some computer files were added to yield the novel that results. Clearly the final shape of the book was not determined by Bolaño, despite editorial assurances that the author's wishes were respected at every point along the editorial process. Curiously, as the editor states, the unusual title was present from the beginning and was never amended. But it seems that only the title was ready for publication since the novel was left in an unfinished state. Was the "intertextual" material of *Woes of the True Policeman* taken from or incorporated into other works by Bolaño? This question could only be answered by knowing the exact dates of composition of the relevant material and of its migration to and from other works. How can it be known, for example, when J. M. G. Arcimboldi turned into Benno von Archimboldi, if that is actually what happened? Intuitively it might be felt that most of *Woes of the True Policeman* is an early draft of *2666,* which does not obviate the possibility that Bolaño may have written some of it concurrently with his final masterpiece. The best that can be said is that *Woes of the True Policeman* mirrors other works by the author and that the novel was written at different times between 1989 and 2003—but this latter statement is merely guesswork.

For all these reasons it is hard to judge *Woes of the True Policeman* on its own merits. There's no question that it is concocted and fragmentary and must be read in relation to other works that constitute its life-support system. The novel may be mostly fit for Bolaño connoiseurs, but there are at least three reasons it should be given some attention on its own terms: it contains many pages of inspired writing, Bolaño stuck with it, and the editorial effort involved in its composition was considerable. Furthermore there is something of Bolaño himself in its two main characters, Padilla, the young poet afflicted with a fatal disease, and Amalfitano, the Chilean man of letters who shortly after the military coup in Chile "was arrested and brought in blindfolded to be interrogated," after which he "was tortured half-heartedly but believed that he had endured the worst and was surprised by his resistance" (196)—a statement that reiterates a well-known passage from Bolaño's biography.[5]

The novel is framed by the relationship between Amalfitano, a widower and literature professor, and Padilla, his student at the University of Barcelona. The older man discovers his homosexuality through his student, and after word of his affair makes the rounds, he is forced to resign his position and find a new job in the remote Mexican town of Santa Teresa, to which he moves with his daughter Rosa. Rosa eventually finds out about her father's newfound sexual inclination, and homosexuality becomes a taboo subject between the two of them. Amalfitano is disconsolate: "At the root of his argument was an attempt to console himself . . . by reasoning that if the Eastern Bloc could crumble, so, too, could his thus far unequivocal heterosexuality" (130).[6] The opening section of the novel is teasingly called "The Fall of the Berlin Wall." The prominence of the homosexual theme marks a sharp difference between *Woes of the True Policeman* and *2666*, a novel in which homosexuality literally haunts Amalfitano but does not characterize him to the extent that it does in the novel's "alternative" version. *Woes of the True Policeman* is dedicated to Manuel Puig, the Argentine writer whose signature novel was *The Kiss of the Spider Woman*, the story of a gay man imprisoned in a common cell with a revolutionary guerrilla during the Argentine Dirty War. (Some of the novel's more experimental writing—such chapter 9 of the first part and chapter 19 of part 2—if not all of part 3—may be read as homage to Puig's groundbreaking narrative style.)

Amalfitano leaves for Mexico but throughout the novel keeps up a correspondence with Padilla, who meanwhile has turned to writing a novel— much like Bolaño did in the early 1980s—called *The God of Homosexuals*.

Amalfitano wants to know what the title means, and Padilla responds that the god of homosexuals is "the god of beggars, the god who sleeps on the ground, in subway entrances, the god of insomniacs, the god of those who have always lost" (41)—the god, in other words, of poets and the lumpen. (But also the god of the terminally ill, since only a few pages later this divinity is explicitly identified with AIDS.) It should not be surprising that Amalfitano identifies Padilla's idol with revolutionary and visionary poets. In admiration he exclaims that Padilla "is describing the god of poets, the god of the poor, the god of the Comte de Lautréamont and Rimbaud" (41).

Later on Amalfitano, as if he himself were a poète maudit, attributes the root of all his ills to his admiration for Jews, homosexuals, revolutionaries, junkies, delinquents, whores, blacks, and the mentally disturbed, among other exemplars of stigmatized groups and individuals. It has been said that Bolaño was not a psychological novelist (and it should be added that he did not mean to be) and was not good at creating well-rounded characters. But, on the other hand, *Woes of the True Policeman* depends to an important extent on the characterization of Amalfitano, who is not a particularly convincing character. At times he seems to be two or three characters stuffed into one. He is more convincing when viewed from afar than when speaking in his own voice about his intimacy. It is worth noting that his life is recounted in mirror form: in chapter 5 of the opening section, the character's life is deployed as autobiography, whereas in chapter 5 of the closing section the same biographical facts are rendered in the third person. Most of the novel is focalized through Amalfitano, but the narration consistently oscillates between the first- and the third-person pronouns. One particular moment when Amalfitano appears exceedingly detached from the narrative instance occurs on page 96: "What Amalfitano would never know was. . . ." He also appears distanced and remote in the passages when he is shadowed by a policeman in the final section of the novel.

Woes of the True Policeman is not a continuous narrative but proceeds fitfully, by jumps and starts. The five different parts of the novel—all of which take the liberty to include extraneous material and jump back and forth in time— are separated by obvious sequential gaps. The last part, for example, opens with the story of a totally new character and seems to belong to another novel. And the third part specializes in digression: the story focuses on Rosa Amalfitano's existence in Santa Teresa but includes chapters on the girl's education many years earlier and easily veers off to comment on the French intervention in Mexico in 1864 and on the activities of a local bullfighter who died in 1933, "a few months before Hitler came to power" (119). These fragments, however, are not as discordant as they appear at first sight, even if their organizational principle is sometimes hard to detect. In this instance the French invasion is a thread that leads to Rosa's love of French poetry and to the hypothetical rape of Rimbaud, which is recounted in another section of the novel. The story is that one of the French soldiers who returned to France in 1867 after the failed invasion of Mexico ran into Rimbaud as the poet headed to Paris to join the Communards and raped him, an event that resulted in the composition of the poem "Le Coeur volé." In the final part of the novel the French invasion is a thread that eventually (and through several generations) leads to the birth of Pancho Monge, a local policeman who starts out as the bodyguard of a Santa Teresa businessman's wife. In turn Pancho overhears his fellow bodyguards talking about illness and death as if they were highly literate: "They knew everything, from the different kinds of flu and adult-onset measles to AIDS and syphillis" (175), a comment that connects this dimension of the novel ("Killers of Sonora") to the disease that is killing Padilla. And, in another example of these secret connecting threads, part 4 picks up—though belatedly and with interruptions—on the end of part 2, when Amalfitano states his intention to read all of Arcimboldi's novels.

The novel ends with a further exchange of letters between Amalfitano and Padilla. (The epistolary strategy is also used in the third section of the novel where the characters exchanging letters are Rosa and her former Barcelonan date Jordi Carrera, an exchange that sets up a structure of parallelism in the novel.) Padilla's last letters are heartbreaking: as he is dying of AIDS, he settles into a new relationship with a woman called Elisa, a small-time heroin dealer who is also infected with AIDS. He goes to see her at the hospital where she is interned and reads her poems by Leopoldo María Panero, a recently deceased Spanish poet who spent long stretches of his life secluded in the Mondragón psychiatric hospital, the same institution to which Elisa undertakes a therapeutic "pilgrimage" at an earlier point in the novel. Elisa is ultimately discharged and surprises Padilla—who did not think he would see her again—by showing up late one night at his building and waiting for him as he comes home drunk and high. The couple end up living together in a "delightful holding pattern" (248). Amalfitano's response is full of concern for his former lover and perhaps too optimistic, as it relates "the giant steps that science was taking in its fight against AIDS" (248). Amalfitano himself undergoes AIDS testing earlier in the novel, but its findings are not disclosed.

Finally an explanation of the title is in order, since some commentators have found it weirdly naive for a Bolaño novel. In Spanish *Woes of the True Policeman* is *Los sinsabores del verdadero policía*, a title in which the word "sinsabores" can mean woes, worries, ups-and-downs, troubles, heartaches, and the like. The translation, therefore, is very much to the point and captures the juvenile connotations of the Spanish original. Explaining the title, furthermore, does not require speculation on who the true policeman is or what his woes are. The last part of the novel does feature several policemen, but their woes are not important. (The policeman—or detective—could actually be the author or reader or even editor of the novel trying to find a way through its jumble of fragments.) What is important is a passage about Arcimboldi's *The Endless Rose,* the only novel by the fictitious French author that Amalfitano translates and one that Padilla encounters by chance in a secondhand bookstore: "Arcimboldi . . . had overnight become a fashionable author in Spain, where they were publishing or about to publish everything he'd written. . . . Even *The Endless Rose* . . . —a difficult and deceptive work despite its apparent simplicity, to the point that sometimes it seemed a book for morons—was already in a second printing" (217). This passage is not only prophetic—since Bolaño would experience the same editorial fate as Arcimboldi does—but also self-referential, since *Woes of the True Policeman* too is a difficult novel masquerading—if one is to judge by its title—as "a book for morons."

Understanding 2666

Like *Woes of the True Policeman,* 2666 was published posthumously and required the expertise of an editor to come into being, but the editor in question, Ignacio Echevarría, confirms that the work was nearly complete when Bolaño died and that very few editorial touches were needed. The one big decision that the editor (and presumably Bolaño's heirs) had to make was whether to publish the 2666 manuscript in bulk or in five separate installments, as the author had suggested shortly before dying. The editorial decision to publish 2666 in one volume (in the hardcover edition) was the correct one, as Bolaño had always wanted to write a mammoth novel and had been working toward that end for years. (Besides, the different parts of the novel can always be reissued separately in the future.) There is an oft-quoted passage in the novel itself that speaks to that intention: "What a sad paradox, thought Amalfitano. Now even bookish pharmacists are afraid to take on the great, imperfect, torrential works, books that blaze paths into the unknown" (227). Bolaño had already written and published several perfect minor works (his equivalent of Kafka's *Metamorphosis* and Melville's *Bartleby*), and now he wanted to try his hand at a work larger even than *The Savage Detectives.* He wanted to write his *Trial* and his *Moby-Dick,* and this is partially what he achieved with 2666. Bolaño always considered literature a dangerous calling and an all-or-nothing proposition.

According to him writers in everyday life had to be prepared to endure the privations that were part and parcel of the business, but also in their work they had to be ready to accept the potential failure or general misunderstanding attendant on risk taking. 2666 is indeed a risky novel, from its cryptic title— a date that never appears in the novel—to its open ending, a trajectory of almost nine hundred pages in which readers have to supply implicit connections and negotiate multiple shifts of tone, characters, settings, and narrative focalization. They also have to tune in to a dark vision of history. The novel is dedicated to Bolaño's two children—his heirs in this world—and has an epigraph by Baudelaire: "An oasis of horror in a desert of boredom." The quote comes from Baudelaire's "Le Voyage," a poem that Bolaño glosses in a mock lecture included in *The Insufferable Gaucho:* "In that line alone there is more than enough. In the middle of a desert of ennui, an oasis of fear, or horror. There is no more lucid diagnosis of the illness of modern humanity. To break out of ennui, to escape from boredom, all we have at our disposal . . . is horror, in other words, evil" ("Literature + Illness = Illness" 138).

The novel is divided into five loosely interconnected books, each of which could stand on its own and belongs to a different genre. "The Part about the Critics" is a variation on the campus novel; "The Part about Amalfitano" is a philosophical thriller; "The Part about Fate" is a Beat road novel; "The Part about the Crimes" is detective fiction; and "The Part about Archimboldi" is a mix of historical fiction and *Künstlerroman* (Deckard 356).[7] The different sections of the novel are of different lengths, and narrative time passes unevenly in them. The part about Fate takes place in only a few days, whereas the parts about the critics and the crimes last years, but not as many as the last part of the novel, which takes place over the protagonist's lifetime going back to 1920. Most of *2666* takes place in the 1990s, except for the many incidents in the part about Archimboldi that return to the beginning of the twentieth century and others that focus on the Second World War. But at the end of the novel Archimboldi's sister ends up in Santa Teresa visiting his imprisoned son Klaus. The year is 2001.

This temporal organization is complemented by a corresponding spatial pattern: the main characters of the novel all converge on Santa Teresa during the rash of women's murders. It is often said that *2666* is Bolaño's stab at the total novel, a form that was at its height during the Latin American Boom of the 1960s and that was practiced and theorized by Mario Vargas Llosa, among others. At this time novels like Carlos Fuentes's *The Death of Artemio Cruz* (1962), Vargas Llosa's *The Green House* (1965), and García Márquez's *One Hundred Years of Solitude* (1967) were put forward as a critical synthesis of Latin American history and culture. The 1970s novels like Fuentes's *Terra Nostra* (1975) and Augusto Roa Bastos's *I the Supreme* (1974) retained the totalizing ambition but pried open the closed systems of their predecessors: heteroglossia replaced synthesis. As for *2666* there's no question that the novel intends to trace an image of evil on a global scale, but totality here comes in parts. The reader is reminded of Amalfitano's reflections in *Woes of the True Policeman* after reading and teaching Hegel, Marx, Plato, Aristotle, and others: "he realized something that in his heart he had always known: that the Whole is impossible, that knowledge is the classification of fragments" (196).

"The Part about the Critics" is mostly about the search for an elusive post-war German writer who goes by the improbable name of Benno von Archimboldi, a pseudonym for Hans Reiter, as some of the characters who are looking for him (together with the readers of the novel) find out when the shadowy quarry is spotted in Mexico City. To the extent that he is sought after by a band of followers, Archimboldi is an avatar of the Cesárea Tinajero of *The Savage Detectives.* But whereas Cesárea is a forgotten poet from an earlier period of the avant-garde (with only one surviving poem to her credit), her German counterpart is a prolific novelist and perennial candidate for the Nobel Prize. Archimboldi keeps publishing one novel after another, but his figure is veiled in mystery: no one knows where he lives, there is no biography dedicated to his person, and his books are published without the standard author photographs on the flaps or back cover. What is known is that he was born in Prussia in 1920, that he is a deserter from the Second World War, and that he is old, tall, and blue-eyed. No one knows why he is in Mexico, and in fact only one witness claims to have seen him. This witness—a Mexican writer-bureaucrat called Almendros and nicknamed "El Cerdo" ("The Pig")—furthermore claims that he took the mysterious guest to the airport and watched him get on a flight to Hermosillo, the capital of the state of Sonora. From there Archimboldi planned to travel to Santa Teresa. When El Cerdo asks the traveler why he is going to that part of the country, the latter responds that he wants to know the place. Or perhaps, El Cerdo speculates, "what he actually said was that he was going to learn something" (104).

The first part of *2666* in particular, and the whole search for Archimboldi through the novel, recalls Borges's "The Approach to Al-Mu'tasim," a story written in 1935 and eventually collected in *Ficciones.* The story pretends to be a review of a real book by a real author but is an elaborate and perfectly executed hoax that convinced at least one of Borges's friends to order a copy from London. The story's outline is described in the text itself: "the tireless search for a human soul through the barely perceptible reflections cast by this soul in others. . . . Al-Mu'tasim's immediate predecessor is a Persian bookseller, an exceptionally happy, courteous man; the one before him, a saint. Finally, after many years, the student comes to a corridor 'at whose end is a door and a cheap beaded curtain, and behind the curtain a shining light'. The student claps his hands once or twice and asks for al-Mu'tasim. A man's voice—the unimaginable voice of al-Mu'tasim—invites him in. The student parts the curtain and steps forward. At this point, the novel ends" (41). Bolaño's version of the story is secular and not mystical. The idea of finding an enlightened prophet by threading one's way through a maze of the mystic's reflections in others is substituted by the conventions of detective fiction. In "The Part about the Critics" searching for Archimboldi involves following clues dropped by people who at some point in time have been briefly in touch with the missing author or who have heard stories about him from others.

Archimboldi's searchers are a quartet of international literary critics who for one reason or another have become obsessed with the writer's work and have resolved to spend their time and resources locating the man behind the novels. The quartet is made up of three men and one woman: the French Pelletier, who discovers Archimboldi as a graduate student in 1980 and eventually becomes the most renowned French specialist on his work; the wheelchair-bound Morini, Archimboldi's Italian translator; the Spaniard Espinoza, who writes a dissertation on Archimboldi in 1990; and the Englishwoman Liz Norton, who becomes the pivot in the literary-romantic kaleidoscope that characterizes much of "The Part of the Critics." All four meet for the first time as a group in Bremen in 1994, the year after the murders begin in Santa Teresa. The "Archimboldian apostles" (99) spend the next few years going from conference to conference and city to city displaying their critical expertise and hoping to find out more about their chosen author, but also working out the romantic feelings that develop among themselves. Both Pelletier and Espinoza are in love with Norton and have sex with her, sometimes simultaneously. In the end, though, the only woman in the group chooses to give herself to the disabled Morini, to the great consternation of her two other lovers. The section actually ends with a letter from Norton to both Pelletier and Espinoza announcing her decision and not with the finding of the ghostly Archimboldi. The search for the missing writer and the love triangle among the critics (three men and a woman) are mutually implicated throughout the first part of *2666*. It's difficult to say which story is embedded in which. At times Pelletier and Espinoza forget Archimboldi because of Liz Norton wheras at others their full attention is focused on their appointed task or on other women they casually meet. At a certain point in the novel, when the stress of the relationship and the frustration of the search get to be too much to handle, Pelletier and Espinoza lose sight of what they are looking for and cease to care (76).

The pursuit of Archimboldi is indeed frustrating. At one of the meetings the critics attend, they become acquainted with a shadowy Swabian writer who had met Archimboldi in some Frisian town just after the war but who does not have any fresh news concerning his present whereabouts. Regardless the critics stay on Archimboldi's trail and pay a visit to the writer's publisher in Hamburg, but after an interview with the owner of the publishing house—Mrs. Bubis—they discover that their quarry had vanished many years earlier and that the money owed him was deposited in a Swiss bank account. Later they receive copies of an article by a Serbian critic tracing a possible itinerary of Archimboldi through several European countries and possibly Morocco but concluding nothing in particular. The most promising clue comes from the above-mentioned El Cerdo, a piece of information that places Archimboldi in Santa Teresa and that motivates the Archimboldians—minus Morini—to fly to Mexico City and later to Hermosillo, thus retracing the possible steps of their quarry. The last fourth of "The Part about the Critics" takes place in Santa Teresa and involves an ultimately fruitless search for Archimboldi, though Pelletier and Espinoza agree that the German hovers like a ghost over the town.

The last fifty pages of the opening section of *2666* feature at least three distinctive narrative clusters that relate to both the search for Archimboldi and the love triangle among the critics: the critics' sojourn in Santa Teresa, the introduction of Amalfitano (the protagonist of the second part of the novel), and Norton's letter to Pelletier and Espinoza explaining her new choice of lover.

Santa Teresa is not a pretty sight for natives or visitors alike. (Norton finds it to be a "horrible place" and leaves early, though she has personal reasons of a different kind to return to Europe.) The narrator maps the city thoroughly: "The western part of the city was very poor, with most streets unpaved and a sea of houses assembled out of scrap. The city center was old, with three- or four-story buildings and arcaded plazas in a state of neglect. . . . To the north were abandoned factories and sheds, and a street of bars and souvenir shops and small hotels, where it was said no one ever slept, and farther out there were more poor neighborhoods . . . , and vacant lots out of which every so often there rose a school. To the south they discovered rail lines and slum soccer fields surrounded by shacks . . . , and, in the distance, the silhouettes of industrial warehouses, the horizon of the maquiladoras" (128–29). A large part of the city's identity, of course, is its location as a border town: "To the north they saw a fence that separated the United States from Mexico and they gazed past it to the Arizona desert" (129). In the novel the border is porous and allows characters to come and go, though in reality the situation is far more restrictive. It should be remarked that Bolaño's notes for *2666* include a detailed and obviously fictional map of the city. (The map is reproduced in the *Archivo Bolaño* 106–7.)

Upon their arrival in the city, Norton, Pelletier, and Espinoza are introduced to Amalfitano, who becomes their guide for a few days. Like Pelletier and Morini, Amalfitano is an Archimboldi translator. He also teaches philosophy at the local university. At first he does not make a good impression on the visitors, who find him stressed out and in a state of nervous exhaustion. He appears as a "castaway, a carelessly dressed man, a nonexistent professor at a nonexistent university" (114). They are also concerned because he is often seen in the company of a handsome young man who happens to be the dean's son, but their fears are assuaged when they realize that the relationship between professor and student is more Socratic than homosexual. Espinoza in particular is concerned about the possibility of a scandal that might lead to shots being fired. They are also flabbergasted when they visit Amalfitano's house and catch sight of a book hanging from a clothesline in the backyard. They whisper among themselves about it, and after realizing that the book is not there to dry, they decide to leave it alone. Espinoza is acquainted with the book, which is by actually existing Galician poet Rafael Dieste. The book, however, is not a collection of poems but the author's *Testamento geométrico,* which makes the whole situation even more puzzling. In the second part of *2666* the scene is somewhat clarified by having the narrator explain its connection to one of Marcel Duchamp's artistic concepts.[8]

Amalfitano takes the searchers around town looking for clues and information about Archimboldi's possible whereabouts, which eventually points them in the direction of the Circo Internacional, one of whose performers is a German magician called Doktor Koenig. Amalfitano suggests the extravagant idea that the magician could be Archimboldi in disguise. The critics look at him "the way students look at the class idiot" (131), but their spirits are so low that they agree to visit the improbable magician, who after all is the first German who has come their way. Doktor Koenig, however, turns out to be an American called Andy López. Readers of Cortázar's *Hopscotch* are bound to remember the circus scenes in that novel and suspect that more is afoot in *2666* than meets the eye. And indeed the circus visit is not there for comic relief. Pelletier asks the magician what he does in his magic act, and the response he gets is that the magician starts by making fleas disappear, then pigeons, then cats, and finally a kid (133). The magician could have expanded his catalog of disappearances by including the women of Santa Teresa, at least two hundred of which had already been murdered when the critics arrive in town. (In an ironic twist, the four critics disappear from *2666* after the first part is over.)

The first reference in the novel to the killings in Sonora occurs early on, long before the Archimboldians have any inkling that they themselves will be visiting the region in their search: "Around this time, Morini was the first of the four to read an article about the killings in Sonora, which appeared in *Il Manifesto* and was written by an Italian reporter who had gone to Mexico to cover the Zapatista guerrillas" (43). At that time the "dead numbered well over one hundred." The Zapatista insurgency took place in Chiapas (at the southern end of Mexico) on January 1, 1994, a date that helps pinpoint the novel's internal chronology. The magnitude of the killing spree hits home with the critics when Pelletier and Espinoza go out partying with a group of students after delivering a talk on Archimboldi and in a fog hear the story of the murdered women: "Then Espinoza remembered that the night before, one of the boys had told them the story of the women who were being killed. . . . First you can't believe it and then you think it's incredible. That was probably what he and Pelletier had said the night before when the boy . . . told them that more than two hundred women had died. But not over a short period of time, thought Espinoza. From 1993 or 1994 to the present day" (137).

The informant adds that there are many suspects in jail but that the murders keep on happening. Someone in the group also speaks the name Albert Kessler, a character that will appear in the third part of the novel and that is the fictionalized version of FBI investigator Robert Ressler, the agent who is credited with coining the term "serial killer." The dark cloud that hangs over the city is very much present in Espinoza's mind during the rest of his sojourn in Santa Teresa. In one of his meanderings through the city Espinoza comes upon an attractive woman who sells rugs in the local crafts market and makes her his lover. One of the places they visit during their affair is a downtown club directly related to the murders: "As they drank Cuba libres, Rebeca told him that two of the girls who later showed up dead had been kidnapped on their way out of the club. Their bodies were dumped in the desert" (151). Obviously Espinoza considers it a bad omen that the killer is a regular at the club. The story about the serial murders is considerably expanded in the fourth part of 2666—Bolaño's acknowledged tour de force—whereas the mystery surrounding the figure of Archimboldi is cleared up in the fifth and final part of the novel, which is an extended account of the writer's life and times.

Before leaving Santa Teresa, Pelletier and Espinoza receive a letter from Norton—the same letter sent separately—informing them of her decision to move in with Morini. In that same letter she also informs them that the painter Edwin Johns has died recently from a fall near the mental facility in Switzerland where the three male Archimboldians had visited him before their trip to Mexico. Johns appears at an earlier point in the novel as a painter whose work puts a run-down London neighborhood on the map and makes it fashionable for artists to move in. Johns achieves his culminating moment of fame when he cuts off his right hand and pastes it on a self-portrait, a kind of collage that sends the painter's stock skyrocketing. Johns is an ambiguous figure in the novel. On the one hand (no pun intended), he admits he mutilated himself for money, but, on the other, he is the painterly version of the poète maudit, of the artist seized by madness who extracts his vision from looking down the abyss. (Johns literally dies from a fall into the abyss: *abismo* in the Spanish original but "ravine" in the English translation, 150.) A standard formulation in Bolaño's discourse on literature is that writing is a dangerous calling and that poets and artists walk on the edge of the abyss.

In *2666* even a translator like Amalfitano is subjected to the dangerous aura of literature, a pursuit that in the novel cannot be separated from the murders happening in Santa Teresa. There is a significant moment in "The Part about the Critics" when Pelletier's and Espinoza's lectures and master class on Archimboldi—staged for the benefit of the local audience—are described in *viscerally* violent terms. The lectures are a *carnicería* in Spanish (but a mere "massacre" in English, 136), and the master class is imparted with a disposition "less like butchers than like gutters or disembowelers" (136).[9] It is as if the real visceralists from *The Savage Detectives* had been reincarnated (like the civilized counterpart of Hahn's butchers) in *2666* to remind the reader that literature exists in the thick of barbarism and is not exempt from its violence. The critics are amazed and moved that their conferences made a few young readers of Archimboldi in the audience cry: "So miracles were possible, after all. The Internet bookstores worked. Culture, despite the disappearances and guilt, was still alive" (136). But these are the same critics that in an early scene of the novel, and for no apparent reason, beat a Pakistani taxi driver to a pulp. It's true that they are shocked by the violence of which they are capable, but the point has already been made: culture contains the seeds of its own negation. As Walter Benjamin famously wrote, there is no document of civilization which is not at the same time a document of barbarism. The dialectic between civilization and barbarism is constantly played out in Bolaño's mature fiction because it's not a simple matter of literature being on the right side and evil on the wrong one. This dialectic, so clearly present in *Distant Star,* reaches its most elaborate formulation in *2666,* a novel in which a scholarly search for a missing author is viscerally linked to a police search for the murderer or murderers of the women of Santa Teresa. The four critics of *2666* are the *civilized* counterpart of the *savage* detectives of Bolaño's previous novel precisely because there is no a priori difference between civilization and barbarism when it comes to the wordly existence of art and literature.

"The Part about Amalfitano" is only about half as long as "The Part about the Critics" and is narrated by the same omniscient narrator who is responsible for the opening section and for the rest of the novel. (In "The Part about the Critics," however, the omniscient narrator at times deposes his objectivity and becomes very cozy with the reader, threatening to become one more character in the novel.)[10] The second part is heavily focused (or focalized) on Amalfitano, and characters like his daughter Rosa and his estranged wife, Lola, are viewed from an external point of view or reveal their interiority through letters. This part of the novel is a concatenation of semiautonomous episodes punctuated and unified by occasional references to the murders. At the beginning of this section it is revealed that Amalfitano has spent only one week in town, which may explain why there are no references anywhere in the second part of the novel to the critics who visit Santa Teresa in the opening section.

The book of Amalfitano is made up of at least four distinctive narrative strands. The first and longest concerns the protagonist's life in Barcelona when he was a professor at the university and was married to Lola. This part of the narrative is mostly told through Lola's letters and focuses on the aftermath of the marriage, a period when Lola (who leaves her husband when their daughter is only two years old)[11] takes to wandering through parts of Spain and France with her friend Imma. Lola's wanderings are an actual pilgrimage. Initially Lola directs her steps to the Mondragón asylum, where her favorite poet (a fictionalized version of Spanish poet Leopoldo María Panero) has been interned for a long time. When she finally gets to see the poet, she blurts out her far-fetched plan to help him escape from the asylum and cross into France "like pilgrims" (172). Then they can live like "mendicants or child prophets" (172), an implicit reference to Schwob's *The Children's Crusade* (1896). Lola's pilgrimage to Mondragón—a place located in Spain's Basque Country—echoes the critics' "pilgrimage" to Santa Teresa in the first part of 2666. Both the mad poet and Archimboldi are the objects of a cult. The critics are in pursuit of Archimboldi because to them he is a living myth who is getting old and nearing death. Lola has a different motivation to get close to the poet. She sees him as a lost child and wants to mother him, though at other times she wants to be his lover despite the rumors that the poet is homosexual. Later, at any rate, Lola makes it to France, and specifically to Lourdes, where she helps the disabled, blind, and terminally ill pilgrims get off the train as if she were "a nun in jeans stationed there by the church" (180). Lola's name—short for Dolores, the Mater Dolorosa—inscribes the character's vocation for Christian charity. (Her friend's name—Imma, short for Inmaculada—reinforces the Christian connotations.) As an auxiliary figure, Lola recalls the Auxilio Lacouture of *Amulet,* the mother of Mexican poetry. Like a heroic nun assisting lepers in earlier times, Lola contracts that modern form of leprosy which is AIDS and goes back to Barcelona to say her final goodbye to Amalfitano seven years after leaving him. Lola's letters are a veritable road novel, a narrative form that will reappear in "The Part about Fate."

The transition between the Lola sequence and the next one is a brief, two-line paragraph, the first part of which is: "The University of Santa Teresa was like a cemetery that suddenly begins to think, in vain" (185). Not by chance Lola has been sleeping in a niche in the Mondragón cemetery and making love to a local acquaintance that enjoys taking her in the grave where his mother is buried. When Amalfitano reads this in a letter he can think only that madness is contagious. Lola is not a mother to her daughter—whom she briefly sees only before going off to die—but behaves like a mother with the mad poet, the desperate throng at Lourdes and—symbolically—with the necrophiliac Basque. On the other hand, asylums, hospitals, and cemeteries figure abundantly in Bolaño's writing.

The second extended sequence of "The Part about Amalfitano" seems extravagant at first sight but is easily integrated into the symbolic fabric of Bolaño's writing, where notions such as *intemperie* (the elements) and visceralism play a significant role. The narrative concerns a geometry book by poet Rafael Dieste (1899–1981) that Amalfitano unexpectedly finds in a box after his move to Santa Teresa and hangs from a clothesline in his yard in order to expose it to the elements. The narrator attributes the idea to Marcel Duchamp, who visited Buenos Aires between 1918 and 1919, and who wrote a letter to his sister and her brand-new husband in Paris instructing them to hang a geometry book by a string on the balcony of their apartment so that the wind could choose its own problems and tear out the pages. This was Duchamp's wedding gift for the couple, a ready-made that exists only in a photograph and a painting. At this point in the novel Bolaño is quoting New York art critic Calvin Tomkins, who in turn quotes Duchamp when he says that "he had liked disparaging 'the seriousness of a book full of principles,' and suggested that in its exposure to the weather, 'the treatise seriously got the facts of life'" (191). So Dieste's book hangs in Amalfitano's yard like a cryptic philosophical symbol until the elements have their way with it. The geometric figures of Dieste's book migrate to Amalfitano's own class notes where they get mixed up with all manner of philosophers and philosophical schools, from Scholasticism to phenomenology. (Amalfitano teaches philosophy at the university.) The list of philosophers (and theologians, psychoanalysts, and artists) that buzz around the edges of Amalfitano's weird geometrical constructs includes St. Bonaventure, Saint Augustine, Schopenhauer, Husserl, Merleau-Ponty, Freud, Lacan, Wittgenstein, and many others.

One main point about this bizarre narrative sequence is that the book is really the work of a poet and poets in Bolaño's conception are never more admirable than when they live their lives *a la intemperie* and without any material resources, just their bravery and their own particular brand of heroism. A related point is that the book exposed to the elements is a moral lesson about the fusion of art and life and a reminder that art draws its roots from "the facts of life," and cannot settle for mere formalism. This is the same lesson imparted by the real visceralists in *The Savage Detectives* and by their real-life counterparts, the Mexican infrarealists of the mid-1970s. Despite its obvious debt to surrealism, infrarealism was a program for living life in the underbelly of the real, not above reality, as the term "surrealism" implies; a program for living on the edge, where life "happens" with greater intensity than in settled mainstream communities. Santa Teresa, of course, is both a city on the (northern) edge (of Mexico) and a city "on edge" as a result of the serial killings that resonate throughout the whole novel and in each of its parts. Despite all this, however, geometric reason plays an important role in restoring Amalfitano's always precarious mental balance as he copes with the experience of living in Santa Teresa: "When they got home it was dark but the shadow of Dieste's book hanging from the clothesline was clearer, steadier, more reasonable, thought Amalfitano, than anything they'd seen on the outskirts of Santa Teresa or in the city itself, images with no handhold, images freighted with all the orphan-hood in the world, fragments, fragments" (206). In this sense the book is a *vox clamantis in deserto*, like that of John the Baptist in the New Testament.[12] Like the city Amalfitano too is a character on edge—always worried about losing his mind and about the safety of his daughter Rosa when she goes out in Santa Teresa—but also on *the* edge between homosexuality and heterosexuality.

Amalfitano starts to hear voices in another of the narrative strands of this section. The haunting voice is an inner voice that originates in the character's Chilean past (those "cracks in the psyche," 201), one that aggressively brings up the topic of his possible homosexuality, and one that Amalfitano interprets as an auditory hallucination or a schizophrenic breakdown. Readers may interpret the intrusion of the fatherly voice as a reference to Shakespeare's *Hamlet*. This ghostly phenomenon haunts the character for days—or nights—on end. At one point the voice identifies itself as Amalfitano's father and questions his son's life choices—his sexual orientation, his move to Santa Teresa, his agitation. But throughout the sequence the voice is in a consistent counterpoint with the image of Dieste's book hanging from the clothesline, a counterpoint that signals an implicit contest between reason and madness.

Two points should be made regarding the homosexual theme in this section of the novel. The first is that the inquisitive voice claims not be homophobic but, on the contrary, to feel "boundless admiration for certain poets who had professed such sexual leanings" (207–8); and the second is that readers of *Woes of the True Policeman* have a different interpretation of how Amalfitano lost his job at the University of Barcelona and ended up at the University of Santa Teresa. (Those who have read only *2666* have to settle for Amalfitano's vague explanation of the event, namely that his contract had expired.) Homosexuality is not a deluded invention of the voice but is suggested in "The Part about Amalfitano" through the ambiguous relationship between Amalfitano and dean Guerra's son, though the gay theme is considerably attenuated in *2666* in comparison with its explicit development in *Woes of the True Policeman*. Amalfitano is bothered by the voice's ostensible homophobia but denies being homosexual. This theme, however, is inscribed in the cryptic and compounded nature of the character's name, which may be decoded as a portmanteau word containing several units of meaning: *Amalfi* (the southern Italian location from where the protagonist's family emigrated to Chile), *mal* (evil), Malfi (as in John Webster's 1612 play *The Duchess of Malfi*, a macabre tragedy in which there is a severed hand, as there is in "The Part of the Critics"), *tano* (an Italian from Neapolitan—*napolitano*—background in South America), and *ano* (anus). The voice, at any rate, is a device that shows the struggle between Amalfitano and his inner demons, a struggle that is concurrently staged in the wasteland of Santa Teresa, a place haunted by its own demons.

The "cracks of the psyche" that propitiate the traumatic return of the protagonist's nationality—now no longer exclusively rooted in a family genealogy but in Chilean history itself—are explored further in the last sequence of "The Part about Amalfitano." This sequence concerns a bizarre book and story that strikes Amalfitano as "extremely odd" (217). The story features telepathic Mapuches (the Indians of southern Chile, also known as Araucanians), a far-fetched kinship between Mapuches and ancient Greeks, and an extravagant theory that Bernardo O'Higgins, Chile's independence hero, was the legitimate offspring of his historically recognized father (Ambrosio O'Higgins, governor of Chile and viceroy of Peru) and an Araucanian woman. (Official history describes the father of the Chilean nation as the illegitimate son of Don Ambrosio and a Spanish woman called Isabel Riquelme.) The source of these deranged fantasies is a dubious but actually existing book by a certain Lonko Kilapán who presents himself as "Historian of the Race," "President of the Indigenous Confederation of Chile," and "Secretary of the Academy of Araucanian Language." The book is called *O'Higgins es araucano* and was published in Santiago by Universitaria in 1978, a year when the military were very much in power and bent on passing legislation that would make them immune to prosecution for the human rights abuses committed since the coup of 1973. Amalfitano is cognizant of the fact that Kilapán's book was published during the military dictatorship and deduces from that fact "the atmosphere of triumph, loneliness, and fear in which it was published" (223). Although it's easy to hear Bolaño's voice speaking through his character in this section of the novel, the gloss on Kilapán's book contains two motifs that relate it to the fictional plane. One is the reference to telepathy, which explicitly evokes the auditory hallucinations of the previous narrative sequence; and the other, the hypothetical Araucanian ceremony of Gapitun (an abduction ceremony), which strikes Amalfitano as a macabre joke pointing to rape and as a "further mockery staged by fat Ambrosio to fuck the Indian woman in peace" (217). The allusion to rape evokes the rape and murders of the women of Santa Teresa that so disturb the city's law-abiding citizens.

Kilapán's delusions concerning the origin of the Chilean nation are contagious. After a while Amalfitano speculates that the Indigenous Confederation of Chile and the Academy of the Araucanian Language were fictitious entities, and that the real author of *O'Higgins es araucano* was not the equally fictitious Lonko Kilapán but perhaps General Pinochet himself posing as a native writer. At one point in the story the narrator says that the book's footnotes "made it very clear in what kind of drunken ship Kilapán had set sail" (222), a passage that should've been translated as "drunken boat" in order to trigger the reference to Rimbaud's visionary poem intended by the original Spanish. Later the narrator invokes Cortázar's notion of the active reader to justify the wild speculations that Amalfitano engages in when he is entranced by Kilapán's equally outrageous historical fantasies. The reference to Cortázar is not haphazard since chapters 129 and 133 of *Hopscotch* discuss the delirious writings of a certain Ceferino Piriz, a Uruguayan counterpart of the Chilean Kilapán, both enlightened madmen. When *Hopscotch* was initially published in 1963 many readers assumed that the extravagant author of the treatise admired and simultaneously mocked in those chapters had to be fictitious given the obsessiveness of his meticulously detailed project to organize world affairs and achieve universal peace. But it turned out that Ceferino was not as fictitious as the remote authors of the Chinese encyclopedia "quoted" by Borges in his essay on John Wilkins,[13] whose classification of the animal kingdom was no less demented than the Uruguayan philosopher's attempts to classify every aspect of human behavior that had any possible bearing on geopolitical organization. Bolaño's Kilapán sequence is nothing less than an intertextual mirror of certain passages from *Hopscotch,* a novel that Bolaño unconditionally admired.

"The Part about Fate" introduces a new character in the novel, an African American journalist who writes about black culture and black politics but who is sent to Mexico to cover a boxing match when the sportswriter for the newspaper where he works is killed by a jealous husband. The section opens with the death of Fate's mother from natural causes followed by Fate's trip to Detroit to interview Barry Seaman, a fictionalized version of Bobby Seale, founder of the Black Panthers in the 1960s. During the interview Seaman talks about the Panthers' deceased cofounder, a certain Marius Newell, a fictional stand-in for Huey Newton, who was shot to death in 1989. The Black Panthers may be considered the U.S. version of the Latin American guerrillas that operated throughout the region in the 1960s and that are noticeably absent in *2666*. But Bolaño's approach to black revolution blunts the violence associated with the revolutionary movement: Barry Seaman is viewed as a peacetime preacher and author of a cookbook (that in actual fact is called *Barbeque'n with Bobby*); both Seaman and Marius are explicitly linked to the sea, even through their names; and the former states that a mother is worth more than the black revolution. But, as the reader knows, the violence in *2666* cannot be deferred for long.

Before buying a ticket for Tucson and driving from there to the Mexican border to cover the boxing match, Fate falls asleep watching TV in a hotel room and misses a news report from Santa Teresa about a disappeared American woman. (The name of the victim—Lucy Anne Sanders—will be revealed in the fourth part of the novel, starting on page 406.) On the road to Mexico Fate stops to eat at a restaurant and overhears a conversation about serial killers. The speaker expounding on the topic is a white-haired man who is referred to as Professor Kessler by his interlocutor. Kessler is the fictionalized version of

Robert K. Ressler, the FBI criminologist who—as was mentioned earlier in this chapter—coined the term "serial killer." At the invitation of the local authorities, Ressler made two consulting trips to Ciudad Juárez in 1997 and 1998 and was impressed with the diligence of the Mexican investigators but also with their lack of experience regarding the kinds of cases they were called on to investigate. Kessler too is on his second trip to Bolaño's fictional version of Ciudad Juárez, but his recomemndation is that everyone in town head out into the desert and cross the border in a northern direction (267). (The fictionalization of real names and the use of pseudonyms and homonyms for imaginary characters is a constant in Bolaño's fiction. Thus "Kessler" is Ressler; "Santa Teresa" is Ciudad Juárez; the murdered women of Ciudad Juárez have made-up names in the fourth part of the novel; the "real" name of Oscar Fate is Quincy Williams, just as Archimboldi's "real" name is Hans Reiter; Oscar Fate shares his first name with Oscar Amalfitano; and there are two Rosas in the third part of *2666*.)

Upon arriving in Santa Teresa, Fate makes contact with local journalists and other personages who introduce him to the city and soon starts to develop a greater interest in the murders than in the fight he's supposed to cover. Two of the locals are Chucho Flores, a journalist who tells Fate about the serial murders, and Charly Cruz, who owns a chain of video stores and discusses movies like Robert Rodríguez's *El mariachi* and *From Dusk Till Dawn* with the guest journalist. (The reference to the latter movie is ironic because Fate writes for a Harlem publication called "Black Dawn.")[14] Fate also meets Guadalupe Roncal, a journalist from the capital who is in Santa Teresa to write about the crimes. After the fight Fate goes out with a group of Flores's friends and meets Rosa Amalfitano, with whom he develops a trusting relationship. The group makes its way from nightclub to nightclub and ends up at Cruz's house, which resembles a porno movie studio. As the revelers watch a vicious porno movie, Fate senses danger, knocks down a pair of bodyguards, and flees with Rosa Amalfitano to her father's house. He promises Amalfitano to help Rosa cross the border to the United States so that she can eventually take a flight to Barcelona and resettle there, which is what Amalfitano had wished for his daughter in the second part of the novel.

On the way to the border with Rosa, Fate stops by the local prison accompanied by the journalist from the capital to interview one of the murder suspects, a German "albino giant" who surreptitiously introduces the Archimboldi theme in a part of the novel where the German author is noticeably missing in action. The reader will not know the prisoner's identity until the next part of the novel—where he is identified as Klaus Haas, Archimboldi's nephew—but it is clear already that the serial murders cannot be atributed to any one single killer since Kessler himself states that they have different signatures. Regardless the suspect is described in larger-than-life terms. He is brought out of his cell in the middle of a rare electric storm, and his approaching footsteps are like those of a giant: "When Fate heard footsteps approaching he thought they were the footsteps of a giant. . . . And then an enormous and very blond man came into the visitors' room, ducked his head . . . , and smiled as if he had done something naughty, singing the German song about the lost woodcutter and fixing them all with an intelligent and mocking gaze" (348–49).

The last few fragments of "The Part about Fate" are an oneiric montage that alternates between Fate and Rosa's trip to Tucson and their visit—along with Guadalupe Roncal, the reporter—to the Santa Teresa penitentiary where Roncal is set to interview the foreign inmate. The interview is left in suspense at this point in the novel (its substance will be revealed over two hundred pages later), but the reporter's words are an ominous interpretation of the crimes: "No one pays attention to these killings, but the secret of the world is hidden in them" (348).

"The Part about the Crimes" is the great tour de force of *2666* and one of the most intense and sustained pieces of writing in Latin American fiction. Forensic prose is not a complete stranger to Latin American narrative—we may remember precursors such as García Márquez's *Chronicle of a Death Foretold* and Sergio Ramírez's *Castigo divino* ("Divine Punishment")—but the compulsive repetition, deadpan style, and meticulous detail with which Bolaño renders the serial killings of Santa Teresa deserve credit for breaking new narrative ground. To expand on some points made earlier in this book, "The Part about the Crimes" is a fictional rendition of the "femicides" that began—or began to be documented—in January 1993 in Ciudad Juárez, Chihuahua, and that have continued into the twenty-first century. Bolaño never visited Juárez, but his reconstruction of the city as "Santa Teresa" in *2666* is utterly convincing. Even though Bolaño's imaginary city is not located in the state of Chihuahua but in the neighboring state of Sonora, Juárez and Santa Teresa are border cities (the former lying across from El Paso and the latter across from Tucson) that struggle with similar issues: they both attract hundreds of thousands of young women from all parts of Mexico to work in the assembly factories; they are both a magnet for many other Mexicans—men and women—who come to border towns hoping to cross the border into the United States; and they are both riddled with drug traffickers powerful enough to corrupt the local police, government officials, and judiciary. Previously existing border violence, fueled by a constant supply of weapons coming in from the United States, misogyny, machismo, the fluid nature of the local population, and criminal impunity are among the causes adduced by the experts who attempt to explain the crimes, which by 2003 had reached the figure of 328. The victims were young maquiladora workers, students, single mothers, waitresses, strippers, and prostitutes, and they were often tortured and raped (anally and vaginally) before being killed. A few of these women were victims of domestic violence, but the majority was murdered by unknown assailants, possibly including two or more serial killers.

Santa Teresa, furthermore—and by extension Ciudad Juárez—is not just the border between Mexico and the United States. It is also the border between the third world and the world of globalization. As Fate tells his boss in the third part of the novel, writing about the women being killed in Santa Teresa is tantamount to drafting a "sketch of the industrial landscape of the third world . . . , a *reportage* about the current situation in Mexico, a panorama of the border [and] a serious crime story" (295) In *2666* Bolaño absorbs and dispatches in his own way two popular subgenres of contemporary Mexican literature: the literature of the drug trade (*narcoliteratura*) and border fiction. Despite its historical reach, *2666* is very much a novel of the present in which the year 2000 is qualified by the number 666, the "cipher of the Antichrist," as one critic puts it (Elmore 261). Thus Bolaño's chronicle of the present time acquires a visionary dimension. Because of the time of composition, *2666* is a millennial novel, and Bolaño takes advantage of the symbolic transition from one millennium to another to endow his novel with an apocalytic vision.

It has been shown that Bolaño changed the names of the hundred plus victims whose deaths are recounted in this section of the novel, but it is also a matter of record that he kept and adapted many of the actual details of the murders of each one of them (Andrews 205–29).[15] Bolaño's main source of information was the research into the murders carried out by Mexican journalist Sergio González Rodríguez, whose book *Huesos en el desierto* ("Bones in the Desert")—the final result of years of investigation—appeared when Bolaño was busy working on his final novel. The last chapter of *Huesos en el desierto* includes an extensive list of victims together with the police reports detailing their deaths. This chapter is the literal source of Bolaño's serial narration of the crimes. (An updated adaptation of the book in English that excludes the final chapter was published by the MIT Press in 2012 with the title *The Femicide Machine*.) Bolaño had started a correspondence with González years before the reporter's book came out and finally had a chance to meet him in November 2002 when González went to Barcelona to attend the launching of his book (Valdés 33). According to González, Bolaño was particularly interested in the minutest details of the murders, in the ways the narcos operated in Ciudad Juárez (down to what cars they drove and what weapons they used), in the way murder cases were written up, and in the mentality of the local police. According to the same source, Bolaño would have preferred that a rational mind like that of Robert K. Ressler had been able to solve the case, as he preferred that there would have been only one serial killer (Valdés 29–32). As it is he was forced to adapt his novel to reality and vice versa without ever losing sight that he was writing a fiction based on the murders and not a nonfiction piece of investigative journalism similar to that of his informant.[16]

Sergio González Rodríguez appears with his full name as a character in "The Part about the Crimes" (376–79), but it would be naive to mistake him for the actual author of *Huesos en el desierto*. In the novel he is sent by the newspaper that he works for in Mexico City to Santa Teresa in order to write the story of the Penitent, a minor criminal who specializes in desecrating churches and whose story is interspersed in this part of *2666* with the larger story of the femicides. When González arrives in town he gets a room at a cheap hotel called El Oasis—an obvious reference to the epigraph by Baudelaire that precedes the text of the novel. He sets up an interview with the detective in charge of the Penitent's case, an honest policeman by the name of Juan de Dios Martínez—a name that happens to be a heteronym of Chilean poet Juan Luis Martínez (1942–93), the almost secret author of an experimental poetic work from the late 1970s ironically called *La nueva novela* (Santiago: Ediciones Archivo, 1985).

Thus González's function in the novel is to guarantee not its veracity but merely its verisimilitude. Bolaño introduces him in "The Part about the Crimes" because of his real-life credentials but uses his biographical existence and journalistic profession for an opposite purpose, namely to separate fact from fiction. The Penitent too is a fictional creation—like many of the novel's secondary characters—that helps contextualize the serial killings and makes part 4 of the novel more diverse and less monotonous. Yet the background information provided in this part of the novel is far from digressive. Everything relates to the central motif of the femicides. Thus the Penitent is a character who incarnates collective guilt—not just the guilt of the murderers but also that of the citizens and authorities who accept the status quo. Lalo Cura, on the other hand, is an orphan (his maternal name is Expósito—"foundling," in English) that represents the Mexican *desmadre*—the general condition of orphanhood that leaves the "children" of the nation in a permanent state of helplessness. In the specific case of Lalo Cura, furthermore, the character is *exposed* to violence, since his fate is to be first the *sicario* (henchman) of a drug lord and later a policeman. (His name is also a pun on the madness that reigns in Santa Teresa—"la locura.") Another secondary character is the seer Florita Almada, a septuagenarian who goes on endlessly about diets, herbs, and the mortal condition but who on a TV show is suddenly possessed by a vision of the murders of Santa Teresa: "It's Santa Teresa! It's Santa Teresa! Women are being killed there. They are killing my daughters. My daughters!" (436). Even the one suicide victim to be found among the 109 women who die of violent causes in "The Part about the Crimes" is related to the murders because she leaves an unaddressed letter in her desk explaining her action as a response to what's going on in Santa Teresa with all "those dead girls" (517).

Perhaps it is not necessary to stress that the structural integrity of Bolaño's fiction is not limited to this section or, indeed, to this novel. His work as a whole is a chamber of resonances, a system of echoes, watchfulness, and affinities—to quote Borges's definition of tightly controlled fiction in his essay "Narrative Art and Magic." Thus the Lalo Cura episode that culminates on page 399 is an alternative version of the Pancho Monge episode related in *Woes of the True Policeman*; and the seer Florita Almada—also referred to as La Santa—is a structural avatar of Amalfitano's estranged wife, Lola, in the second part of *2666:* "La Santa understands Hermosillo's unfortunates better than anyone, La Santa has a feeling for those who've been hurt, for sensitive and abused children, for those who've been raped and humiliated . . . , the freaks feel like divas when she speaks to them, the scatterbrained feel sensible, the fat lose weight, the AIDS patients smile" (434). In "The Part about Amalfitano" Lola undertakes a pilgrimage and becomes a healing figure; in "The Part about the Crimes" Florita's followers approach her like "a procession of penitents" (433) in search of healing. Penitents and penitentiaries, of course, are closely related. Last but not least, one of the murders takes place in a subdivision just past Colonia Lindavista, the neighborhood where Amalfitano and Rosa live in the second part of the novel—a neighborhood, furthermore, where a mysterious black "Peregrino"—a nonexistent brand of car or SUV—roams at night and keeps a threatening watch on the dwellers' activities. This car shows up in other parts of the novel as well. *2666* is full of these kinds of echoes and connections that crisscross its nine hundred pages in the English translation and that often extend beyond the confines of the novel.

The last two hundred pages of "The Part about the Crimes" are structured as a counterpoint between the main story of the chapter—the serial killings of women—and various other narrative strands focused on the investigation but taking an angular approach to it, mainly those of the presumed criminal Klaus Haas, the reporter Sergio González, and the former FBI investigator Albert Kessler. The reader has to presume that the events making up these interlaced narratives occur prior to the time when the critics from the first part of the novel visit the city, since in 1997 the Archimboldians are still in Europe. And by the time Morini reads about the crimes in Santa Teresa, these have already surpassed the one hundred mark, which is close to the total number of deaths recorded by Bolaño's narrator until December 1997. Needless to say none of the critics appear in "The Part about the Crimes." Neither does Fate, who visits Santa Teresa when Lucy Anne Sanders is reported missing. Her body is found in the early months of 1994, which must be the year when Rosa Amalfitano leaves

Santa Teresa for Barcelona and thus disappears from the story. Her father stays in town but fails to reappear in the rest of the novel.

Any one of the 109 semifictionalized medical examiner reports that make up the narrative substance of this part of the novel would serve to illustrate its dominant style, for example this one: "Four days later, the mutilated corpse of Beatriz Concepción Roldán appeared by the side of the Santa Teresa–Cananea highway. The cause of death was a gash that sliced her open from navel to chest, presumably inflicted with a machete or big knife. Beatriz Concepción Roldán was twenty-two, five foot five, thin, and dark-skinned. She had long hair half-way down her back. She worked as a waitress in Madero-Norte and she lived with Evodio Cifuentes and his sister" (494). The first thing to note is the temporal indication of the murder or—more commonly—of the finding of the body, which in other passages of the novel consists of the specific date and time when the victim's case became part of the police record. In a sense, "The Part about the Crimes" is a grisly chronology of life and death in Santa Teresa from January 1993 until December 1997. The narrator even includes dates when no crimes were reported and no bodies were found: "In July 1994 no woman died, but a man showed up asking questions" (414).

This "toggle" approach to positive and negative dates—to dates, in other words, when victims did or did not disappear, or when bodies were or were not found—is another way in which Bolaño introduces variations on a fixed scheme and avoids the monotony of serial narration. At the same time, his emphasis on chronology brings the novel closer to the *crónica roja* (police blotter) format—the section in newspapers reporting on the crimes of the day. This is a limited format that Bolaño skillfully stretches to the maximum and complements with other kinds of information—the side stories and what goes on behind closed doors—to create a dense narrative fiction. The ending of "The Part about the Crimes" is particularly effective both as crónica roja and fictional construct. The narrator details the last case of 1997 and ends the chapter by subtly interpreting the preceding three hundred pages through the metaphor of the black hole: "The Christmas holidays in Santa Teresa were celebrated in the usual fashion. There were *posadas* [a Mexican Christmas tradition remembering Mary and Joseph's wanderings through the streets of Bethlehem in search of lodging], piñatas were smashed, tequila and beer were drunk. Even on the poorest streets people could be heard laughing. Some of these streets were completely dark, like black holes" (633). This description evokes the scene in *Amulet* where the date 2666 makes its only appearance in Bolaño's writing other than in the title of his final novel.

The murder of a raped and strangled seventeen-year-old provides clues that lead one of the local investigators to Klaus Haas, the chief suspect of "The

Part about the Crimes" and a fictionalized version of an Egyptian man called Abdul Latif Sharif, who was the chief suspect of the Mexican police during a particularly intense stretch of the crime epidemic. Like Klaus Haas, Sharif was tall, had green eyes (Haas does not specifically have green eyes but is blond and has white eyebrows), spoke Spanish with a foreign accent, and had lived in Florida, where he had been convicted of rape and done time in prison (Haas is accused of attempted rape in Tampa). And Like Bolaño's fictional suspect, the real suspect of the Mexican police called for a press conference in which he accused a pair of rich Mexican cousins of committing the Juárez murders. Both Haas and Sharif, furthermore, were accused of delegating killings to a gang of teenagers: the Bisontes, in the case of the fictional German, the Rebels in the case of the Egyptian. The gangs were the authorities' way of explaining why the killings continued while the chief suspects were in prison.

The story of Klaus Haas belongs to the genre of prison narratives and is characterized by several episodes of sadistic cruelty, as well as by the paradoxical "freedom" the character enjoys to set up his own press conferences and air his point of view on the femicides. At one of these conferences Haas declares his innocence, and at a later one—as remarked above—he inculpates a pair of rich Mexican cousins as the material authors of the crimes. These conferences are scandalous since Haas is a prison inmate. He gets away with them because he has the protection of a powerful drug lord who is also incarcerated and is the true boss of the prison. This inmate continues to manage his affairs from inside with complete impunity. Narcos, policemen, and government officials are all part of the same spider web in Santa Teresa, but Bolaño is careful to give credit to the investigative work and honesty of some of the members of the local police force, thus retaining a glimmer of hope that the atrocities of the city can produce a redeeming hero or some kind of moral regeneration. Despite the character's protestations to the contrary, the narrative is handled in such a way that the reader cannot but suspect that Haas has some involvement in the murders, though its extent is never disclosed. *2666* does not provide the closure delivered by shorter novels like *Distant Star* and *By Night in Chile*. Bolaño is less interested in the solution of a criminal puzzle than in exposing the "secret of evil." Klaus is eventually convicted in a trial that lasts twenty days but only of the murder of four women. A year later, the trial is annulled, a new trial is scheduled and postponed, and ultimately the case is in a deadlock. Sharif died in prison waiting for trial that never materialized.

González and Haas run into each other at the time of the latter's first press conference, but their paths soon diverge. The reporter is committed to collecting information on the crimes in order to write an article exposing them in one of the newspapers of the capital. Apart from attending Haas's conference, he interviews a police inspector, the mother of one of the victims, the head of

Santa Teresa's Department of Sex Crimes (who points out that the male-female ratio of killings in Mexico is ten to one whereas in Santa Teresa it's ten to four), and the seer Florita Almada, a "charlatan with a heart of gold" (571). Later, and back in Mexico City, González is contacted by a feminist PRI congresswoman (the PRI was the Mexican ruling party until 2000) who takes him to her house and tells him a long rambling story about a childhood friend who is reported missing in Santa Teresa after getting mixed up with a powerful banker who launders money for drug traffickers. This character introduces the political theme in the chapter, though she does so belatedly. The PRI is viewed as another source of power whose adherents are often mixed up in the networks of corruption that stretch throughout the territory of Mexico. Of greater significance the feminist congresswoman incarnates the spirit of revenge associated with the Furies of Greek mythology and reawakened by the extent of the Santa Teresa atrocities: "As I learned about other cases . . . , as I heard other voices, my rage began to assume what you might call mass stature, my rage became collective . . . , my rage . . . saw itself as the instrument of vengeance of thousands of victims" (626).

Sergio González is not portrayed as a detective or private investigator in these pages and is, therefore, not charged with finding the criminal or criminals. This is true of both the real and fictional character. (In fact González's fictional background includes writing a novel and an article on Latin American fiction.) Kessler is more involved with the search for the criminal, but he is officially invited to the city to give a professional training course to a select group of officers and not to solve the serial killings. In some circles the invitation—precisely dated at the end of July 1997—raises questions about the competence of the Mexican police and stirs nationalist resentment. Kessler promises a local woman that he will try to stop the killings, but most of the detective's activities in Santa Teresa are of a social, gastronomical, or academic nature, even if at one point he hires a taxi driver to do some field work in the slums and in the desolate areas around the maquiladoras. Kessler gives a standing-room-only keynote address on crime detection at the University of Santa Teresa that recalls the lecture or master class on Archimboldi given by the critics in the opening section of the novel. His prestige in town—unlike those of the critics, who impress only the university's academic audience—is that of a visiting movie star. And yet Kessler's lecture and the critics' pronouncements on Archimboldi are parallel activities that restate the unifying theme of *2666*, namely the correlation between the search for a disappeared author and the tracking down of the unknown criminal responsible for the disappearance and murder of hundreds of women. The same theme is reinscribed in the facts associated with the Negrete twins, one of which is the chief of police of Santa Teresa while the other is the rector of the local university. The intellectual and criminal spheres of social life are intertwined in their story. (Pedro and Pablo Negrete, incidentally, are Bolaño's version of the Pedro and Pablo Vicario of García Márquez's *Chronicle of a Death Foretold*.)

For the most part, the figures of cult author and criminal approach each other only asymptotically in the novel but at one point they come dangerously close to being one and the same. This happens in the passage (in "The Part about Archimboldi," a few pages before the end of the novel) where Klaus's grandmother confuses her grandson with her own son Hans, Klaus's uncle (Benno von Archimboldi, to the readers of German literature). Granted that this is only a hallucination produced by morphine, but also Lotte sees Klaus as a miniature version of her brother: "They called him Klaus . . . , although at some point Lotte thought about calling him Hans, after her brother. . . . Sometimes she looked at him and saw a resemblance to her brother, as if Klaus were Hans's reincarnation in miniature" (872). Klaus himself is not immune to envisioning his uncle as some kind of giant coming to deliver him, as the following passage from "The Part about the Crimes" demonstrates: "a giant is coming and a giant is going to kill you. . . . A big man, very big, and he's going to kill you and everybody else. . . . Haas called out to say he heard footsteps. The giant was coming. He was covered in blood from head to toe and he was coming now" (481–82). This giant, which may derive from a fairy tale by Hans Christian Andersen, is none other than Archimboldi, who has killed a man and experienced the holocaust of World War II, which is why he is covered in blood from head to toe. Throughout the novel it seems that the second coming is at hand or has already arrived. But Bolaño never elucidates the identity (or identification) of author and criminal. The former disappears behind his work; the latter, behind his crimes.

Carmen Pérez de Vega, Bolaño's companion in the last years of his life, affirms that Bolaño wrote "The Part about Archimboldi" first and that he suspended work on *2666* in February 2003, just a few months before he died in July of that year (Maristain, *Bolaño: A Biography* 212). She implies, furthermore, that Bolaño was working on "The Part about the Crimes" when he was forced to stop work on the novel as a result of his deteriorating health, and that he left it unfinished. Although Bolaño had enough strength left to write two more stories and complete *The Insufferable Gaucho* before he died, he could not survive the last relapse of his chronic illness and ran out of time to revise and finish *2666*, as he had intended. We can surmise, therefore, that though *2666* remained unfinished, "The Part about Archimboldi" is complete.

The last book of *2666* closes the circle opened at the outset of the novel. It recounts in detail the whole biography of Archimboldi, beginning in Prussia in 1920 when the future author and soldier of the Reich is born (as Hans Reiter) and ending over eighty years later as the protagonist—now known for decades as Benno von Archimboldi—makes ready to get on a flight from Germany to Mexico. The biographical details exhaust the meaning of the character because it is impossible to compose a coherent profile of Archimboldi's second self, a profile, that is, of Archimboldi as the author of a number of narrative works that reflect not one but many—and many disparate—images of their author.

Hans is born to a couple made up of a veteran of the First World War—who comes home missing a leg—and a one-eyed mother. Are these characters modern incarnations of Oedipus and a cyclops? There are more than enough references to Greek mythology scattered throughout Bolaño's works to endorse this interpretation. The cyclops was a member of the primeval race of giants, and Hans is described precisely as a forest giant throughout the novel. The Oedipus myth, on the other hand, is related to the incest taboo; the avoidance of incest explains why Hans's friend Hugo Halder, the son of Prussian Baron Von Zumpe, rushes away from his father's country estate every time his cousin Anna shows up with her festive friends. (The passages that take place at the baron's manor beginning on page 652 are intertextually woven with two notable novels of Boom writers: *A House in the Country* by José Donoso, and *One Hundred Years of Solitude* by Gabriel García Márquez. Halder could easily be the Aureliano Babilonia of García Márquez's masterpiece, and Anna his incestuous lover Amaranta Úrsula.)

In 1933, the year Hitler rises to power, Hans drops out of school and is put to work as a servant in Baron Von Zumpe's country estate. There he meets the Baroness Anna von Zumpe, who makes several reappearances throughout the novel, the last few of which take place when she is already married to Jacob Bubis, Archimboldi's publisher. In 1936 the country manor is shut down, and Hans and Hugo continue their friendship in Berlin until the war breaks out three years later and Hans is drafted and assigned to a light infantry regiment posted near the Polish border. Later Hans's battalion is transferred to the Carpathians, and Hans is asked to carry out menial tasks for German and Romanian officers who sojourn at a local castle during a lull in the war. Naturally talk turns to Dracula, who seems to be reincarnated in the figure of General Entrescu, whose drained lover is none other than the Baroness Von Zumpe. Later still Hans is wounded in action and receives the Iron Cross. As he convalesces in Soviet territory, he discovers the hidden papers of Boris Ansky, a Russian Jew who was once a member of the Red Army and whose notes end when Hitler invades Poland and "he sketches a map to join the guerrillas" (736). In Ansky's diaries Hans for the first time comes upon the name of Italian painter Giuseppe Arcimboldo, whose technique strikes Ansky as "happiness personified," "Arcadia before the coming of man" (734). At the end of the war Hans surrenders to the Americans and ends up sharing a tent in a prisoners' camp with a former Nazi called Sammer, who tells him how he was forced to dispose of a trainload of Jews during his command in a Polish town. Hans later tells his eventual wife Ingeborg that he strangled Sammer between the tents and the latrines and that he followed advice to change his name to Archimboldi in case the Americans were looking for him.

The adoption of the pseudonym, however, coincides with Hans's discovery of his literary vocation: "Around this time Reiter finished his first novel. He called it *Lüdicke* and he had to roam the backstreets of Cologne in search of someone who would rent him a typewriter . . . , in other words no one who knew his name was Hans Reiter" (783). For the first time in the novel Hans introduces himself as Benno von Archimboldi. The omniscient narrator accepts this change of name and begins to refer to his character by his pseudonym, but Archimboldi's eventual publisher has some trouble with it, especially with the name Benno, which reminds him of Benito Mussolini. Improbably Archimboldi retorts that he's called Benno in honor of Benito Juárez, the Mexican president of Indian extraction who is credited with turning back a French invasion in the 1860s and whose legacy resonates in the name of Ciudad Juárez. The publisher overcomes his resistance and agrees to publish his new client's first novel. Archimboldi meets Bubis's much younger wife and discovers to his amazement that she is the same Baroness Von Zumpe of his chidhood and of his war experience. They become lovers and lifelong confidantes. Archimboldi continues to write and publish but becomes reclusive when the health of his wife, Ingeborg, deteriorates and she eventually dies. Then Mr. Bubis dies, and his widow takes over the management of the publishing house. Archimboldi throws away the typewriter that the publisher had given him in order to encourage him to write and timorously buys a laptop in one of the many computer stores he has been nosing around in. (Klaus owns a computer business in Santa Teresa.) In one of Mrs. Bubis's letters to Archimboldi, she confesses that she has not read any of his novels because she does not like "difficult" and "dark" novels such as the ones he wrote (863).

The narrative focus shifts in the last thirty pages of the novel. Now Archimboldi is revealed from the perspective of his sister Lotte who, by the time the crimes of Santa Teresa come into view, is a widow living in Germany. She gets a telegram from Santa Teresa in 1995 informing her that her son Klaus is in jail and accused of the murder of some women. Despite the fact that Klaus was a troubled youth and spent time in a reformatory after being charged with sexual assault, Lotte refuses to believe that her son could be a murderer of women. She had lost track of him when he decided to try his luck in the United States. She hires an Atlanta detective to find him, but by then Klaus is in Mexico. Lotte undertakes several trips to Santa Teresa to be near her son, the last of which is in 2001. During that trip she casually picks up a novel at the Los Angeles airport called *The King of the Forest* by an unknown author (unknown to her) called

Archimboldi, and as she reads it in the plane she realizes that the novel tells the story of her whole family, including her crippled father and one-eyed mother. Then it comes to her that Archimboldi could be no other than her vanished brother Hans, who meets up with her once again in Germany and agrees to take on the Klaus matter. Her trips to Santa Teresa make Lotte dream of the desert: "She saw Archimboldi walking in the desert, dressed in shorts and a little straw hat, and everything around him was sand" (878).[17] In the dream she tells her brother that the desert is hostile and unfathomable, to which Archimboldi— echoing the novel's epigraph—responds that "it's just boring, boring, boring" (879). The novel ends the night before Archimboldi is set to board a plane and head to Mexico. The last scene has him talking to a gentleman by the name of Alexander Fürst Pückler, one of whose forebears was an enlightened minor author interested in botany and gardening. The scene itself takes place in a sort of oasis in the woods. The garden stands in sharp symbolic contrast to the desert, as the ocean does near the beginning of the third part of the novel.

Finally who narrates 2666? The editor states that in his notes for the novel Bolaño indicates that its narrator is Arturo Belano, an Argentine author, and personal friend Rodrigo Fresán (who makes a cameo appearance in the novel, page 60) adds that the narrator of the novel was supposed to have been "a kind of superbeing, transmitting the entirety of 2666 à la Kubrick, like a kind of floating fetus in a space station" (Maristain, *Bolaño: A Biography* 154). Bolaño may have dropped this bit of information in a casual conversation with Fresán when he was thinking about Kubrick's *2001*. All that is known from the novel as it was published is that its five books are narrated by an omniscient and therefore heterodiegetic narrator that sometimes becomes partially homodiegetic and less than omniscient. Two examples from "The Part about Archimboldi": "And at last we come to Archimboldi's sister, Lotte Reiter" (864); and "What did they live on? Probably Archimboldi . . . turned to petty theft" (835). In the end the matter of the narrator is left unresolved, but it seems reasonable to speculate that the narratological aspect of the novel needed further work.

As for the possible identification of Archimboldi with Bolaño, there is some textual evidence to support it. Archimboldi views literature "as divided into three compartments," one containing the writers and books he deems magnificent, another one composed of the works of his enemies, and a third compartment made up of his own published and future works, which he sees as a game, "insofar as he derived pleasure from writing, a pleasure similar to that of the detective on the heels of the killer" (817). This same compartmentalized view of literature can be ascribed to Bolaño. A later passage brings out the difference between a writer like Archimboldi—and Bolaño—and a more sedate author like Italian novelist Alberto Moravia, the latter being "bourgeois and practical and worldly," wheras the former "was . . . an artist in a state of permanent incandescence" (839). Despite these occasional resemblances it must be remembered that Archimboldi is fundamentally an intertextual creation with only the most precarious footing on social and historical reality. The source of the character and the details of his biography will more likely be found in the works of German and Austrian novelists like Joseph Roth, Robert Walser, Alfred Döblin, Robert Musil, Ernst Jünger, and Thomas Mann—without forgetting Kafka—than in the pages of history (Elmore 285).

Conclusion

Bolaño was a Chilean-born writer who started his career as a little-known poet in Mexico, became a novelist and short story writer in Spain, and a few years before his early death began to achieve the recognition that his talent and dedication deserved, first in the context of Latin American fiction and finally in that of world literature. The meaning of his achievement differs according to the context in which his work is placed. For Latin American critics and fellow writers Bolaño quickly became the center of a new post-Boom generation that until his arrival was dispersed and engaged in valuable literary ventures that, however, seemed centrifugal in the absence of a cultural and historical center of gravity. Such observers credited Bolaño with reconstituting Latin American writing, which he did by returning to the canon consolidated in the 1960s—the decade of the Boom of Latin American fiction—and revising and updating it to make it relevant in contemporary times. Bolaño's work is read throughout Latin America and gives the impression that it belongs to an actually existing Latin American literature that is not merely the invention of academic critics working in the United States and in European universities. At times Bolaño could pass for a Chilean writer and at others for a Mexican or Spanish or an Argentine one, but he explicitly defined himself as Latin American.

Bolaño achieved this feat of continental relevance not only by dint of his raw talent and the audacity of his imagination but also by responding to the political concerns that defined his generation. Politically he came of age with the massacre of students by the Mexican army in 1968, and he projected the martyred students' protest on behalf of a more equitable and less authoritarian society onto the struggle of Central American revolutionaries and opponents of the Southern Cone military dictatorships in the years that followed. Bolaño not only synthesized contemporary politics with the modern tradition of Latin American narrative but also fused fiction and poetry within the same tradition. He was certainly not the only fiction writer who acknowledged the importance of poetic discourse for narrative experimentation, but he may have been the one who most consistently carried out the task of fusing poetry and prose in his work. Last but not least, Bolaño also bridged the transatlantic gap between Spanish and Latin American literature. All his major work was published in Spain but carried an unmistakable Latin American stamp.

For observers situated beyond the confines of the Hispanic world Bolaño was remarkable because he utterly transformed the stereotype of Latin American writing, until then dominated by the magic realism of García Márquez and his epigones. Even though a mythical Bolaño emerged from the ashes of magic realism in the United States and Britain, the transformation he operated on the tropical stereotype has opened a window on a Latin American cosmopolitanism that has always been present in Latin American literature but that has rarely been acknowledged abroad. Latin American literature and culture have characteristically been far more open to external influence than any of the major European traditions. Poetry, fiction, and essays have been a veritable crucible of cross-cultural influences going back at least to the end of the nineteenth century.

Bolaño also made his mark on world literature because of the contemporary feel of his style and the transcultural nature of his themes. Bolaño (who was said to write while plugged in to his Walkman listening to rock or heavy metal) was able to adapt his reading of "literary" authors to the formats of contemporary mass culture in print and film: police thrillers, science fiction, Gothic horror, even pornography. It is not rare to find in his works references to Hollywood movies mixed in with allusions to obscure French poets, as it is not that surprising to find a mix of tones in some passages where more conventional authors would limit themselves to high seriousness or low comedy. In the middle of the daunting 2666, for example, a passage appears in which Nazi officers and their Rumanian allies spend a social evening in a castle that might have belonged to Dracula, at the end of which soirée a well-endowed Rumanian general impales the lady of his desires.

Bolaño's themes, furthermore, are large and consequential in scope: war, criminal and political violence, and the "secret of evil" in general, which may also be at the bottom of certain kinds of erotic passion and of literature itself. But Bolaño conveys these themes through the mediation of writers who are placed in the position of facing the enormous burden of history or of the violence that lies at the bottom of the social order, a violence that society is hardly able to repress. So it may be said that Bolaño's central theme is the confrontation between the writer and power, whether that power derives from the state, from those who engage in violence with impunity, or from the literary institution itself. Or, as a critic puts it, Bolaño's main subject is the relationship between art and infamy (Valdés 10).

Chilean novelist Roberto Brodsky includes Bolaño as a semifictitious character in his novel *Veneno* ("Poison") and says of him that he loved literature but that above all he loved the *real* situation of literature in the world to which he was condemned to live (149). The real situation of literature puts it on a collision course with the powers that be, not only the powers of the state and society but also the omnipotent clout of the market, which turns every value into a commodity. For Bolaño writing had to have consequences, and since he did not believe in posterity, those consequences had to manifest themselves in the here and now. He paid for his eventual fame during the long years when he labored in obscurity, as other writers pay for their métier with their disappearance, imprisonment, or exile. The fact that he ended up as a character in the novels of his contemporaries (he also appears in Javier Cercas's *Soldiers of Salamis*) means that Bolaño succeeded in becoming a prime example of what the ends of literature can be in our convulsed era.

Notes

Chapter 1: Understanding Roberto Bolaño

1. See "The Corridor with No Apparent Way Out" in *Between Parentheses* and the story "I Can't Read" in *The Secret of Evil*.

2. See Maristain, *Bolaño: A Biography*, 209–13. Bolaño's wife, Carolina, was also present at the hospital when the writer died. The couple had remained on friendly terms after their separation (at the end of 1992, according to the poem "Roberto Bolaño's Devotion," included in *The Unknown University*); their daughter Alexandra was conceived during one of their occasional encounters. The 1992 separation was perhaps one of many, since author and friend Enrique Vila-Matas records that on the morning of December 6, 1998, Bolaño "moved house in Blanes, going to live with Carolina and Lautaro at number 13, carrer Ample, Flat 1, Second Floor ("Blanes" 160).

3. The War of the Flowers refers to the Aztec custom of waging war in order to capture (and not kill) enemies who would later be ritually sacrificed. Cortázar popularized the term in his story "The Night Face Up." Bolaño uses the term to signify revolutionary idealism and sacrifice.

4. The references to mass graves and the bottom of the sea recall the fate of many victims of the Argentine Dirty War and the Pinochet regime in Chile. Mass graves have been found in Argentina and Chile (also in El Salvador and Guatemala), and a number of people were dumped into the sea from military helicopters. Violeta Parra was a noted Chilean folk singer and powerful symbol of popular culture who commited suicide in 1967. Her brother Nicanor, one of Bolaño's favorite poets, was the founder of Chilean antipoetry in the 1950s.

5. Unfortunately, Fuentes did not reciprocate Bolaño's early admiration. In his *Gran novela latinoamericana* (Mexico City: Alfaguara, 2011) the author of *Where the Air Is Clear* unaccountably leaves Bolaño out of contention. Fuentes's first novel is often described as a biography of Mexico City.

6. One of Bolaño's novels, *Una novelita lumpen,* is an ironic reference to Donoso's *Tres novelitas burguesas,* translated into English as *Sacred Families.* Donoso appears fleetingly and anonymously in *The Savage Detectives* (230).

7. See, for example, Wallace Fowlie, *Rimbaud and Jim Morrison: The Rebel as Poet* (Durham, N.C.: Duke University Press, 1994).

8. nytimes.com/2008/1/09/books/review/Lethem-t.html?pagewanted=all and_r=0>, accessed January 8, 2015.

9. Chiara Bolognese's *Pistas de un naufragio* (Santiago: Editorial Margen, 2009), for example, fails to include a single reference to any critical article on Bolaño published in English, even though the book purports to be a comprehensive analysis and interpretation of the author's work. The same is true of *Territorios en fuga,* an uneven collection of Chilean responses to Bolaño's works edited by Patricia Espinosa.

10. Jorge Volpi has called Bolaño the last Latin American writer, or the "last total Latin American," the last author, in other words, who was able to stand for a whole generation of writers engaged in the same work (*El insomnio de Bolívar* 176). In Volpi's view there are no writers after Bolaño who feel part of the Latin American tradition to the extent that Bolaño did, and no writers who are willing and able to respond in their work to canonical influences.

Chapter 2: Bolaño the Poet

1. Many of the poems from the original edition of *Los perros románticos* were simultaneously published in Mexico as *El último salvaje* (Al Este del Paraíso, 1995). All the poems of this collection are included in *The Unknown University.*

2. Other poems of his also appeared in two different issues of *Punto de partida,* a student magazine sponsored by the National University of Mexico (UNAM): "Overol blanco y otros poemas" was published in the November 1976 issue of the journal, and "Reinventar el amor y otros poemas" in the following issue, January 1977. The latter was also published separately as a book.

3. letras.s5.com/ms090107.html, accessed January 7, 2015.

4. The story of Bolaño's friendship with Mario Santiago is told in "The Old Man of the Mountain," one of the stories included in *The Secret of Evil.*

5. http://www.letraslibres.com/revista/convivio/del-surrealismo-al-infrarrealismo -un-atajo, accessed January 7, 2015.

6. The information regarding the original publication of the manifesto is included in the bibliography. The manifesto is reprinted in Spanish on http://garciamadero.blog spot.com/2007/08/djenlo-todo-nuevamente-primer.html (accessed on 7/3/2015), and in English on https://launiversidaddesconocida.wordpress.com/manifesto-of-infrarealism/ (accessed on 7/3/2015). No page numbers are given in either case. The passages quoted in the text are from Tim Pilcher's translation.

7. Maples Arce was the leader of the *estridentistas,* the most important avant-garde group of poets and artists in Mexico in the 1920s. Their name alludes to the typically loud attitude of avant-garde groups as they try to break into the cultural mainstream. The estridentistas advocated a cosmopolitan approach to Mexican art and celebrated the technological inventions and material achievements of the twentieth century: automobiles, bridges, radio, skyscrapers, locomotives, ocean liners, modern communications, etc. A much older and jaded Maples Arce is one of the characters in the middle part of *The Savage Detectives.*

8. It also excludes a few poems scattered in difficult-to-find anthologies (like Soledad Bianchi's *Entre la lluvia y el arcoiris*) and in ephemeral publications like *Berthe*

Trépat, a short-lived magazine edited by Bolaño and Bruno Montané after the poets, also friends, moved to Spain.

9. Another "daybreak" poem (but with friends) is "Those Mexican City dawns appear this time of day," 207.

10. "She could have been a great poet / the most loving / beloved / of mine," "Generación de los párpados eléctricos" (142), from the *Muchachos desnudos* anthology.

11. In her faux memoir of her relationship with Bolaño, Lieberman recounts how the writer used to lock her in his apartment when he went out to work or meet friends. "Tempestuous"seems to be a good word to describe their brief relationship.

12. See David Jasper, *The Sacred Desert: Religion, Literature, Art, and Culture* (Oxford: Blackwell, 2004) and Raúl Zurita, *Purgatorio* (Santiago: Editorial Universitaria, 1977).

13. "The Last Love Song of Pedro J. Lastarria" also features a "South American in Gothic land." "Gothic" is a translation of "godos," which in South America has been used as a pejorative term for Spaniards since the wars of independence against Spanish domination in the first quarter of the nineteenth century.

14. Bolaño always admired Chilean "antipoet" Nicanor Parra, who in the 1950s introduced conversational irony into a poetic system dominated by Pablo Neruda's portentous rhetoric.

15. The name "Gaspar" has other relevant connotations: Aloysius Bertrand's prose poems in *Gaspard de la Nuit,* Verlaine's poem "Gaspard Hauser chante," and Georges Perec's "Gaspard Winckler" in *Life: A User's Manual.*

16. On page 321 he admits that he "can't string two words together. I can't express myself coherently or write what I want."

17. In one of his interviews Bolaño tells a childhood story about an experience of people walking away that for him meant the first concrete intimation of death. See Braithwaite 82–83.

18. See Espinosa and Blume in *Territorios en fuga.*

19. Dogs and poetry come strangely together in a prose text by Bolaño on Chilean poetry: "The picture I have of Chilean poetry is like my memory of my first dog, Duke" (*Between Parentheses* 95).

20. The Peruvian César Vallejo was one of the key Latin American poets in the first half of the twentieth century. *Trilce* is his most radical avant-garde work. He appears in *Monsieur Pain,* the novel that Bolaño wrote in 1981 and published in 1993 with the title *La senda de los elefantes.*

21. Perec is also the author of *La Boutique obscure,* a collection of 124 dreams that may have served as an inspiration for Bolaño's "Stroll."

Chapter 3: The Turn to Fiction

1. Maquieira published two experimental collections of poetry in the 1980s in Chile but has published very litle since then. On Lihn, see chapters 1 and 2.

2. Toward the end of the novel, the narrator remarks that he is reading Marcel Schwob's *Children's Crusade,* a short narrative told by many different speaking voices. Bolaño transfers this formal model to his novel's epilogue. Schwob's book was first

published in English two years after its original publication (Boston: Small, Maynard, 1898).

3. Georgette de Vallejo's memoirs were published in 1978 as *Vallejo: Allá ellos, allá ellos, allá ellos*. The account of Vallejo's death may be found on pages 117–31.

4. For these topics see Stephen M. Hart's *César Vallejo: A Literary Biography* (Rochester, N.Y.: Tamesis, 2013), chapter 5.

5. The death theme also explains the original title of the novel ("The Elephant Path"), which refers to the myth of the elephant cemetery.

6. In a sense all of Paris is a labyrinth in the novel, but the Arago Clinic is marked out as the preferential site of confusion and disorientation, especially in the sequence beginning on page 108, where Pain is trapped in one of its rooms and alienated from his surroundings. He is possessed by the "fascination of the labyrinth" (110). If he is the minotaur, however, he is Borges's version of the monster in "The House of Asterion," a pathetic beast who yearns for the redeemer who will slay him and save him from his solitude. (Borges's story may be found in *The Aleph and Other Stories* collection.) Trapped in his life and locked deep within himself, however, nobody can hear Pain's anguished screams, least of all Madame Reynaud, his would-be redeemer.

7. *Neruda and Vallejo: Selected Poems*, trans. Robert Bly (Boston: Beacon Press, 1971).

8. Porta, "La escritura a cuatro manos," 10.

9. The exquisite corpse was a parlor game in which improvised sentences were passed around a table in a folded sheet of paper for the next player to generate a story. This surrealist technique was used to explore the role of chance in artistic creation.

10. As stated in chapter 1 above, "sudaca" was a pejorative term used in Spain in the 1970s to refer to South American exiles and immigrants. There is a thin line in the novel separating criminal activity from political terrorism and revolution. But the novel stops short of fully exploring this connection.

11. See Michel Lafon and Benoit Peeters, *Nous est un autre: Enquête sur les duos d'écrivains* (Paris: Flammarion, 2006), for a study of literary collaborations. This book was translated into Spanish as *Escribir en colaboración* (Rosario: Beatriz Viterbo, 2008). The translator is César Aira, one of the most notable contemporary Argentine writers.

12. Jim Morrison, of course, was himself a poète maudit on a grand scale. See chapter 1, note 7 for the reference to Wallace Fowlie's study of Morrison and Rimbaud.

13. Bolaño refers to this person in one of his newspaper columns collected in *Between Parentheses*: "The owner's name is Santi and he's my friend and I owe him three thousand pesetas" (125). On the occasion of that visit to the game store Bolaño buys a computer game called *Settlers,* which he thinks must be similar to the more familiar *Age of Empires*. For PC formats, see http://diario.latercera.com/2013/03/10/01/contenido/la-tercera-el-semanal/34-131772-9-los-pasos-de-bolano-en-cataluna.shtml, accessed January 9, 2015.

14. http://www.avalanchepress.com/game3R.php, accessed January 9, 2015.

15. Page references are to the Natasha Wimmer translation of the novel.

16. Goethe's *Sorrows of Young Werther* is not too far removed from Bolaño's novel. Neither is Thomas Mann's *Death in Venice*. El Quemado may in fact be read as a monstrous version of Tadzio.

17. All references to the novel are to the Chris Andrews translation.

18. For the term "narratee" see Gerald Prince's *Dictionary of Narratology* (Lincoln: University of Nebraska Press, 1987).

19. The topic originated in a 1930 book (*El retorno de los galeones* [Madrid: Compañía Ibero-Americana de Publicaciones]) by literary critic Max Henríquez Ureña, who was studying the influence of Latin American writers like Rubén Darío and José Enrique Rodó on Spanish literature.

Chapter 4: Siamese Twins

1. www.lrb.co.uk/v31/n04/michael-wood/more-like-a-cemetery, accessed January 9, 2015.

2. The novel was published in English in New York as *Michael: A Novel* by Amok Press in 1987.

3. As Lentricchia and McAuliffe point out, in our time real bombs have replaced the cultural bombs that the literary imagination has been dreaming up since romanticism. See their *Crimes of Art + Terror* (Chicago: University of Chicago Press, 2003).

4. More in tune with Serrano's anti-Semitic obsession, "The Fourth Reich" is also the title of a saga in *Nazi Literature in the Americas* whose last installment is "a surreptitious manifesto directed against African Americans, Jews and Hispanics" (106).

5. Pauwels and Bergier's *Morning of the Magicians* ("Le Matin des magiciens" [Paris: Gallimard, 1960]) is playfully suggested as a kind of correlate to the book in *Distant Star* (108). The translation, however, is misleading. The title *The Warlocks Return* does not convey the meaning of *El retorno de los brujos* (Barcelona: Plaza and Janes, 1962), which is the title of the Spanish translation of Pauwels and Bergier's best seller.

6. See Irma Zangara, ed., *Borges en Revista Multicolor* (Buenos Aires: Editorial Atlántida, 1995).

7. Other stories by Borges included in *Ficciones* and *El Aleph* show marked affinities with Bolaño's *Nazi Literature in the Americas*, especially "Deutsches Requiem," "The Secret Miracle," and "An Examination of the Work of Herbert Quain."

8. Bolaño has also mentioned Mexican author Alfonso Reyes's *Retratos reales e imaginarios* (Mexico City: Lectura Selecta, 1920) as a source of his "novel."

9. Social class is another feature that distinguishes among characters and creates variety. Thus, while the Schiaffino brothers come from a "humble family" (157), Ignacio Zubieta is the "only son of one of Bogotá's best families" (31).

10. "Copi" was the pseudonym of Raúl Damonte Botana, an Argentine playwright and cartoonist who produced most of his work in Paris. He was the grandson of a famous newspaper editor (Natalio Botana) and died of AIDS at an early age. Natalio Botana was the founder of *Crítica*, the journal where Borges first published the stories of his *Universal History of Infamy*.

11. See Jeremías Gamboa for a fuller study of this topic.

12. An excellent study of this topic is Aníbal González's *Killer Books* (Austin: University of Texas Press, 2002).

13. The participation as witness of the Garmendias' Mapuche maid prefigures the trial of General Ríos Montt in Guatemala that began in January 2013. The Guatemalan dictator was indicted for genocide, and many of the victims and witnesses in his

trial were Mayan Indians whose testimony had to be translated into Spanish. When the Mapuche maid spoke in court, writes Bolaño's narrator, "every second word was in Mapuche, and the two young Catholic priests who escorted her like bodyguards . . . had to serve as interpreters" (110–111).

14. A further perversion results from the connection between Wieder's photographs (which often represent victims of forced disappearance) and the photos brandished by the Mothers of the Plaza de Mayo in Argentina, picturing their own disappeared children and husbands.

15. Zurita's text may be found in his *Anteparadise* (Berkeley: University of California Press, 1986), which also includes photographs of the text before it dissolves in the sky.

16. The Third Reich is, of course, the name of a war game.

Chapter 5: Bolaño's Breakthrough

1. These quotes are from Daniel Zalewski, James Wood, Benjamin Kunkel, and Alex Abramovich, respectively, writing, in the same order for the *New Yorker,* the *New York Times,* the *London Review of Books,* and *Bookforum.* All these reviews may be found on the web.

2. And perhaps like Ambrose Bierce, who disappeared in Mexico at the time of the Mexican revolution and who is the protagonist of Carlos Fuentes's *Old Gringo* (New York: Farrar Straus Giroux, 1985, trans. Margaret Sayers Peden).

3. Except in Mexico City, where Cesárea lived in the 1920s before returning to her homeland in the Sonora desert.

4. See Cobas Carral and Gariboto (166). Apollinaire's calligrams are a prime example of typographic experiments in avant-garde poetry, but many Latin American poets (like Vicente Huidobro, José Juan Tablada, Manuel Maples Arce, and others) tried their hand at such innovations.

5. As if to demonstrate that *The Savage Detectives* can be read as a game, the poets' trip to the desert in search of Cesárea Tinajero takes some ironic and playful turns, such as the reference to Caesar's assassination (539) and the name of the Peña Taurina Pilo Yáñez (542), which refers to Chilean avant-garde writer and painter Juan Emar, whose real name was Álvaro Yáñez but was known to friends and family as "Pilo."

6. Cesárea herself is an orphan (251).

7. For Octavio Paz, all Mexicans are orphans. In *The Labyrinth of Solitude* (1950) he argues that Mexicans cannot identify either with the aggressive Spanish conquistador nor with their passive Indian mother as a result of the violence of the Conquest.

8. Cristóbal Pera has written at length on the Latin American myth of Paris in *Modernistas en París* (Bern: P. Lang, 1997).

9. See Miguel Huezo Mixco for a chronology of events. Unfortunately the author gets the dates wrong because he confuses the details of Bolaño's trip from Mexico City to Chile with the trip back from Santiago to the Mexican capital. Bolaño traveled by land to Chile in August or September 1973 but returned by plane in January 1974. (See also "Exiles," in *Between Parentheses.*)

10. Writers from many parts of the world traveled to Nicaragua to show support for the revolution or to learn more about it. William Styron, for example, recorded his

intention to visit Nicaragua with Carlos Fuentes in a letter to his daughter dated August 1982 (*Selected Letters* [New York: Random House, 2012], 558). In a later letter, dated January 1988, he restates his plans to travel to Nicaragua, again with Fuentes (593). And in August of that year he writes that he is trying to finish a piece based on a trip to Nicaragua with his Mexican friend and fellow writer. Cortázar, Vargas Llosa, and García Márquez also wrote about their experiences in Nicaragua.

11. Retamar appears in *The Savage Detectives* in the guise of the "great lyric poet of the Revolution" (302). Nicolás Guillén might also be considered as the "great lyric poet of the Revolution," but the reference to Caliban on the following page makes it more likely that the personage implied in the novel is Fernández Retamar, whose most influential work was the essay "Calibán: Apuntes sobre la cultura en nuestra América." (See *Caliban and Other Essays* [Minneapolis: University of Minnesota Press, 1989].)

12. The peasant poets of *The Savage Detectives,* who came together in the decade immediately following the Cuban revolution, have their own Marxist theoretician. The suggestion of an ideological straightjacket for poetry suffices in the novel to disqualify such a group from literary legitimacy.

13. The *cristero* war was a bloody conflict that took place in western Mexico between government forces and Catholic guerrillas incensed by the application of the anticlerical provisions of the Constitution of 1917. It lasted three years and took thousands of lives. Juan Villoro's 2004 novel *El testigo* ("The Witness") revives the conflict in the context of contemporary Mexican politics.

14. The name of Archimboldi does appear on page 155, but it refers not to the German novelist who is at the center of *2666* but to a French writer whose full name is J. M. G. Archimboldi. The initials unmistakably recall the winner of the 2008 Nobel Prize in literature, Jean-Marie Gustave Le Clézio. This French Archimboldi, however, appears in the same situation as his German avatar in the first part of *2666*, arriving at the Mexico City airport.

15. The burlesque duel staged in chapter 22 of *The Savage Detectives* between Belano and the literary critic Iñaki Echevarne is a parody of the knife fight in Borges's story.

Chapter 6: Two Dramatic Monologues

1. The multiple-voiced narrative strategy of this book was probably one of the models for the style of the middle section of *The Savage Detectives.*

2. La Maga ("The Magician") is an expatriate free-spirit in Paris who was born in Montevideo, as was Alcira. They are both fluent in French. Alcira's poet friends sometimes speak in "Gliglish," a funny language invented by Cortázar in one of the chapters of *Hopscotch.* La Maga is, to some extent, Cortázar's version of André Breton's Nadja in the novel of the same name (1928).

3. See Schweppenhauser, *Theodor W. Adorno: An Introduction* (Durham, N.C.: Duke University Press, 2009) for the Frankfurt critique of society.

4. Like Pedro Garfias, León Felipe was a Spanish poet exiled in Mexico, where he died on September 17, 1968, the day before the Mexican army took over the campus of the National University.

5. Information on Lilian Serpas is scarce and contradictory. Some of it is available on three websites: http://www.mcnbiografias.com/app-bio/do/show?key=serpas-gutierrez-lilian; http://www.cultura.gob.sv/biblioteca/images/pdf/octubrelilianserpas.pdf; and http://nunezhandal.blogspot.com/2010/04/lilian-serpas-tras-el-velo-del-olvido-y.html, the last of which is authoritative if the author quoted in the blog is actually David E. Galindo; accessed January 9, 2015.

6. The earliest Spanish-language translation of this novel dates from 1965 and was published in Mexico by Joaquín Mortiz.

7. The reference to mirrors may be clarified by an earlier passage in which Auxilio contemplates herself in the bathroom mirror at Coffeen's place: "when you're happy or sense that happiness may be imminent you're not afraid to look at yourself in mirrors" (136). The death march of the ghost-children is imbued with love: "although the children were clearly marching to war, the way they marched recalled the superb, theatrical attitudes of love" (184).

8. Interview cited in Bogue 127.

9. Susana Draper quotes this definition from Schelling (quoted in turn by Freud) when discussing *By Night in Chile* in the context of postdictatorial discourse, 128.

10. Silva's poem was published posthumously in 1908. The poet died in Colombia—his native country—in 1896 at age thirty. Silva's portrait and the poem's imagery has illustrated the front and back of the Colombian five-thousand-peso bill since 1995.

11. Opus Dei ("God's Work") is a conservative Catholic organization founded in Spain in 1928. Its membership is both clerical and secular. The contemporary film *There Be Dragons* narrates the story of a journalist who discovers that his father was close to José María Escrivá de Balaguer, the founder of Opus Dei.

12. This surname already appears in *Distant Star* (with a different given name) but the character bearing it—also an eminent literary critic—dies at the end of the 1970s and thus cannot be identified with the Ibacache of *By Night in Chile*.

13. Vargas Llosa analyzes this kind of narrative device as a shift in the spatial point of view. See *Letters to a Young Novelist* 44–57.

14. The novel's various scenes are not as arbitrary as they may seem. They can all be integrated into a common design, and they are linked by functional terms. Even within them what at first seems arbitrary can easily be made coherent. A good example is the conversation between Chilean author Salvador Reyes and German writer and war hero Ernst Jünger in the novel's second sequence. The conversation takes place in the attic of an anorexic and melancholy Guatemalan painter. The Chilean writer asks about German art. His German interlocutor talks only about Dürer. The choice of artist is not arbitrary, even if it is not disclosed by the author-narrator. One of Dürer's most famous works is "Melencolia I (1514)," which functionally relates to the painter's malaise.

15. Sophia Martelli, www.theguardian.com/books/2009/may/24/la-bas-huysmans-classics-review, accessed January 9, 2015.

16. www.habsburger.net/en/chapter/heldenberg-monument-patriotism, accessed January 9, 2015.

17. "Ta gueule" in French is roughly equivalent to "Shut your trap" in English (or, more emphatically, "Shut the fuck up"). The falcon Ta Gueule at one point flies over the

fields of Provence, "where . . . Sordello . . . wandered once" (72). El Cid is the national hero of Spain, a Castilian nobleman who fought the Moors in the eleventh century and became the subject of a great epic poem. El Cid was born near Burgos and is buried in that city.

18. Quoted by Caroline Lepage, "Littérature et dictature" 89.

19. A homodiegetic narrator is present in the story he or she tells, whereas a heterodiegetic narrator is not a character in the situations he or she recounts (Prince, *Dictionary of Narratology*). *By Night in Chile* may also be considered an autodiegetic narrative because its homodiegetic narrator is the protagonist of the story and not just a character in it.

Chapter 7: The Stories and a Short Lumpen Novel

1. Some stories are entirely written in dialogue form and eliminate the narrative function altogether ("Detectives," "Murdering Whores"). Others are not really stories but rough drafts or actual drafts of lectures ("Sevilla Kills Me," "Vagaries of the Literature of Doom," "Literature + Illness = Illness," and "The Myths of "Cthulhu").

2. This story is an expansion of the scene in *Distant Star* (starting on page 125) when detective Abel Romero (who remains nameless in "Joanna Silvestri") visits the ailing porno star in search of clues regarding Wieder's aliases and whereabouts. In the novel it is the detective that recounts the interview with the presumed witness. In the story the same interview is rendered from the opposite point of view, that of the interviewee.

3. It is worth remembering here that "Sensini" won first prize in a short story competition held in the Basque Country in 1996.

4. "The Devil's Spittle," though the title can be contextually translated as "The Devil's Web." See Julio Cortázar, *Blow-Up and Other Stories*.

5. *Martín Fierro* (1872, 1879) is the signature work of gauchesque literature, which was literature about the gauchos written by urban intellectuals. Nicolas Shumway characterizes it as consisting of "first-person narratives written in a language filled with ruralisms of varying degrees of authenticity, local color, type characters, and forced imagery that purportedly reflect lower-class rural life and speech" (68). *Martín Fierro* is a long narrative poem published in two parts. Its hero is a gaucho outlaw who, in later interpretations by nationalist intellectuals, evinces the courageous qualities and individualism of the true Argentine *criollo*. In the 1910s these interpretations were motivated by the massive arrival in Buenos Aires of southern European immigrants, whom writers like Lugones referred to as the "plebe ultramarina," the hordes from across the ocean.

6. Narratologists might call Bolaño's "*contraire*" the hypotext.

7. "Tesis sobre el cuento," *Formas breves* (Barcelona: Anagrama, 2000). Chekhov, Hemingway, and the Joyce of *Dubliners* are two of the authors mentioned by Piglia in relation to the development of the modern short story.

8. The film version of *A Little Lumpen Novelita* is called *Il Futuro*. It was filmed in Italian, directed by Chilean filmmaker Alicia Scherson, and released in 2013.

9. http://prodavinci.com/blogs/santiago-gamboa-y-roberto-bolano-bosquejo-de-una-amistad-literaria/, accessed on January 9, 2015.

10. Another way to read the epigraph is to notice that it points to an unusual absence of writers in the novel. The characters are all immersed in a world of popular and video culture and seem to have little time for reading. Maciste is blind so it's not surprising that his library has no books. But it can be said that Bolaño's novel as a whole is a library without books.

Chapter 8: 2666

1. The *maquilas* or *maquiladoras* are border factories that employ cheap (mostly female) labor and import tax– and duty-free materials to assemble products sold in the world market. The NAFTA agreement signed by the U.S. and Mexican governments that went into effect in January 1994 was responsible for a substantial increase in the number of these assembly plants operating in border towns. *Femicide* is a term that came into being to describe the murder of hundreds of women in Ciudad Juárez beginning in 1993. Sometimes these femicides are considered to be serial killings and, at other times, an instance of mass murder. There is no serial murderer responsible for the phenomenon, which must be regarded as a complex social phenomenon and not exclusively as a police matter.

2. http://elsilenciero.com/2011/07/roberto-bolano-el-mejor-herrero-de-la-palabra/, accessed January 9, 2015.

3. http://www.nytimes.com/2012/12/20/books/woes-of-the-true-policeman-by-roberto-bolano.html?_r=0, accessed January 9, 2015.

4. There is evidence that Bolaño was working on *Woes of the True Policeman* in 1995. See Valdés 11.

5. In *Woes of the True Policeman* Amalfitano is said to have been born in 1942, but in *2666* he is born in 1951, closer to Bolaño's own birth date.

6. In one of his interviews, Bolaño clarifies his approach to homosexuality: "My father was a courier. He was also a professional heavyweight boxing champion in southern Chile. The only thing fit to do before that man was to be stronger than him—otherwise it was to opt for homosexuality. If [it] had depended on me, I would have opted for homosexuality, which seems to me a magnificent aesthetic escape, but it wouldn't have been natural. I'm heterosexual" (Álvarez 72).

7. A Künstlerroman is a bildungsroman (or education novel) in which the protagonist is an artist.

8. There is a passing reference to Duchamp's *machine célibataire* in "The Part about the Critics" (56).

9. The word *carnicería* evokes the aforementioned poem by Oscar Hahn that shares Bolaño's apocalyptic vision of history in *2666*.

10. Examples: "But it's Number 46 that matters to us" (11). "As for what passed through Liz Norton's head, it's better not to say" (16). "But before coming to the crux of the matter, or of the discussion, a rather petty detail that nonetheless affected the course of events must be noted" (17). "So the days in Salzburg were generally pleasant, and although Archimboldi didn't receive the Nobel Prize that year, life for our four friends proceeded smoothly" (40). Perhaps deliberately, perhaps ironically, Bolaño here is using a pre-Flaubertian third-person narrative style—a modest instance of the intrusive

narrator, a narrative device that José Donoso systematically uses in his postmodern novel *A House in the Country.*

11. Bolaño and his wife also separated when their first child was two years old.

12. It shouldn't be forgotten that the title of Dieste's book is actually *Testamento geométrico* (La Coruña: Ediciones del Castro, 1975). Perhaps for Bolaño, who was dying when he wrote *2666*, the novel was his testament. At any rate Amalfitano is a witness who *attests* to the violence that surrounds Santa Teresa and of which he is himself a (psychological) victim.

13. "El idioma analítico de John Wilkins" was originally published in *La Nación* (Buenos Aires) in February 1941, and collected in *Otras inquisiciones* (Buenos Aires: Sur, 1952).

14. Later in the section Fate discusses David Lynch's movies with the motel receptionist, who particularly likes *Twin Peaks.* There is a scene at the motel right before Fate and Rosa take refuge in Amalfitano's house that seems taken from a movie like *Wild at Heart.*

15. A comic instance of name changing involves the case of "La Vaca," "a solidly built woman, five foot five, dark-skinned, with short curly hair" (417) who is killed by two male acquaintances when they all stage a fight after a drinking bout. In González Rodríguez's account, La Vaca is La Burra.

16. The Juárez murders have generated an abundant bibliography, of which *Huesos en el desierto* remains the prototype. Interested readers may also consult *Cosecha de mujeres* (Mexico City: Editorial Océano, 2012), by Diana Washington Valdez, and *Las hijas de Juárez* (New York: Atria Books, 2007), by Teresa Rodríguez et al. There is also a video bibliography comprising documentaries (like Lourdes Portillo's *Señorita extraviada*, 2001; Alejandra Sánchez's *Ni una más*, 2001; and *La batalla de las cruces*, produced and directed by Rafael Bonilla Pedroza and Patricia Ravelo Blancas, 2005) and fiction movies (*Bordertown, Backyard*).

17. Strictly speaking the narrator cannot be narrating from Lotte's point of view in this passage because she doesn't yet know that her brother is known as Archimboldi. Even if the notion that Bolaño completed this part of the novel long before he went on to write the next four can be granted, the suspicion is still that he might have revised this kind of narrative inconsistency had he had enough time to do so.

Bibliography

Works by Roberto Bolaño

"Déjenlo todo, nuevamente: Primer manifiesto del Movimiento Infrarrealista" (1976). *Correspondencia infra, revista menstrual del Movimiento Infrarrealista* 1 (Oct.–Nov. 1977): 6–11.

Reinventar el amor. Mexico City: Taller Martín Pescador, 1976.

Muchachos desnudos bajo el arcoiris de fuego: once jóvenes poetas latinoamericanos antologados por Roberto Bolaño. México: Editorial Extemporáneos, 1979.

"El contorno del ojo." *Encuentro en Praga.* Valencia: Prometeo, 1983.

Consejos de un discípulo de Morrison a un fanático de Joyce. Barcelona: Antropos, 1984.

Fragmentos de la universidad desconocida. Toledo: Ayuntamiento de Talavera de la Reina, 1993.

La pista de hielo. Alcalá de Henares: Ayuntamiento, 1993.

La senda de los elefantes. Toledo: Ayuntamiento de Toledo, 1993.

Los perros románticos. Irún: Fundación Kuxta, 1995.

La literatura nazi en América. Barcelona: Seix Barral, 1996.

Estrella distante. Barcelona: Anagrama, 1996.

Llamadas telefónicas. Barcelona: Anagrama, 1997.

Los detectives salvajes. Barcelona: Anagrama, 1998.

Amuleto. Barcelona: Anagrama, 1999.

Monsieur Pain. Barcelona: Anagrama, 1999.

Nocturno de Chile. Barcelona: Anagrama, 2000.

Tres. Barcelona: Acantilado, 2000.

Putas asesinas. Barcelona: Anagrama, 2001.

Una novelita lumpen. Barcelona: Mondadori, 2002.

Amberes. Barcelona: Anagrama, 2002.

El gaucho insufrible. Barcelona: Anagrama, 2003.

2666. Barcelona: Anagrama, 2004.

Entre paréntesis. Barcelona: Anagrama, 2004.

"Diario de bar." *Consejos de un discípulo de Morrison a un fanático de Joyce.* Barcelona: Acantilado, 2006.

216   Bibliography

La universidad desconocida. Barcelona: Anagrama, 2007.
El secreto del mal. Barcelona: Anagrama, 2007.
El tercer Reich. Barcelona: Anagrama, 2010.
Los sinsabores del verdadero policía. Barcelona: Anagrama, 2011.

English Translations of Roberto Bolaño's Works

By Night in Chile. New York: New Directions, 2003.
Distant Star. New York: New Directions, 2004.
Amulet. New York: New Directions, 2006.
Last Evenings on Earth. New York: New Directions, 2006.
The Savage Detectives. New York: Farrar, Straus and Giroux, 2007.
The Romantic Dogs. New York: New Directions, 2008.
Nazi Literature in the Americas. New York: New Directions, 2008.
2666. New York: Farrar, Straus and Giroux, 2008.
The Skating Rink. New York: New Directions, 2009.
Antwerp. New York: New Directions, 2010.
Monsieur Pain. New York: New Directions, 2010.
The Return. New York: New Directions, 2010.
The Insufferable Gaucho. New York: New Directions, 2010.
The Third Reich. New York: Farrar, Straus and Giroux, 2011.
Tres. New York: New Directions, 2011.
Between Parentheses. New York: New Directions, 2011.
The Secret of Evil. New York: New Directions, 2012.
The Woes of the True Policeman. New York: Farrar, Straus and Giroux, 2012.
The Unknown University. New York: New Directions, 2013.
A Little Lumpen Novelita. New York: New Directions, 2014.

Works Cited

Abrams, H. M. *Glossary of Literary Terms.* 9th ed. Boston: Wadsworth Cengage Learning, 2005.
Actis, Walter. "Argentinos en España." *Inmigración latinoamericana en España.* Ed. Anna Ayuso and Gemma Pinyol. Barcelona: Bellaterra, 2010. 147–65.
Aira, César. *La liebre.* Buenos Aires: Emecé, 1991.
Álvarez, Eliseo. "Positions Are Positions and Sex Is Sex." *Roberto Bolaño: The Last Interview and Other Conversations.* Brooklyn: Melville House, 2009. 69–91.
Andrews, Chris. *Roberto Bolaño's Fiction: An Expanding Universe.* New York: Columbia University Press, 2014.
Archivo Bolaño. Barcelona: Centro de Cultura Contemporánea de Barcelona, 2013.
Ayala, Matías. "Notas sobre la poesía de Roberto Bolaño." *Bolaño salvaje.* Ed. Edmundo Paz Soldán and Gustavo Faverón Patriau. Barcelona: Editorial Candaya, 2008. 91–101.
Bañuelos, Juan. *La espiga amotinada.* Mexico City: FCE, 1960.
———. *Ocupación de la palabra.* Mexico City: FCE, 1965.
Basti, Abel. *Tras los pasos de Hitler.* Buenos Aires: Planeta, 2014.

Bell-Villada, Gene. *Borges and His Fiction: A Guide to His Mind and Art*. Austin: University of Texas Press, 1999.

Bianchi, Soledad. *Entre la lluvia y el arcoiris*. Rotterdam: Instituto Para el Nuevo Chile, 1983.

Bizzio, Sergio. *En esa época*. Buenos Aires: Emecé, 2001.

Blume, Jaime. "Roberto Bolaño, poeta." *Territorios en fuga: Estudios críticos sobre la obra de Roberto Bolaño*. Ed. Patricia Espinosa. Santiago: Frasis Editores, 2003. 149–66.

Bogue, Ronald. *Deleuzian Fabulation and the Scars of History*. Edinburgh: Edinburgh University Press, 2010.

Borges, Jorge Luis. "The Aleph." *The Aleph and Other Stories*. Trans. Norman Thomas di Giovanni. New York: E. P. Dutton, 1970. 15–13.

———. "The Approach to al-Mu'tasim." *Ficciones*. Trans. Anthony Kerrigan. New York: Grove Press, 1962. 37–43.

———. "Conjectural Poem." *A Personal Anthology*. Ed. Anthony Kerrigan. New York: Grove, 1967. 192–93.

———. "The Gospel According to Mark." *Doctor Brodie's Report*. Trans. Norman Thomas di Giovanni. New York: Dutton, 1972. 15–22.

———. "Imaginary Lives." *On Writing*. Ed. Suzanne Jill Levine. New York: Penguin, 2010: 108.

———. "Narrative Art and Magic." *Selected Non-fictions*. Trans. Eliot Weinberger. New York: Viking, 1999. 75–82.

———. "The South." *Ficciones*. Trans. Anthony Kerrigan. New York: Grove, 1962. 167–74.

———. *A Universal History of Infamy*. Trans. Norman Thomas di Giovanni. New York: E. P. Dutton, 1972.

Boullosa, Carmen. "Reading Is Always More Important Than Writing." *Roberto Bolaño: The Last Interview and Other Conversations*. Brooklyn: Melville House, 2009. 53–67.

Bourriaud, Nicolas. *The Radicant*. New York: Lukas and Sternberg, 2009.

Boyle, Claire. *Consuming Autobiographies: Reading and Writing the Self in Post-war France*. Leeds: Legenda, 2007.

Braithwaite, Andrés, ed. *Bolaño por sí mismo: Entrevistas escogidas*. Santiago: Ediciones Universidad Diego Portales, 2006.

Breton, André. "Second Manifesto of Surrealism." *Manifestoes of Surrealism*. Trans. Richard Seaver and Helen R. Lane. Ann Arbor: University of Michigan Press, 1969: 119–94.

Brodsky, Roberto. *Veneno*. Santiago: Mondadori, 2012.

Bryce Echenique, Alfredo. *Guía triste de París*. Madrid: Alfaguara, 1999.

Cabral, Tristan. *Du Pain et des pierres*. Paris: Éditions Plasma, 1977.

Cabrera Infante, Guillermo. *Vidas para leerlas*. Madrid: Alfaguara, 1998.

Cercas, Javier. "Bolaño in Girona: A Friendship." *Archivo Bolaño*. Barcelona: Centro de Cultura Contemporánea de Barcelona, 2013. 149–53.

———. *Soldiers of Salamis*. Trans. Anne McLean. New York: Bloomsbury, 2004.

Cobas Carral, Andrea, and Verónica Garibotto. "Un epitafio en el desierto: Poesía y revolución en *Los detectives salvajes*." *Bolaño salvaje*. Ed. Edmundo Paz Soldán and Gustavo Faverón Patriau. Barcelona: Editorial Candaya, 2008. 163–89.

Cortázar, Julio. *Blow-Up and Other Stories*. Trans. Paul Blackburn. New York: Pantheon, 1985.

———. *Hopscotch*. Trans. Gregory Rabassa. New York: Pantheon Books, 1966.

Deckard, Sharae. "Peripheral Realism, Millenial Capitalism, and Roberto Bolaño's *2666*." *Modern Language Quarterly* 73.3 (2012): 351–72.

Délano, Jorge. *Kundalini, el caballo fatídico*. Santiago: Zig-Zag, 1957.

Dés, Mihály. "Entrevista a Roberto Bolaño." *Jornadas homenaje Roberto Bolaño (1953–2003)*. Ed. Ramón González Férriz. Barcelona: Casa América de Cataluña, 2005. 135–53.

Di Benedetto, Antonio. *Zama*. Buenos Aires: Centro Editor de América Latina, 1967.

Donoso, José. *The Garden Next Door*. Trans. Hardie St. Martin. New York: Grove, 1992.

———. *Hell Has No Limits*. Trans. Suzanne Jill Levine. Los Angeles: Sun and Moon, 1995.

———. *A House in the Country*. Trans. David Pritchard and Suzanne Jill Levine. New York: Knopf, 1984.

———. *The Obscene Bird of Night*. Trans. Hardie St. Martin and Leonard Mades. New York: Knopf, 1973.

———. *Sacred Families: Three Novellas*. Trans. Andrée Conrad. New York: Knopf, 1977.

Dorfman, Ariel. *Death and the Maiden*. New York: Penguin, 1992.

Draper, Susana. *Afterlives of Confinement: Spatial Transitions in Postdictatorship in Latin America*. Pittsburgh: University of Pittsburgh Press, 2012.

Dunstan, Simon, and Gerrard Williams. *Grey Wolf: The Escape of Adolph Hitler*. New York: Sterling, 2011.

Elmore, Peter. "*2666*: La autoría del tiempo en el límite." *Bolaño salvaje*. Ed. Edmundo Paz Soldán and Gustavo Faverón Patriau. Barcelona: Editorial Candaya, 2008. 259–92.

Espinosa, Patricia. "*Tres,* de Roberto Bolaño: El crac a la posmodernidad." *Territorios en fuga: Estudios críticos sobre la obra de Roberto Bolaño*. Ed. Patricia Espinosa. Santiago: Frasis Editores, 2003. 167–75.

Espinosa, Patricia, ed. *Territorios en fuga: Estudios críticos sobre la obra de Roberto Bolaño*. Santiago: Frasis Editores, 2003.

Falconer, Bruce. "The Torture Colony." theamericanscholar.org/the-torture-colony/#.VGPBDTTF_h4. Accessed January 9, 2015.

Faverón Patriau, Gustavo. "El rehacedor: 'El gaucho insufrible' y el ingreso de Bolaño en la tradición argentina." *Bolaño salvaje*. Ed. Edmundo Paz Soldán and Gustavo Faverón Patriau. Barcelona: Editorial Candaya, 2008. 371–415.

Fonseca, Rubem. *High Art*. Trans. Ellen Watson. New York: Harper and Row, 1986.

———. *Vast Emotions and Imperfect Thoughts*. Trans. Geoffrey E. Landers. New Jersey: Ecco, 1998.

Fresán, Rodrigo. "Dos hombres en el castillo." *Bolaño por sí mismo: Entrevistas escogidas*. Ed. Andrés Braithwaite. Santiago: Ediciones Universidad Diego Portales, 2006. 133–38.

Frye, Northrop. *Anatomy of Criticism*. Princeton, N.J.: Princeton University press, 1957.

Fuentes, Carlos. *The Death of Artemio Cruz*. Trans. Sam Hileman. New York: Farrar, Straus and Giroux, 1964.

———. *Distant Relations*. Trans. Margaret Sayers Peden. New York: Farrar Straus Giroux, 1982.

———. *Terra Nostra*. Trans. Margaret Sayers Peden. New York: Farrar, Straus, Giroux, 1976.

———. *Where the Air Is Clear*. Trans. Sam Hileman. New York: Farrar, Straus and Giroux, 1960.

Gallegos, Rómulo. *Doña Bárbara*. Trans. Robert Malloy. New York: Peter Smith, 1931.

Gamboa, Jeremías. "¿Dobles o siameses? Vanguardia y posmodernismo en *Estrella distante*." *Bolaño salvaje*. Ed. Edmundo Paz Soldán and Gustavo Faverón Patriau. Barcelona: Editorial Candaya, 2008. 211–36.

García Márquez, Gabriel. *Chronicle of a Death Foretold*. Trans. Gregory Rabassa. New York: Knopf, 1983.

———. *One Hundred Years of Solitude*. Trans. Gregory Rabassa. New York: Harper Collins, 1970.

Gardner, Martin. *Fads and Fallacies in the Name of Science*. New York: Dover, 1957.

González Rodríguez, Sergio. *Huesos en el desierto*. Barcelona: Anagrama, 2002.

Herralde, Jorge. *Para Roberto Bolaño*. Santiago: Catalonia, 2005.

Iñigo Madrigal, Luis. "Primeras noticias de *Una novelita lumpen*." *Roberto Bolaño: Una literatura infinita*. Ed. Fernando Moreno. Poitiers: CNRS, 2005. 187–97.

Jencks, Charles A. *The Language of Postmodern Architecture*. New York: Rizzoli, 1977.

Kingston, Maxine Hong. "The Novel's Next Step." *Mother Jones*. December 1989: 37–41.

Lafourcade, Enrique. *Palomita blanca*. Santiago: Zig-Zag, 1971.

Lepage Caroline. "Littérature et dictature: Lecture croisée de trois romans de Roberto Bolaño." *Les Astres noirs de Roberto Bolaño*. Ed. Karim Benmiloud and Raphaël Estève. Bordeaux: Presses Universitaires de Bordeaux, 2006. 67–89.

Logie, Ilse. "Un bestiario transatlántico: Reminiscencias de Kafka en la obra de Roberto Bolaño." *Roberto Bolaño: La experiencia del abismo*. Ed. Fernando Moreno. Santiago: Lom Ediciones, 2011. 281–94.

López-Vicuña, Ignacio. "The Part of the Exile: Displacement and Belonging in Bolaño's *Putas asesinas*." *Hispanófila* 164 (2012): 81–93.

Lowry, Malcolm. *Under the Volcano*. Philadelphia: J. B. Lippincott, 1965.

Madariaga Caro, Montserrat. *Bolaño infra 1975–1977: Los años que inspiraron 'Los detectives salvajes.'* Santiago: RIL Editores, 2010.

Manzoni, Celina. "Recorridos urbanos, fantasmagoría y espejismo en *Amuleto*." *Roberto Bolaño: Una literatura infinita*. Ed. Fernando Moreno. Poitiers: CNRS, 2005. 173–86.

———. "Reescritura como desplazamiento y anagnórisis en *El amuleto* [sic] de Roberto Bolaño." *Hispamérica* 32.94 (2003): 25–32.

———, ed. *Roberto Bolaño: La escritura como tauromaquia.* Buenos Aires: Corregidor, 2002.

Marías, Javier. *Los dominios del lobo.* Barcelona: EDHASA, 1971.

Marinetti, "Manifesto of Futurism." *Paths to the Present: Aspects of European Thought from Romanticism to Existentialism.* Ed. Eugen Joseph Weber. New York: Dodd, Mead & Co, 1960: 242–46.

Maristain, Mónica. *Bolaño: A Biography in Conversations.* Brooklyn: Melville House, 2014.

———. "The Last Interview." *Roberto Bolaño: The Last Interview.* Brooklyn: Melville House, 2009. 93–123.

Miles, Valerie. "A Journey Forward to the Origin." *Archivo Bolaño.* Barcelona: Centro de Cultura Contemporánea de Barcelona, 2013. 136–41.

Mixco, Miguel Huezo. "Roberto Bolaño en El Salvador." *Cuadernos hispanoamericanos* 23.731 (2011): 9–19.

Moíño Sánchez, Pablo. "Novela-nieve, poema-río: Sobre *Amberes* y "Gente que se aleja." *Roberto Bolaño: Estrella cercana.* Ed. Augusta López Bernasocchi and José Manuel López de Abiada. Madrid: Editorial Verbum, 2012. 299–316.

Neruda, Pablo. *Elementary Odes.* Trans. Carlos Lozano. New York: G. Massa, 1961.

Pastén, Agustín. "De la institucionalización a la disolución de la literatura en *Los detectives salvajes,* de Roberto Bolaño." *Revista Canadiense de Estudios Hispánicos* 33.2 (2009): 423–46.

Paz, Octavio. *The Labyrinth of Solitude.* Trans. Lysander Kemp. New York: Grove, 1962.

———. *Sunstone.* Trans. Eliot Weinberger. New York: New Directions, 1991.

Perec, Georges. *La Boutique obscure: 124 Dreams.* Trans. Daniel Levin Becker. Brooklyn: Melville House, 2012.

———. *Life: A User's Manual.* Trans. David Bellos. Boston: D. R. Godine, 1987.

———. *W, or the Memory of Childhood.* Trans. David Bellos. Boston: D. R. Godine, 1988.

Pollack, Sarah. "Latin America Translated Again: Roberto Bolaño's *The Savage Detectives* in the United States." *Comparative Literature* 61.3 (2009): 346–65.

Poniatowska, Elena. *Massacre in Mexico.* Trans. Helen Lane. New York: Viking, 1975.

Porta, A.G. "La escritura a cuatro manos." *Consejos de un discípulo de Morrison a un fanático de Joyce.* Barcelona: Acantilado, 2008: 7–14.

Prince, Gerald. *A Dictionary of Narratology.* Revised edition. Lincoln: University of Nebraska Press, 2003.

Puig, Manuel. *Kiss of the Spider Woman.* Trans. Thomas Colchie. New York: Knopf, 1979.

Quezada, Jaime. *Bolaño antes de Bolaño.* Santiago: Catalonia, 2007.

Ramírez, Sergio. *Castigo divino.* Madrid: Mondadori, 1988.

Richard, Nelly. *Margin and Institutions: Art in Chile since 1973.* Melbourne: Art and Text, 1986.

Schiffman, Robyn L. "*Werther* and the Epistolary Novel." *European Romantic Review* 19.4 (2008): 421–38.

Schmidt, Paul. *Arthur Rimbaud: Complete Works.* New York: Harper and Row, 1975.

Schwob, Marcel. "La Croisade des enfants." *Oeuvres*. Paris: Belles Lettres, 2012.

———. *Imaginary Lives*. Trans. Lorimer Hammond. New York: Boni and Liveright, 1924.

Sepúlveda, Magda. "La narrativa policial como un género de la modernidad: La pista de Bolaño." *Territorios en fuga: Estudios críticos sobre la obra de Roberto Bolaño*. Ed. Patricia Espinosa. Santiago: Frasis Editores, 2003. 103–15.

Serrano, Miguel. *Adolfo Hitler: El* último avatãra. Santiago: Ediciones la Nueva Edad, 1984.

———. *El cordón dorado: Hitlerismo esotérico*. Santiago: Edicioneself, 1978.

Shumway, Nicolas. *The Invention of Argentina*. Berkeley: University of California Press, 1991.

Solotorevsky, Myrna. *El espesor escritural en novelas de Roberto Bolaño*. Rockville: Hispamérica, 2012.

Soto, Héctor Soto, and Matías Bravo. "Literature Is Not Made from Words Alone." *Roberto Bolaño: The Last Interview*. Brooklyn: Melville House, 2009. 41–50.

Stolzmann, Uwe. "Entrevista a Roberto Bolaño." *Roberto Bolaño: Estrella cercana*. Ed. Augusta López Bernasocchi and José Manuel López de Abiada. Madrid: Editorial Verbum, 2012. 364–76.

Stone, Marla. *The Fascist Revolution in Italy: A Brief History with Documents*. Boston: Bedford–St. Martin's, 2013.

Toro, Vera, et al. "La auto(r)ficción: Modelizaciones, problemas, estado de la investigación." *La obsesión del yo*. Ed. Vera Toro et al. Madrid: Iberoamericana, 2010. 7–29.

Valdés, Marcela. "Introduction: Alone among the Ghosts." *Roberto Bolaño: The Last Interview*. Brooklyn: Melville House, 2009. 9–40.

Valenzuela, Andrea. "La muerte de César Vallejo." www.habanaelegante.com/Winter 2007/Dicha.html. Accessed January 9, 2015.

Vallejo, Georgette de. *Vallejo: Allá ellos, allá ellos, allá ellos*. Lima: Editorial Zalvac, 1978.

Vargas, Rafael. *Octavio Paz: Entre la imagen y el nombre*. Mexico City: Conaculta, 2011.

Vargas Llosa, Mario. *The Bad Girl*. Trans. Edith Grossman. New York: Farrar, Straus and Giroux, 2007.

———. *Conversation in the Cathedral*. Trans. Gregory Rabassa. New York: Harper and Row, 1975.

———. *The Feast of the Goat*. Trans. Edith Grossman. New York: Farrar, Straus, and Giroux, 2001.

———. *Letters to a Young Novelist*. Trans. Natasha Wimmer. New York: Picador, 2002.

———. *The War of the End of the World*. Trans. Helen R. Lane. New York: Farrar Straus Giroux, 1984.

Vila-Matas, Enrique. *La asesina ilustrada*. Barcelona: Tusquets, 1977.

———. "Blanes or the Writers of Yore." *Archivo Bolaño*. Barcelona: Centro de Cultura Contemporánea de Barcelona, 2013. 153–61.

Villoro, Juan. *El testigo*. Barcelona: Anagrama, 2004.

Volpi, Jorge. "Bolaño, epidemia." *Bolaño salvaje*. Ed. Edmundo Paz Soldán and Gustavo Faverón Patriau. Barcelona: Editorial Candaya, 2008. 191–207.

———. *El insomnio de Bolívar.* Barcelona: Debate, 2009.

Wells, Sarah Ann. "Late Modernism, Pulp History: Jorge Luis Borges' *A Universal History of Infamy* (1935)." *Modernism/Modernity* 18.2 (2011): 424–41.

Wilcock, Juan Rodolfo. *The Temple of the Iconoclasts.* Trans. Lawrence Venuti. San Francisco: Mercury House, 2000.

Index